The Modern Falconer

The Modern Falconer

Diana Durman-Walters

SWAN·HILL
PRESS

To Leonard
A Master Falconer

Copyright © 1994 by Diana Durman-Walters

First published in the UK in 1994
by Swan Hill Press
an imprint of Quiller Publishing Ltd

Reprinted 2002

British Library Cataloguing in Publication Data
  A catalogue record for this book
  is available from the British Library

ISBN 1 85310 368 3

Printed and bound in Great Britain by Butler & Tanner Ltd, Frome and London

Swan Hill Press
an imprint of Quiller Publishing Ltd
Wykey House, Wykey, Shrewsbury SY4 1JA, England
E-mail: info@quillerbooks.com
Website: www.swanhillbooks.com

Contents

	Acknowledgements	7
	Foreword	9
	Introduction	11
Chapter 1	The Modern Falconer	15
Chapter 2	The Old and the New	26
Chapter 3	Hawks – the New Wave	34
Chapter 4	Falcons – the New Wave	38
Chapter 5	Veterinary Advice on Raptor Keeping	47
Chapter 6	Game Hawking	55
Chapter 7	Tame Hacking	67
Chapter 8	Upland Game Hawking	70
Chapter 9	Lowland Hawking	74
Chapter 10	Rook Hawking	78
Chapter 11	The Game Fair and Display Hawk	83
Chapter 12	Dogs for Falconry	89
Chapter 13	Puppies	101
Chapter 14	Advanced Training	109
Chapter 15	Dogs and Hawks: Working Together	115
Chapter 16	Breeding or Raptor Propagation	119
Chapter 17	Aviaries	123
Chapter 18	The Occupants of the Aviary	128
Chapter 19	Incubation and Rearing	135
Chapter 20	Growing Up: Fledging and Dispersal of Young	140
Chapter 21	Artificial Insemination	156
Chapter 22	Conservation and Education	158
	Bibliography	160
	Glossary	162
	Game Seasons	167
	Useful Addresses	169
	Index	172

Acknowledgements

Falconers and falconry cannot exist without the support of landowners and like-minded enthusiasts. In this capacity I would like to give my sincere gratitude and thanks to the following: Willie and Sadie Phillips, Jimmy Johnson, Miles Pole, Robert Bewlay, George Bewlay, Susie Richards, James and Debbie Playfair-Hannay, John Jackson, Mary Dudgeon, Michael Dudgeon, Olivia and John Oakes, Mr and Mrs Douglas Cairns, Wilson Young, Bob Clarke, Bruce and Louise Graham-Cameron.

Falconers worldwide: Steve Baptiste, Dave Jamieson, Bill Shinners, Mike Yates, Phil Di-Maggio, Riccardo Velarde, Edmund Oettle, Bennie van de Merwe, Trevor Oertle, Ron Hartley, Paul Ventor, Greg Simpson, Dirk Verwoerd, Arshed Ahmed, Roland Leroux, Pierre Pele, Gilles Nortier, Patrick Morel, Stephen Frank, Christian Saar.

To the memory of Tom Martin and Jack Rogerson.

Special thanks and recognition of help received in the finer points in the field of AI to Dr Peter Lake.

Illustration Credits

All the photographs are by the author unless otherwise credited. The diagrams are by John Holmes.

Foreword

Falconry – the sport of flying trained raptors at wild quarry – is one of the most ancient of all field sports, preceded only by the innate impulse of dogs to chase hares and other quarry. Yet, after more than 4,000 years of established practice in Europe and Asia, the falconer's art has undergone astonishing new advances since the 1960s, especially in captive breeding techniques. In the 1920s and 1930s, perhaps the golden age of British game hawking, who would have dreamt that by the 1980s the vast majority of falconers' birds would be captive-bred, many by methods of artificial insemination?

In the aftermath of the 1981 Wildlife & Countryside Act, when Parliament decreed a radically new basis for the central licensing of falconry, I had the complex but often rewarding task of setting in motion the new procedures for the Department of the Environment. Despite the tiresome red tape and bureaucracy of the new system, I forged many firm friendships among falconers, including that of Diana Durman-Walters and her husband, Leonard. At Bonchester Bridge, where the high road southwards to England rises towards the border at Carter Bar, and where they now run the Scottish Academy of Falconry, they welcomed me in as a stranger from the darkness and rain of a Borders night in 1982, to see their newly constructed mews and breeding aviaries, and to talk enthusiastically into the wee small hours about modern falconry.

Eleven years on, the Durman-Walters' enterprise has grown to command international respect at the leading edge of modern falconry developments, not only in training raptors and schooling their handlers, but in the skills of selective breeding and hybridising of hawks and falcons, in breeding and training dogs for falconry, and in reviving the picturesque and highly effective practice of hawking from horseback, a unique blend of the traditional and the modern. A medieval falconer would recognise the birds and the horses' tack, but would be puzzled by the telemetry radios on the birds' tails!

The Modern Falconer offers a clear, practical and enthusiastic introduction to all the fundamentals of breeding, training and flying hawks and falcons, and shows how best to mould man, hawk and dog into an effective hunting team in the 1990s. Born out of the author's lifetime dedication and enthusiasm, and infused with the most modern proven techniques for success, this is an essential guide for newcomer and practitioner alike.

Colin McKelvie
Dumfriesshire

Introduction

For a quarter of a century my days have been immersed in and enriched by birds of prey. It is probably difficult for many falconers to be sure when the seed is sown that determines their irrevocable path to hunt with birds of prey, but for me it was the moment when as a student I was walking towards the art complex one evening to complete some work. A wild kestrel flew down in front of me and took a sparrow. I was obscured temporarily from his vision by mounds of earth from construction work as I ran over to get a better view. For a few tantalising seconds both of us gazed at each other, unable to move. The kestrel, no doubt shocked, gathered his wits and flew immediately onto the nearest roof with his prize. From that moment I longed to know something more about birds of prey, their hunting styles and techniques. Falconry would be the key.

That same year I applied to the Home Office for a licence to take a kestrel from the wild, in fact from the grounds of my college, and so began the foundation for my all-consuming passion. A goshawk was my first hunting bird. It was a tiercel haggard gos with coal-red eyes, superbly manned by his previous owner. This gos was to teach me many of the finer points of fieldcraft and hawk behaviour. His undying desire was for small birds whether jays, moorhens or magpies. He knew instinctively where he could find these and would endeavour to position himself in woods to his advantage. Often he would hunt at quite a distance from me, so the prospect of a pointing dog became important – I thought I might see much more of his hunting ability at close quarters if he flew at lowland gamebirds.

One item he never cared for was a rabbit, of which we had a good few on our ground. He was in fact quite set in his ways which made me decide to purchase an eyas female. This Finnish female and I spent the next decade hunting together. By the time she arrived the dogs (which were German short-haired pointers) were well versed in the field and able to create the working partnership that enabled her to become accomplished on fur and feather.

During the ensuing years, the ability of these magnificent hunters, whether hawk, falcon or eagle, never failed to keep me in awe of them. The disemination of information and the chance to compare hawks in the field at club meetings was then the means of keeping one's finger on the pulse; indeed the clubs were the principal source of acquiring goshawks, the mainstay of the majority of falconers.

In this period I was obsessed with flying short-wings while my husband Leonard flew only long-wings. Our individual interests in specialised hawking provided the unique pool of knowledge which has been effectively applied to all the species mentioned in this book. The dogs have changed over the years from short-haired pointers to wire-haired pointers and for some considerable time field trials with the wire-hairs (just another extension of exploring the talents of these working animals) were an important part of our calender.

At the British Falconers Club International Field meeting at Woodhall Spa in 1977, Leonard and I met Kent Carnie and Frank Bond from the USA. Among many aspects of falconry, they talked to us about the new wave of breeding programmes in the States. This was one of the most exciting new issues that had entered the falconry arena, the prospect of being able to breed your own falcons for hunting, particularly as peregrines were at such a premium and it was difficult to acquire licences to take them from the wild.

In 1979, in conjunction with Cornell University breeding facility, the French Falconry Club utilised the skills of specialist Steve Baptiste to assist with their breeding project. Through the kind efforts of Kent Carnie, Leonard and I were invited to join Steve for three weeks to be taught the current techniques and methods used in raptor breeding. It was a revelation. The methods were well taught and well learned. American breeding techniques were highly advanced, having already produced pure species and hybrids of many of the falcons. A powerful additional tool had been the development of artificial insemination in the production of raptors where projects contained females that would never breed naturally.

In 1980 we produced the first of our 'American' hybrids, the prairie x peregrine. Their reputation in the US and the opportunity to fly a peregrine type was all important in our breeding programme. They were and still are consistently one of the most successful in their field for all known types of hawking in this country.

Visits to the USA in 1982 and '87 to see falcons of various species and hybrid types flown at the North American Falconers Association (NAFA) meets and in alternative field gatherings confirmed for us the strength of the falcons being bred and the breadth and wealth of knowledge that falconry had yet to offer.

In the UK obtaining falcons and hawks from the wild under licence was about to become a thing of the past. From a conservation point of view this is a considerable plus to falconry, but it makes an enormous difference to the falconer's view of the natural world. The knowledge that would in the past have made him or her a keen naturalist, purely because it was of paramount interest to know where birds were nesting and what their habitat and geographical status were in order to fulfil the requirements for a licence, is no longer necessary. Nowadays the birds all come from domestic breeding projects.

Today's new-wave falconer may well feel this is of little importance. Many novice falconers rapidly acquire the opportunity to hunt with an amazing array of raptors. This may have undeniable attractions, but the stages of development in the falconer's skill become obscured through having too many birds too quickly and never being thoroughly conversant with their behaviour or that of quarry species. Too little time is spent in observation and making use of the knowledge thus acquired to the benefit of the hawk or falcon.

This book brings together the aspects of training of hawk, dog and horse. With its brief, informative look at raptor habitat and quarry species, it is designed to give background knowledge that will provide greater scope for developing the ability of the new-wave falconer and hawk.

From a veterinary point of view, there is guidance on how to be more observant when going about the daily management routines. Raptor veterinary care and treatment with its ever-increasing field of knowledge is a vital part of falconry, yet somehow the basic requirements of simple routine observation are often discarded in favour of seeking veterinary help when it may be too late. In Chapter 4 there is some excellent help and prompts as to what to look out for on a daily basis.

Today as I look at the new falcons on the lawn, which are now gyr-hybrids, I consider myself fortunate to have evolved in a period of such great change. To be able to fly the enormous wealth of domestic raptors in this country is possibly quite unique, worldwide. Other countries that legislate for falconry elect to control through the falconry clubs. They have their own three-year apprenticeship schemes, in which novices are affiliated to experienced falconers. They remain at all times governed and controlled by their clubs or association. In our 'free' society, where anyone can own a hawk or falcon, it is to the credit of many individual falconers in the UK today that the standard, skills and sense of responsibility are of a very high standard. There are a rapidly growing number of novice falconers for whom much of this book will be invaluable, with its new look at the variety of hawks and falcons available and what we have found can be done with them in the field.

Like so many other like-minded people I have met throughout the world, falconry is my heartbeat. It is there in the morning and in the evening. Its demands of input, skill, dedication and its continuous learning curve mean that I am always able to be close to the natural interchanging world of predator and prey and yet in the developing modern world assist in the vital role falconry has to play in the conservation of declining species. It has incorporated into its culture dedicated people who may be scientists, academics, aviculturalists, business executives or plain out of work. It spans a classless group of society that has as its horizon and goal the all-consuming desire to fly a hunting hawk to the highest standard of excellence.

Chapter 1
The Modern Falconer

Origins

Where did it all begin? This question has been asked many times throughout the history of falconry but the answer remains a matter of great speculation. Evidence suggests that it originated among the nomadic peoples of Asia, that they cultivated it from the most remote period of history. In fact the great plains which these people inhabited lent themselves excellently to the practice of falconry because they were plentiful in birds of prey and game of all kind (which would have been difficult to approach in these open areas). Birds of prey are faster than horses and other domestic animals which man can use for hunting and essentially the style of life of these people contributed greatly towards making the practice of falconry necessary as well as pleasurable. From central Asia it spread to Japan on one side and on the other into India, Persia, western Asia, North Africa and Europe.

One Japanese work says that in China the falcon was among the gifts which princes gave to each other from the time of the Hia Dynasty, which is believed to have begun in 2205 BC. We know that falconry was already cultivated in China by the reigning emperors in the 7th Century BC and that it was about 400 BC that Ctesias picked up, at the court of the Kings of Persia, ideas on the art as it was practised at the time by certain peoples who inhabited the northern parts of India and Persia.

As falconry diverged along its many routes it was remarkable how the falconers of the east and west agreed on almost every point. Although the communication between them had been interrupted for centuries, their general system of treatment and the many ingenious contrivances either discovered or handed down from posterity were very similar. Both made use of jesses, leashes, bells and hoods, varying only in pattern and material. Broken feathers were imped in the same way and they bathed and weathered their hawks, fed and gave castings likewise.

In the history of falconry in Europe, one figure stands out: that of Emperor Frederick II of Germany, who died in 1250. He had seen hawking in the east and in 1229, on his return from a Crusade which he had undertaken the year before, when he was crowned King of Jerusalem and Sicily, he brought with him from Syria and Arabia several expert falconers with their hawks. He began to spend much of his leisure time in learning from them the secrets of their art. His excellent treatise *De Arte cum Avibus* ('On Skill with Birds'), was the first to appear in the West and is undoubtedly still one of the best in existence.

Frederick II was equally passionate about architecture. Like his grandfather King Roger II of Sicily he was an energetic builder. In his favourite province of Apulia he erected more than twenty large castles, one of the better known being Castle del Monte, where he spent many hours pursuing falconry. However, castles were too large and imposing and were surrounded by day-to-day business, which encroached on his falconry. In connection with the larger castles Frederick built a number of minor dwellings, the *loca solatiorum* of his correspondence, the pleasure retreats to which he could retire at frequent intervals and forget the affairs of state, simply to pursue his all-absorbing passion.

The hawks chiefly used by imperial followers of falconry were the gyrfalcon, saker, peregrine, lanner, goshawk and sparrowhawk. Frederick was acquainted with the use of other birds for sport, but he regarded these as the most practical. Unlike most concepts of emperors, he had no interest in eagles, which were too heavy to be carried about on the fist and consequently valueless for his hunting purposes.

In his writings Frederick described at length the furniture and other devices employed in training the hunting falcon. These included leash, jesses, bell and swivel, much as one would expect to see in textbooks today. The bell, however, was often seen attached to one or more of the caudal feathers (tail feathers) which were secured by perforating the shaft or quill and fixing it in place.

The content of the *De Arte* shows that Frederick was also something of a scientist/naturalist. Intrigued by anatomy, he wrote about the form of the sternum, the structure of the lungs and the rump glands, and the pneumaticity of bones. He also covered the mechanics and conditions of birds on migration, experiments into the artificial incubation of eggs and to see whether vultures find their food by sight or smell. Much of this research work revealed a fist-class scientific mind.

His treatise on falconry was intended to be entirely scientific and general; hence he told no hunting stories and made few references to people or places. Indeed a rare man for the 13th century, as he insisted on seeing and hearing for himself: if facts were not available he did not write inaccurate conclusions.

As the Middle Ages progressed, the practice of falconry became commonplace. During this period the Germans were great falconers, as were the French. To a lesser extent the art was practised in Spain and Italy and even to a degree by the Kings of Norway and Denmark, who used gyrfalcons which had been sent to them as gifts.

The precise date of the introduction of hawking to Great Britain is uncertain. We know from various sources that it was practised by our ancestors in early Saxon times (450 AD). So general was the pastime of hawking during the later Saxon period that the monks of Abingdon found it necessary in 821 to procure a charter from King Kenulph to restrain the practice in harvest-time, in order to prevent their crops from being trampled on!

As its popularity grew, it was pursued by many of our kings with the greatest of enthusiasm. Henry VIII's love of hawking is well documented and this devotion was continued throughout the reigns of Tudors and Stuarts by Elizabeth I, Mary Queen of Scots and King James I. James was an enthusiastic sportsman and especially delighted in hawking, on which he spent considerable sums of money every year. It was in his reign that Sir Thomas Monson as Royal Falconer was said to have given £1,000 for a cast of falcons. In fact Sir Anthony Wheldon in his *Court and Character of King James* (1650) reported that the truth was Sir Thomas spent £1,000 before he succeeded in getting a cast of gyrfalcons that were perfect for flying at kite. This he might very well have done, as it might have included the cost of expeditions to Norway or Iceland for them. Naturally such a sum was of interest to the nation, as today it would represent the equivalent of £38,219 of taxpayers' money!

James I's love of hawking and hunting, to which he was passionately addicted; his invitations to foreign princes and noblemen skilled in these pursuits to join him in the hunt; instructing his own countrymen and his frequent imports and purchases of hawks, hounds and horses promoted a sportsman king never seen before or since. By virtue of his complete indulgence he did more to encourage and promote the exercise of these field sports than any other British monarch.

The time for indulgences was drawing to a close for the monarchy. Although all the Stuarts were fond of hawking, after the Restoration it ceased to be popular. The causes which led to its decline were many and varied. The disastrous state of the country during the period of the Civil War naturally put an end to it for a while, but the enclosure of waste lands, the drainage and cultivation of marshes and in particular the advent of the gun contributed to lessen its interest universally.

So the gun had emerged to rival the hawk. Interestingly enough a second factor appeared which was to herald the arrival of the professional falconer. Falconers up until this period had always considered it necessary to carry their own personally trained hawk on their fist. This obviously implied that they were people of leisure and wealth and could devote a vast amount of time to their bird, but as with the changing face of management and government, few could afford to give themselves up so exclusively.

After the Civil War many patrons of the sport simply could not afford to employ a professional falconer, their mews were disbanded and they would adopt the gun as an alternative. Among professional falconers some outstanding men evolved, especially from Scotland and Holland. However, it must be said that one of our most famous falconers, Colonel Thomas Thornton of Thornville Royal (1757-1823) was one of the last of a breed of his era that dedicated themselves wholeheartedly to the art of falconry and for whom the perfection of the hawk lay in their own knowledge and talent. In the pursuit of excellence in the field he had few equals.

Colonel Thornton came from a distinguished family. His father, Colonel William Thornton, with a troop of yeomanry and tenantry one hundred in number served with distinction at the battles of Falkirk and Culloden. He died suddenly leaving Thomas as a youngster at Charterhouse, where he remained until he was fourteen graduating to Glasgow College. Here he developed a passion for field sports, particularly falconry, on which he spent a great deal of time and money. Even at this early age his resolve was to bring the sport as near to perfection as is possible.

He left his college at nineteen and went back to the family home where with well-trained dogs and hawks he formed the basis of a sporting establishment that was later to become famous. He became Colonel of the West York Regiment of Militia and here formed a falconry club.

He was, even by today's athletic standards, incredibly fit. He loved hunting to hounds, racing and inbetween times would organise feats that would test his competitors' abilities to the full. Always ready for a wager he is alleged at different times to have taken part in a walking match, covering four miles in 32 minutes; jumped his own height (5ft 9in) and jumped six five-barred gates in six minutes. At Newmarket on horseback, he ran down a hare, which he picked up in the presence of people assembled to witness the feat. All of course, for a considerable bet. A good shot and fisherman, his greatest ability nevertheless lay in falconry. He was especially skilled in flights at the kite, red grouse and snipe hawking.

At home at Thornton Royal his hawks were flown at hack from the observatory in the park. He hawked all over the moors at Blubberhouse and Grassington and open country around Kirk Deighton. At Beilby Grange there was a heronry, and he flew at the herons 'on passage' as they crossed the moors (heron being a culinary delicacy). While the crops were standing he used to adjourn to the Yorkshire Wolds, where he built a house called Falconers Hall near Scarborough.

In 1808 Colonel Thornton left Yorkshire for Spye Park in Wiltshire. The wolds of Yorkshire which had up until then been open grass country began to be broken up into areas designated for corn crops, making his form of falconry infinitely more difficult. Wiltshire still had vast open territories from which it was still possible to see bustard. Thornton occasionally attempted flights at these, because he felt they looked very slow birds, only to find that his falcons had no chance at them whatsoever.

In 1815 he gave up hawking and retired to France. He died in Paris in 1823 aged seventy-five, leaving his six-year-old daughter as his heir.

Colonel Thornton broke with tradition in that he employed Dutch professional falconers. At around the close of 18th century he and Lord Orford made an effort to revive hawking in this country and introduced the 'Dutch School of Falconry' to England. This system never extended into Scotland, which always had its own native falconers. The Dutch system of hawking was to use only 'passage hawks', whilst the Scottish school used 'eyases'.

All the Dutch falconers came from Valkenswaard, a village near Bois le Duc in Holland. Many of their well-known falconers came to England to be in the employ of the various hawking gentry: such names as John Daims, John Bekkers, Francis van den Heural and John Pells, are to name but a few.

Pells is probably the best known of these. Born in Valkenswaard 1778 he was sent as a boy of eleven to the Landgrave of Hesse Cassel, who was then the greatest falconer on the continent. (A landgrave is a 12th century German title used to distinguish a governor of a province from inferior counts.) Pells came to England in 1800 and spent the years up until 1832 in the employment of various gentry, whereupon he was engaged by the Duke of St Albans. When he died his position as the duke's falconer was carried on by his son John.

The Dutch falconers probably assisted in reviving a taste for the sport in England. They were also immensely knowledgeable on the trapping of wild hawks and their training and management particularly at kites, and herons 'on passage'. In return they learned how to use eyases, which was little understood in their country: as Holland is so flat, peregrines did not nest there.

As fathers passed on their traditions to sons in Holland, so they did in Scotland. Some of the more famous names are William Barr, Peter Ballantine and John Anderson.

John Anderson was quite a character in the sporting world and a master falconer. Born in 1750 at Currie near Edinburgh he became interested in falconry (then commonly practised in Scotland) and from an early age wanted no other profession. He was taken into the employ of Mr Flemming of Barochan, Renfrewshire (near Paisley), who had a chequered career as a falconer, being keeper of the Renfrewshire Subscription Hawks, which were flown chiefly at partridge and woodcock.

Anderson became Flemming's head falconer and took as his assistant Peter Ballantine, who was to become equally famous. On Flemming's death in 1819

Anderson was engaged by the Earl of Morton at Dalmahoy. On the occasion of the coronation of George IV in 1820 he was selected to represent the Duke of Atholl in presentation of a cast of hawks to the king. This was the feudal tenure by which the Dukes of Atholl held the Isle of Man from the Crown.

In his later years he spent some time in the service of Sir Alexander Donne of Ochiltree where he retired on a pension at the age of eighty-two.

Peter Ballantine was born in 1798 at Dumfries House, Ayrshire, where his father, who had formerly been falconer to the Earl of Eglinton, was employed as steward to the Marquis of Bute. He was a great friend of John Anderson and between them they developed a passion and love of falconry. Peter particularly had a gentleness in the handling and training of birds that was to be his trademark throughout his career. At the age of twenty he went to work for John Anderson, then an up-and-coming professional falconer. Here he remained as assistant falconer until Anderson's retirement in 1832. Not long afterwards he entered the service of Lord Carmarthen (later to become the Duke of Leeds) as assistant to John Pells. Their hawks were kept at Huntly Lodge, Aberdeenshire and while old Pells kept a few passage falcons at work, Ballantine trained the Scottish eyases. The former were used at heron, and the latter at every description of game.

The finest sport of all came from the flights to be had at woodcock, which were abundant in the young plantations around Deeside. Here the falcons could combine the stoop of a game hawk or the high, mounting ringing flight of the heron hawk all in one sequence.

It was at this period that Peter Ballantine adopted the principle of making Dutch hoods and the use of traditional jesses and a separate swivel. Up until then varvels and a leash had been used, which was typical of the time and to which the Scots falconer had been educated. Varvels were little flattened silver rings just under an inch in diameter which were seen on the end of each jess. They were not removed as they did not have a swivel and the leash was quickly slipped through them for flight. Being flat they had the owner's name engraved on one side and his address on the other. The main problem with them was that the jesses were apt to get twisted up tightly as the hawk turned round and round on the perch. Eventually the development of a swivel prevented this.

Ballantine then went on to work for Sir James Boswell of Auchinleck, where he had charge of a kennel of greyhounds and was required to train at least one cast of falcons per year. He remained with Sir James for twenty-five years. On his death, he moved once again, this time to Mr Robert Ewen of Ewenfield, Ayrshire. It was in this latter period that Ballantine established himself beyond all doubt as one of the greatest trainers of eyases for gamehawking. In 1870 the score of game was 269 head. The following year it was 346 head and reached the incredible score of 367 head in 1873. Many of the hawks he trained in those years were to become some of the most famous of the period and remained unmatched in the field.

In his later years he once again changed employer (having consistently outlived them) and a Mr Oswald of Auchencruive kept him in his old home, allowing him to pursue falconry to his dying day. In the last three years before his death he flew a splended falcon called Pearl, which was perhaps as good a hawk as he had ever trained. It is a curious fact that when he died in 1884, at the age of eighty-six, the falcon, which had been lost for several days previously, died on the same day as her old master.

Strangely enough, although the UK produced some quite outstanding falconers during this period, the best remembered is from the Dutch School, Aidrian Mollen. He was head falconer to the Royal Loo Hawking Club, near Arnhem, Holland. This club, established in 1838, consisted of fifty members under the patronage of the King of Holland with HRH Prince Alexander of Holland at its head. It had many English members, some of whom were employers to our own professional falconers at this time. Mollen was a native of Falkenswaard and had been a pupil of Jean Botts. In 1837 he entered the service of Prince Trautmansdorff, near Vienna. There he trained not only peregrines he had brought from Holland but also eyas sakers brought from Hungary for flights at partridges, crows and large plovers (probably stone-curlew). In 1841 he decided to leave Vienna to become head falconer at the Loo. What made this club so popular was its abundance of herons. This branch of falconry had stopped in England in about 1838 but was still considered the highest form of falconry that could be achieved. Consequently it had an avid following. Mollen was a successful falconer, and no sooner was he employed at the Royal Loo Hawking Club than he found his time consumed by the training and flying of twenty-one falcons, already in the company of assistant falconers and showing a great deal of sport. As this branch of hawking was conducted over large tracts of ground which had few boundaries, they had also to be competent horsemen in order to be able to keep up with the chase.

Falconry of this ilk was exclusive, as can be seen by the patrons involved. Naturally others who were just as capable wished to fly their falcons at herons. In 1840 a society of amateur falconers was formed with Baron Tindall as president. This group had twenty-two falcons which took 138 herons. The society had club rules with a president, secretary and treasurer, and its members were divided between the two top falconers, Aidrian Mollen and Jean Botts. Their intake of falcons rose to forty-four, with which they took a phenomenal number of heron. The interest and number of falcons remained the same until 1849, when they were reduced to fourteen.

In 1850 the king maintained an interest in hawking and retained Mollen, various under-falconers and their horses at his own expense, which must have been considerable. The society was transferred to the hunting lodge which adjoined the château at the Loo and they were to maintain Jean Botts in similar fashion. However, by 1853, the club had seen its heyday and was composed solely of the professional falconers and their aides. Their royal patron, a devotee of regulated eating habits, dined every day at the same hour – the very hour which was best suited to go hawking! Naturally every member of his entourage was governed by his example and forced to join him. This was no doubt the cause of enormous friction, which was to prove terminal. In that same year the king withdrew his patronage.

Mollen, with his access to trapped passage hawks, became the major source of supply of peregrines in England. With the abolition of the Royal Loo Hawking Club, amateur falconers in this country had begun to take a passionate interest in rook hawking. For this they required passage falcons and Mollen was kept busy throughout his career providing hawks for the sport.

Although falconry had once been popular all over Europe, by the 19th century it was in decline everywhere. English and Dutch falconers had done much to attempt revival, and it is difficult to know exactly what brought about the loss of interest. Many authors writing in the early 19th century believed that the combination of fewer available falcons, the invention of small shot and ever-increasing cultivation of land were all contributing factors. Undoubtedly the changing face of farming requirements altered the *status quo* of certain areas: for instance heronries which were subjected to land drainage and subsequent land enclosure were no longer available for riding and hawking. The use of the gun also drew many people's attention away from hawking, but this could be only part of the answer, as falconry still had its ardent followers worldwide. It was an accepted part of many European communities, encouraged and promoted by its princes and kings. Although it peaked and troughed throughout various reigns it never completely lost its cult following. Up until the time of the French Revolution it was still commonly practised.

But it was at this point in history that sweeping social changes were to wipe falconry almost off the map. The French Revolution and the wars that followed it involved the whole of Europe for more than twenty years. As a result, the wealthy were forced to reappraise their luxuries as universal moves towards equality took place. It became politically embarrassing for royalty and nobility to indulge wantonly in an extravagant sport which openly brought public disapproval, simply because it reflected the gross inequalities of wealth between king and country.

Suddenly there was no more work for professional falconers. As they grew old they were not replaced by their sons, as had been the case in times gone by. The art of training hawks for the chase would have come very close to oblivion had it not been for the fact that several falconers from Valkenswaard were called into service in a country which was not overrun by the great wars of Europe. This country was Great Britain. Protected by their island status from the turmoil in Europe, people could still devote themselves to their favourite pursuit.

It is around this period that what we can describe as modern falconry begins to emerge. It is little wonder that Valkenswaard features so strongly in its history. The art of training birds for the chase and of practising various types of flights would undoubtedly have been lost had it not been for the English patrons of the Dutch experts, whose highly developed skills were to bring falconry into the 20th century.

The idea of clubs to which falconers could gravitate was not a new one, as has been seen, but it was through the emergence of such clubs that falconry in the UK would proceed. So it was that in 1864 the Old Hawking Club was formed. Robert Barr was club falconer and the manager was Edward Clough Newcome. A similar renaissance began in France with the Champagne Hawking Club. This was in the capable hands of John Barr, brother of Robert. Here they hawked rooks, magpies, partridges, stone curlews and little bustards. It was usual to investigate sporting potential wherever that may be. The Champagne Club in 1869 took its hawks to Scotland and here the two Barr brothers met with their respective patrons' hawks. With a mixed group of haggard, passage and eyas they executed some quite outstanding grouse hawking. Hawking as ever was seasonal. Hence Easter time found the clubs rook hawking, and in England this meant on Salisbury Plain; later they moved on to partridge hawking, with magpie hawking in Ireland, then on to Valkenswaard to collect the feshly taken passage hawks.

In 1866 a young Gerald Lascelles spent his Easter holidays rook hawking. Here he met Edward Newcome, an original member of the Royal Loo Hawking Club. They were to remain friends up until Newcome's death in 1871. Just prior to that time the

Old Hawking Club had ceased to exist. Lascelles felt it was important to resurrect it and with the help of Lord Lilford reformed the Old Hawking Club, becoming manager and secretary until the outbreak of the First World War.

The club itself finally came to an end in 1926. The Mollen descendants who had been the mainstay of falconry equipment-makers and master trappers ceased to be involved in this work. The number of hawks required by the Old Hawking Club had dwindled to about eight birds a year and times were changing.

The First World War saw many of the Old Hawking Club members actively engaged. During that period their falconry was naturally in abeyance. However, one familiar name from this time would become the link between the old and the new. This was Colonel Gilbert Blaine. Although he began his hawking career on the heathland of Dorset, hunting partridge, it was for his impressive development of grouse hawking that he would be best remembered; he would set a pace that to this day is the stereotype which many try to emulate.

In 1920 he took over the management of the Old Hawking Club, remaining in this post until the club disbanded. The following year, 1927, he became one of the founder members of the newly formed British Falconers Club.

For a short while falconry within the ranks of the dedicated continued as before. Gilbert Blaine was now concentrating his hawking expertise in Caithness with seasonal regularity and still had in his employ two professional falconers and a professional dog handler. The Downs of the West Country and the open countryside of Lincolnshire still provided uninhibited flying on horseback or by car.

The Second World War marked the great divide between the old and the new and saw the advance of the Modern Falconer. Up until this point in time falconry had been strictly an English/European occupation. No reference was made to Africa, America or Australia. Curiously enough these three continents have a far greater diversity of birds of prey capable of participating in falconry than those to be found in Europe, yet records concerning their use begin post-war. To date Australia does not have legislation that permits falconry.

Africa
Africa has a very active falconry community, almost exclusively in the southern parts. Zimbabwe and South Africa are its most committed participants. In South Africa there are clubs within each province. Each regulates its own members with their own constitutions and code of ethics. The most recently established of these is the Cape Province. The geographical diversity within South Africa is such that some of the most exciting aspects of falconry are practised here, utilising their indigenous raptors over a wide variety of quarry species. South African falconers are equally committed to conservation and breeding programmes which are now able to produce young for the purposes of falconry and capable of sustaining their sport.

Zimbabwe, like South Africa, has vast open spaces which afford enormous scope and potential for falconry. Although it is a relatively young sport in this country, long-wings, short-wings and eagles are flown at a great variety of quarry.

In the early 1950s, falconry in what was then Southern Rhodesia was spearheaded by Major Eustace Poles and his nephew Allan Savory. Between them they flew Ovambo sparrowhawk, African goshawk, peregrine and Ayres hawk eagle. Initially interest from other people was sporadic. During the '60s and '70s falconry began to have a serious profile and in 1970 the Rhodesian Falconers' Club was formed, ensuring that falconry was recognised as a legitimate sport and would be protected in the impending wildlife legislation.

The initial interest was in the flying of short-wings of which the southern regions of Africa have some nine different species. In the late '70s the flying of long-wings became the premier sport. There are a great variety of eagles in this country, but the African hawk eagle has proved to be by far the most suitable and is the only eagle allowed on the general falconry permit.

The Zimbabwe Falconry Club plays a very great part in the education and public awareness concerning birds of prey and in assisting young falconers. Perhaps its greatest achievement is through the establishment of falconry at two private schools, Falcon College and Peterhouse. Membership is restricted to eight at any one time, candidates having been filtered through a stringent selection course. These young apprentices learn with African goshawks and Gabar goshawks.

Veterinary care, research and captive breeding are in-depth studies conducted from the schools and are concurrent with the vast amount of work being done in these specialist fields by the club. The important scientific conservation work being conducted, in particular the inclusion of studies on the Taita falcon, is published quarterly in the club magazine *Talon*.

Such is the development within these fields especially the productive emphasis on captive breeding that much support has been given from their own Conservation Trust, plus valuable liaison between Dr Tom Cade of the Peregrine Fund, USA, and Mrs J Parry-Jones of the National Centre for Birds of Prey, Gloucestershire.

North America
North America has had perhaps the most celebrated rise in modern falconry. The North American Falconry Association (NAFA) was founded in Denver, Colorado, in 1961. Today its membership is well over 2,000. This is considerable: the next largest club worldwide, the British Falconers Club, has only 1,000 members. In 1961, like many clubs of its genre NAFA reflected the growing interest in falconry. The input from its members during the next thirty years was to see many new and exciting concepts undertaken, including flying indigenous raptors and producing hybrids which not only proved highly versatile in falconry, but were a living statement to the success of captive breeding.

I quote from Article 1 Section 2 of the North American Falconers Association:

Our purpose is to provide communication among and to disseminate relevant information to interested Members; to provide scientific study of the raptorial species, their care, welfare and training; to promote conservation of the birds of prey and an appreciation of their value in nature and in wildlife conservation programmes; to urge recognition of falconry as a legal field sport; and to establish traditions which will aid, perpetuate and further the welfare of falconry and the raptors it employs.

Within the above remit, the membership has been blessed with very able scientists, politicians, educationalists and above all particularly talented falconers.

Today NAFA is a vital source of input and feedback to falconers worldwide and its important work is published quarterly in *Hawk Chalk* and annually in the *Journal*.

The Irish Hawking Club

We know that the Old Hawking Club came to Ireland to fly at rook and magpie. We also know that Lord Talbot de Malahide was associated with the forming of a club in 1870, but it was not until 1967 that the Irish Hawking Club was founded. The Club serves two jurisdictions. Eire in the south governed from the Dail and Northern Ireland governed from Westminster, London. This means there are two different sets of conservation and importation legislations which lead to the differing availability of hawks.

In the south, the sparrowhawk is the main bird with one or two red-tails and Harris hawks flown. In the north it is the red-tails with a few Harris hawks and goshawks flown. Not a lot is done either side of the border with large longwings and only one member breeds and flies merlins seriously.

The Welsh Hawking Club

In 1962 the Welsh Hawking Club was formed under international falconer Lorant de Bastyai. Hungarian by birth and President of the Hungarian Falconers Association, he escaped the uprising of 1956 and was in 1962 a taxidermist to Newport Museum and South West District. Whilst there he met members of the Newport Wildfowling and Gun Club who, learning of his falconry history, decided to form a club which could cater for their growing interest in the sport.

A notice in the *South Wales Argus* welcomed interested sportsmen. Twenty people attended and it was proposed that this new group should be called the Welsh Hawking Club. An active committee quickly established priorities and in October 1962 the WHC attended an international meeting in Bavaria, courtesy of the Deutsche Falkenorden.

From this liaison came several goshawks and a female Bonelli's eagle. This favourable meeting was in the early years to be the source of hunting hawks. They came not only from the Continent but also from the United States. Among the early arrivals was 'Mini', the prairie falcon. On a second trip, this time to Austria, they brought back further goshawks and a golden eagle.

Today there are around 400 members and the club has a friendly reputation with a large proportion of its members being keen and active falconers. It has invested a great deal in its breeding programme with a view to supplying hawks to members and currently has hawks and falcons out on loan. Field meetings are held and the affairs of the club can be seen in the annual magazine *The Austringer* and in newsletters throughout the year.

The British Falconers Club

Founded in 1927 with fifteen members, today it has just over 1,000. It is the oldest and by far the largest club in the UK. Since its inception it has achieved and established many firsts which have all been to the benefit of falconry and falconers alike. In 1954 the Bird Protection Act allowed hawks to be taken for falconry under licence, following intensive representation by the BFC. In 1958 it gave the first exhibition of hawks flying to the lure at the first Game Fair. Throughout the 1960s the BFC represented the interests of falconry at national and international conferences and 1973 saw the first of the international field meetings. During the '70s the club continued to host or support international conferences on birds of prey and in 1980, with the British Field Sports Society, mounted a vigorous campaign to safeguard the interests of falconry in the Wildlife and Countryside Bill. It has maintained this level of input and this is reflected in its current breeding successes. Over the past ten years some £20,000 has been invested in specialised breeding facilities, resulting in some sixty-four offspring of six different species of raptor being produced. The goshawk breeding programme has been a triumph of endeavour, producing to date thirty-seven young. In additions a number of merlins, redtails, sparrowhawks, common buzzards and peregrines. Regional groups have their own schemes which are also enjoying good results. The club produces two newsletters per year and *The Falconer* annually.

Today within the UK there are thirteen clubs representing all areas and regions. With so many diverse groups geographically and of differing local requirements they have additional powerful representation from the Hawk Board.

The Hawk Board
This is the only democratically elected advisory board. Members are voted for by the raptor-owning community who are on the electoral role. It is based in London and designed to assist the needs of all groups whether commercial or non-commercial, aviculturalists, zoos and falconers that have an interest in birds of prey. This is done through regular meetings liaising with the Department of the Environment and the Joint Nature Conservancy Council on all issues concerning related legislation and welfare. It maintains a positive relationship with the British Field Sports Society.

The British Field Sports Society
The BFSS was started in 1930 because it was recognised that field sports would be targeted by the 'antis' one by one, starting with the weakest. Although no sport has yet been banned, intentions have not changed. It is the only organisation that defends all field sports in the political arena. Its unique asset is its parliamentary committee, made up of peers and MPs with an interest in country sports. Its public affairs department is backed up by professional consultants.

The BFSS has ensured the retention of field sports as an integral part of the activities of modern society and shown how field sports enrich and conserve the wildlife of our country. It continuously provides information and advice and assistance to members. Its infrastructure is made up from committees representing every facet of country sport, including Scottish, Welsh and Northern Ireland branches.

The Department of the Environment
An individual who keeps a hawk, falcon or eagle needs to have in his/her possession a registration document for that bird. These are issued by the Department of the Environment, as indeed are any requirements and/or licences concerning birds of prey. The department has specific case officers who will deal with enquiries, which allows for continuity and prompt replies.

Laws concerning raptors in captivity are far more likely to change now that we are part of the EC. All relevant issues – quarry licences, import, export, quarantine requirements, movement of birds, ownership or whatever – are under the jurisdiction of the department who are able to advise on current updates and procedure.

Chapter 2
The Old and the New

At the turn of the 19th century the familiar peregrine falcon and goshawk were the mainstay species kept in every respectable mews. Not that falconers weren't aware of other species. Early writings such as those of Emperor Frederick II show that he expertly flew gyrfalcons, peregrines and lanners. Eleanora falcons, hobbies and hawk eagles were flown out of interest. Falconers would no doubt have attempted to fly a wider variety of species, but it would have been largely for amusement. Not a lot seems to have been gained out of flying 'exotics' as little mention is made of performance and when they did write about them it was usually in passing. The main priority was to fly medium-sized birds of prey, as these were capable of the most exciting and demanding forms of falconry. Eagles of any description weren't worth the effort of carrying them and small falcons couldn't take on the quarry which provided the very best flights.

Falconry became steeped in tradition. The opportunities to hawk kite, heron or crane with high-mounting spectacular falcons meant that a highly specialised branch of falconry had evolved. When this style of hawking was eventually phased out, due to land drainage and systematic changes in agricultural policies, it had been an obvious move to adjust peregrine to rook hawking and to fly merlins at lark: these provided the perfect combination of the essence of *haute volerie* or high flying and of course you could still pursue the field on horseback.

Therefore there had been no need to look at varieties of different species. After all, what could you possibly want to achieve with them? What indeed, was the challenge that modern falconers applied themselves to.

As modern falconry in the UK began its growth curve in the early 1960s, other groups were doing the same worldwide. As they began to explore the talents of their indigenous hawks and falcons, a greater variety of raptor were trained in falconry.

At home the increased accessibility of ground to fly on meant more people than ever before had leisure time to pursue their interests in falconry. However, access to hawks and falcons strategic to the sport were not easy to come by. As a result of liaison with falconers from different countries, a small number of exotic hawks, mainly from North America, began to be seen at field meetings here.

The flying of hawks such as the redtail and Harris hawk began to gain popularity among many people who had hitherto flown goshawks. One of their additional advantages was their ability to breed in captivity, which although an undeveloped science at this point was suffcient to warrant further interest. Their adaptability to the geography and climate of the UK also endeared them, as did their suitability to the available prey base. But the introduction of exotics brought a great diversity of raptor to be flown at indigenous quarry and created a breakaway movement from traditional hawking as it was known then in the UK.

Perhaps the ultimate break with tradition was in the early 1980s when the first of the UK hybrids (prairie x peregrine) appeared on the scene. The impact of this bird on conventional falconry gathered momentum as its performance matched and could outperform the peregrine. These trailblazers liberated a new-wave falconer, who could now compete in the traditional manner with an entirely unknown man-made commodity. Such hybrids rapidly became very successful in all orthodox fields of game hawking. They prospered due to their ability to take a high pitch rapidly, combined with a co-operative disposition yet a highly aggressive hunting instinct in the field.

Hybrid falcons have gained a permanent position in modern falconry and many varieties are now flown at traditional and alternative quarry. Despite some people's thoughts to the contrary, pure species will never step aside to hybrids, because their biological role in the environment is determined through gradual evolution. Genetically geared to survival in the wild, they are eminently adapted to the rigours of strong winds, varied terrain and indigenous prey species.

Today a wide variety of non-indigenous falcons and hawks are flown in the UK. Their performance will always be a direct reflection on how they relate to either the goshawk or the peregrine falcon in the field, because they are in pursuit of the same quarry.

More true species are flown than ever before and with the option of hybrids available, the modern falconer has entered an era in which his future is sustained through domestic breeding programmes. From these endeavours has emerged the opportunity to succeed in the pursuit of excellence in a hunting bird.

The Traditional Falcon

Peregrine Falcon *(Falcon peregrinus peregrinus)*
Flying Weight: (F) 1 lb 13½ oz–2 lb 4 oz. (M) 1 lb 4 oz–1 lb 7 oz.
Range: Virtually worldwide. Found on all continents and many island groups.

The Siberian and Arctic peregrines of North America are migratory. Almost exclusively bird-eater, the peregrine takes a wide range of species, which it will attempt to take on the wing, frequently using stooping to catch quarry. It will also take quarry by snatching from tree-top, rock ledge or building. Speed in the stoop is estimated to be 100–150 mph.

Universally the falcon of the gauntlet, its ease of training, consistent performance, speed and style in the field have made this the favoured hawk throughout the centuries. It is flown at all lowland and upland game birds, including woodcock, magpie and snipe. Since the turn of the century falconers have concentrated their skills with notable acclaim on red grouse, which requires a high-mounting falcon that can hit from the stoop. The peregrine is a natural master of this method and will willingly co-operate with training focused on waiting on flights. Slipping out of the hood is another of its specialist traits where it can call upon its impressive powers of flight to overcome the quarry, normally corvids. It also has the ability to 'ring up' above the chosen rook or crow in order to get the upper hand and by half closing its wings stoops at its quarry at speed, forcing its prey downwards.

When striking it delivers a lethal blow with its hind talon, often allowing its prey to fall freely to the ground before going down to collect it.

Superbly adapted to our climatic changes, it will make maximum use of high winds when game-hawking and with its short tail and high wing-loading (which reduces its buoyancy) is ideally suited to spectacular power flying.

Peregrines are by nature extrovert and inquisitive. Their wandering ability is testimony to that. In flight they will naturally explore areas from which they can benefit and they will do this increasingly once they are fit. They are well disposed to people and the term 'falcon gentle' is very well applied to them.

These combinations of characteristics make them exciting falcons to fly and comparatively easy to enter to quarry. They are persistent in chasing anything in front of them. One of our females, whilst waiting-on, became so excited by the dog working below her in the bracken that when a pipit sprung from the cover she was in immediate pursuit. She nimbly caught this morsel and proceeded to eat it on the wing. She then flew back up into position, waiting for something more substantial. Not only did it satisfy her curiosity, it also demonstrated her speed and agility.

This compulsion to chase can be put to good use when rook hawking. A gathering of rook in the fields will attempt to scatter as the falcon speeds towards them. As they rise, having spotted her approach, she will be among them before they have had too much time to form a tight group. She is then in a far better position to make a selection and it will usually be the last one to rise that she will attempt to take. A novice falcon won't know anything about her quarry, but her natural instincts come to the fore; with this ability of 'self training', she is remarkably quick on the uptake as well as being highly co-operative with her falconer.

Tiercels or males are masters of agility and speed. They are better suited to lowland hawking although many capable tiercels have been flown very successfully at red grouse and occasionally ptarmigan. With speed as their natural asset they are highly efficient on partridge and magpie and have been flown effectively on woodcock and snipe. (Rooks are definitely best left to the more powerful females.) With their short tails and high wing-loading they produce powerful, persistent flights at quarry and like the female are more than capable of handling very strong wind: in fact they are well suited to it. Peregrines are not particularly well designed for hot or warm weather flying and because of their wing-loading expend a great deal of energy in wing beats to keep aloft, far more so than desert falcons who are much more buoyant. Cool windy days bring out the very best in them.

The Traditional Hawk

Goshawk *(Accipiter gentilis)*
Range: Distributed right around the northern hemisphere and represented by nine geographical forms. Partially migratory. In North America it is a late autumn migrant; in northern Europe and Asia the species is more sedentary.
Flying weight: (F) 2 lb–2 lb 10 oz. (M) 1 lb 4 oz–1 lb 9 oz.

This is a hawk that is exclusively a bird of forested and wooded areas, particularly conifer woods, though it inhabits deciduous woods as well. Highly skilled at flying through thick forest, it will for preference nest close to the tree-tops where streams, forest rider, fire breaks or glades allow clear access. It was considered virtually extinct in this country during 19th century. Regular breeding was discovered in 1968, partly due to escapees or the release of falconers' birds.

A solitary bird, shy and secretive it is nevertheless a highly aggressive hunter. It takes a wide variety of mammals up to the size of brown hare and birds up to the size of capercaillie. Its usual technique is to take advantage of any cover to make surprise attacks on quarry, which it can take in flight either off nests, from branches or on the ground. It is also capable of stooping from great heights, in exactly the same way as a peregrine, usually at wood pigeon. It will pluck the quarry and eat it on the ground or take it to a low elevated point. It is an opportunist hunter that will take any prey of convenient size.

The goshawk's broad weight range is connected with its area of origin. Goshawks from Hungary and Czechoslovakia tend to be at the lower end of the scale, while the heaviest flown in this country are generally descended from Scandinavian birds. Those in the mid-weight range are of German stock. The quarry base in the wild would depend very much on the size of the hawk and this is reflected in falconry.

This hawk is the master of lowland hunting. Utterly fearless and determined, its powerful sprinting flight, ability to accelerate in the closing speed and its versatility and manoeuvrability in securing its prey put it into a class which has no equal.

However, like any maestro it can be prone to *prima-donna* behaviour and this is one of the reasons that it is sometimes difficult to handle. The goshawk most certainly is not a novice falconer's bird.

Well-manned goshawks are a pleasure to be with. Of all species they are least likely to present a problem in the field by objecting to strangers, or farm objects, or strange dogs. With the growing number of domestic-bred goshawks it is noticeable that these birds are less frenetic than their wild-imported parents and grandparents. Females are used to take a wide variety of quarry although the rabbit is the staple quarry for many. In conjunction with a German wire-hair or hunter-pointer retrievers they will become very efficient and can anticipate that the dog is about to flush. There is a distinct advantage of putting them up into trees. Working with the dog means that the gos, once elevated, will have additional speed to tackle fast powerful birds such as cock pheasants.

I have found that if I keep them on the fist while the dog is on point, they get so tense and excited waiting for the flush (once they know the routine) that they hurl themselves off fist into the cover at the slightest movement, or the mere sound of my voice commanding the dog. This usually ends up with the hawk being completely disadvantaged. It is far better to stand a little distance away from the pointer. If the gos decides to fly then she may well be in contention with quarry when it begins to move.

The flights out of trees are breathtaking. From these prominences the hawk can use the whole glossary of flying skills. With height and speed it can twist and whip through the trees and if the quarry is pheasant, which will normally leave the forest floor vertically, the gos will have the power and thrust to climb up into the canopy in pursuit. Male goshawks are far better equipped for this branch of tactical flying and over the initial 50 yards are faster than any female. With their high manoeuvrability they are capable of quite spectacular moves and in flight will frequently attempt to take bird quarry from underneath in order to immobilise it.

Females have the body weight for sustained power flying; if they cannot close the gap between themselves and their intended bird quarry they will accurately mark where it went in. When they arrive they will either launch an attack straight into the cover, or take stand in the nearest tree or vantage point, hoping that the quarry will reveal itself by moving, so that they can dive in and tackle it from above.

Rabbits are most often taken by females from the fist. As the gos is carried across fields or rough pasture, rabbits can be found lying out in clumps of cover. Flying her at slip affords some excellent long chases which may well tax her skills to the full. Should she miss her quarry she is more than capable of picking herself off the ground and from a standing start sprinting rapidly in pursuit and still catching it. The method of stopping ground quarry is always the same: the conquest is made by flying over the top and grasping the animal with one foot on the shoulder or neck and the other foot on the mask. This is highly effective in so much as it literally halts the prey in its tracks. In such a situation the quarry cannot get up and run any more and if it kicks, the gos with its long legs can simply hold the quarry away from its body. It despatches its quarry through repeated gripping and squeezing of its powerful talons. This action will puncture vital organs and combined with a crushing grip makes the gos capable of dealing with medium to large quarry.

Many males also acquit themselves well at rabbit. However the smaller birds may find this quarry intimidating and refuse to fly it even though the prey is abundant.

Being much smaller than the female, male goshawks are ideally suited to bird quarry, whether pheasant, partridge or duck. Their extra manoeuvrability is eminently more suited to these difficult prey species.

Goshawks are traditionally flown from the fist, mainly because this is their most attentive mode in the bond between falconer and hawk. However they do have another card up their sleeve: soaring and striking quarry from a height. This is not an easy combination to achieve as in this mode the gos is more independent. We have found this alternative method very useful where the gos is flown at a higher weight, is a total imprint, knows the terrain well and is capable of keeping a watchful eye on a dog working below.

Tree-lined cleughs, gullies or glens which hold pheasant and/or rabbit suit this type of method hunting. It should be in open country, not tightly wooded with limited vision. From this height the soaring gos will be in direct pursuit should there be any favourable movement.

Should they spot a departing pheasant or bolting rabbit from altitude, their quick reactions and impulsion have all the benefits of any soaring/hunting flight. By stooping they are just as successful in this approach and with the increased height and speed have a better chance of taking quarry in more difficult terrain. However, they prefer not to sustain their pitch for long and if nothing is happening they will go and sit in the tallest tree and switch to watching the dog from a 'still hunting' stance.

When being hunted in a well-fed state such as this the gos is far more inclined to come to a swung lure than it will to the fist. Lures are important when goshawking at any time, but more so in altitude flying. Dragged rabbit lures do not hold their attention in the same way as 'bird' lures so that by not coming in, the hawk may well drift off downwind. Their responses are keyed to 'flying' movement and the use of a lure designed for large falcons is ideal. Flying in this way is really an extension of following on through trees. An experienced gos will automatically do this when it is familiar with the dog working for it, particularly if it is most often flown through woodland. If you and the gos hunt frequently this way, then soaring flights will follow, especially when there are windy days to assist you.

Minature Traditionals

The merlin and the sparrowhawk have an important place in traditional hawking. Small though they may be, they are experts in specialised branches of advanced hawking which have changed little over the years. The merlin has been compared to the mighty gyr, and not without good reason. Much of her approach to her work is similar, particularly her style of flight. The sparrowhawk is very like her large cousin the goshawk. Her courage and unswerving aggression in the field make her a dashing, spectacular hunter. This falcon and This hawk are both capable of high speed and amazingly agile manoeuvering.

Merlin *(Falco columbarius)*
Range: Across northern North America, Europe and Asia, including Iceland and the British Isles, Scandinavia and Russia to Mongolia and Kamchatka.
Flying weight: (F) 6¾–8 oz. (M) 4½–6½ oz.

The merlin prefers open tracts of low, rough vegetation on uplands and foothills. In certain parts of its range it breeds in trees although it is less attracted to them than other small falcons are. Usually absent from tree habitats, it favours undulating land with wide horizons, especially upland valleys. It usually flies low, travelling near to the ground for hunting purposes. Its diet relies strongly on small birds, usually caught after short distance surprise attack. It is also capable of prolonged, persistent chasing and taking quarry in the stoop. It nests on moorland in heather, using some sites year after year. In some parts of the UK merlins remain resident throughout the year, but generally they seek milder climates in winter, especially around coastal areas and estuaries.

The merlin may at one time have been the lady's hawk, but today far more men fly this diminutive, fast little falcon. The flight that merlins are famed for is 'ringing up' after their quarry. This is a technique which they will readily adopt in the wild and one which eyases are more willing to explore than intermewed hawks. Once they commit themselves they will try to get above the bird they wish to catch; this may involve a direct approach underneath the quarry or a pair of birds ringing up simultaneously in parallel flight lines. If the merlin can force the issue with her quarry, she will have the distance advantage for a stoop as well.

Merlins can be carried unhooded and flown from the fist like hawks. As the majority of their bird quarry will be in rough pastureland, stubble field or heather they will need the advantage of instantaneous sighting in order to begin their pursuit. They will do this instinctively and will begin the chase with short, deep wing beats similar to those of a gyrfalcon. If the flight leaves the horizontal plane and becomes a vertical one, the merlin resembles the larger falcon in its capacity to 'stand' on its tail and pump itself up into the sky whilst in pursuit. In fact in 'power' flight it resembles a gyrfalcon in miniature.

Its small size means it is extremely agile in very tight turning circles and can keep its quarry in sight no matter how many jinks and swift turns it makes.

With its diminutive frame the merlin is usually fed on its quarry as it is capable of metabolising this by the following day. The energy it normally expends on its flights means that it benefits by being kept on as natural a diet as possible. Merlins are comparatively easy to train as they take to manning very quickly. Their trusting nature means that they form very strong bonds with their falconers and will as often as not return to the gauntlet as they will to the lure. Because they are flown directly from the fist, it is usual to carry them unhooded on the glove. In this situation they behave very much like hawks. They use the glove to full advantage in that they have the opportunity to see all around them. They are equally fast off the mark and can rapidly gain ground in straight, level flights. The sparrowhawk can use its longer leg to snatch at quarry, while the merlin has to be considerably closer to its prey; it achieves this by superior powers of flight.

They instinctively dash off the fist at any movement of birds in front of them and experience soon tells them which are going to be worth the effort in the chase. If they repeatedly catch small prey this will inevitably influence their choice when hunting in the future. If larger quarry is the general intention, then the merlin would be better held back on smaller birds and slipped only at the preferred quarry. Jacks (males) are equally adept in the chase. Their slightly smaller frame does not indicate a lack of ability and both male and female are extremely able falcons.

Sparrowhawk *(Accipiter nisus)*
Range: Widespread throughout most of the old world north of the tropics up to the Arctic Circle, from the Canaries across to western China and southern Kamchatka. For the northern part of its range it migrates south for the winter as far as India and Burma and in Africa as far as the Equator.
Flying Weight: (F) 7½–10 oz. (M) 4½–6½ oz.

The sparrowhawk frequents woodland at all altitudes, though for breeding it prefers well grown, undisturbed stands of conifer, or mixed conifer. It is less commonly found in deciduous woodland. Surprise attack is its staple method of hunting. It uses cover to hunt groups of small birds, often bordered by woodland edges, clearings, rides, copses, spinneys and orchards. It feeds almost entirely on birds, which it hunts in woods, in open country and around farms and villages. The female shows a preference for hunting in open fields and similar areas, while the male prefers woodland. Both sexes hunt from a secreted position waiting for prey to approach. They will then fly out fast and low, using cover as a blind to take the unsuspecting prey either in the air or from a perch. In reconnaissance hunting flights the sparrowhawk will more typically be seen flying low along hedgerows, zig-zagging from side to side or on the perimeters of woods, along paths, streams, bushes or buildings. Here it will opt for a speedy snatch, by sticking out one foot as it passes, or it may rise steeply with its quarry and take it from below. Once it has caught its prey it prefers to pluck it in cover, on a tree stump or on the branch of a tree.

These are most certainly not novice falconers' birds and indeed should not be handled or flown unless considerable experience has been gained flying and entering larger species.

Miniature traditional. The merlin.

The ferruginous hawk. One of their disadvantages is their huge gape.

Three imprinted sparrowhawk sisters.

Training the hawk.
Calling to the fist on the crean
(Philip Norgale)

(Above) Telemetry. I carry our equipment in a luminous rucksack. (R. Edmead)

(Below) Upland gamehawking

The falcon literally flies over the horse's neck.

There is often a conflict of desire in rook hawking.

Introduce basic retrieves over shallow water.

'She should be taught to eat her food on the lure next to the dog.'

Artificial incubation using Marsh Roll x incubators.

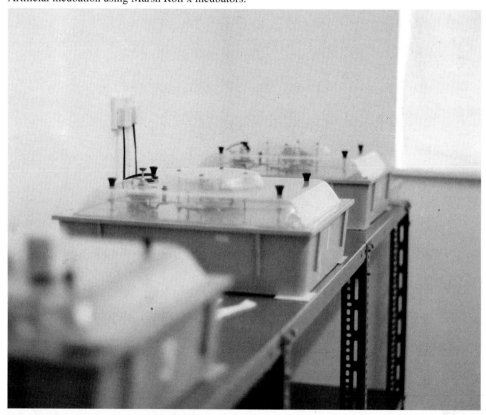

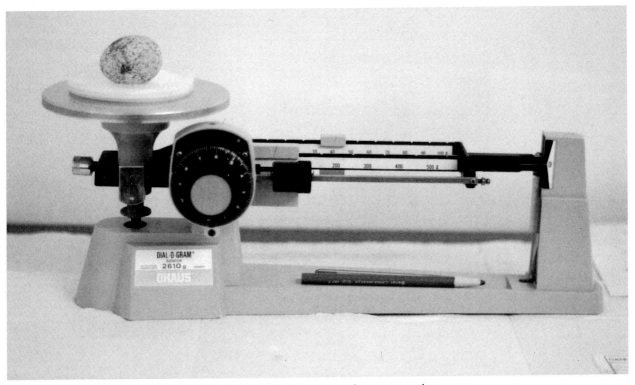

Weighing must be done accurately on gram scales.

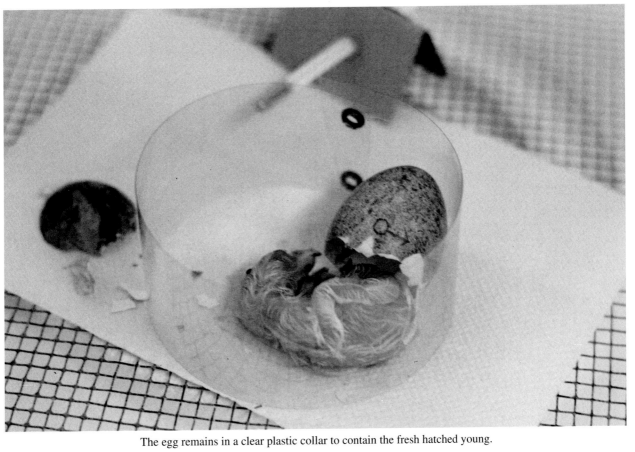

The egg remains in a clear plastic collar to contain the fresh hatched young.

(*Above*) She may immediately attempt to brood them or (*below*) she may automatically begin to feed them.

The female is a much better choice for the falconer than the male or 'musket', as he is simply too small and fragile for practical hawking.

The sparrowhawk is carried unhooded on the fist in the same manner as the merlin. She too is driven instinctively by sudden movement and will leave the fist with tremendous acceleration in pursuit of her quarry. She is almost exclusively a bird-catching raptor and with her long, fine toes she is very well equipped for the job. Hawking will normally be in areas that have hedges and ditches which will suit her style of hunting.

Like the goshawk she will work well with pointing and/or flushing dogs that can get into dense hedges and flush bird quarry for her. She too can be fussy as to whether she wants to fly with a dog in the field and needs to be manned and trained with one from the start; otherwise, imprinted or not, she is likely to go and sit in a tree and not come down until the dog is taken out of the field.

In enclosed country sparrowhawks are amply suited to dramatic, short-sprint flights that involve quick-fire change of direction and movement. Their style of flying uses up so much energy that they are normally out in the field for short periods only. They need to have their weight accurately monitored on a daily basis and in winter a supplementary feed in the morning is important, particularly if they are to be flying in the afternoon in cold weather.

Another method of slipping spars that has been tried is that of throwing. The hawk is held snugly in the palm of the right hand, which is gloved; when quarry is on the wing she is propelled in the same direction, which some say will give her the advantages of additional speed. However my experience of this has been that she gains very little. Normally her quarry is close to hedges and shrubbery, so by the time she is airborne she cannot navigate quickly enough in a tight space, or she simply objects to any situation that takes away her initiative and will go and sit in a tree until she's sure you won't repeat the exercise!

The sparrowhawk's attitude to hunting is such that it is usually safer to fly one at a time in the field, though this is not always the case. We have had three imprinted sisters together in large fields, flying either independently or semi-co-operatively. They were hand-reared imprints who had been raised and flown together from day one. They were quite happy taking stand in the same tree or bush and we observed little or no animosity between them. They would set off in hunting forays of their own choice, with the nearest to the quarry usually making the running. If all three happened to be in pursuit it was often the least successful of the flights as they jockeyed for position and their concentration levels were not as finely honed. However, although they predominantly hunted birds, their reflex actions and courage were such that one of the sisters sprinted after a very young rabbit and caught it. She was triggered by movement and, although she didn't repeat this chase, on that occasion she was rewarded with a larger than usual meal.

Sparrowhawks are capable of flights at pigeons, starlings, moorhens and partridge in the early part of the season, as these are large, testing quarry which can be found in the areas that really suit their style of flying.

Chapter 3
Hawks – The New Wave

The Red-Tailed Hawk *(Buteo jamaicensis)*
Range: North America as far north as the timberline in Canada and Alaska, and south to the mountains of western Panama, the Bahamas and West Indies. Within its range it is a common bird, residing in forest, desert and at a variety of elevations. Migrates from the colder parts of its range.
Flying weight: (F) 2 lb 8 oz–3 lb. (M) 2 lb–1 lb 5 oz.

In the last fifteen years this large member of the buzzard family has become one of the more popular species of hawk in UK falconry. Primarily flown at rabbit it lends itself to flights from the fist or from vantage points such as trees. It is highly aggressive by nature and the span of a female's foot makes her more than capable of tackling brown hare. It will attempt most quarry species that is within range, with males setting off after pheasant with intent. Their buzzard attributes also make them excellent hawks for soaring. Making use of favourable winds and sloping ground a well-trained red-tail enjoys the opportunity to soar above the falconer and from here is just as likely to be successful in a stoop at rabbit or pheasant and indeed has a distinct advantage by making use of height when hunting.

Given the choice they prefer to 'take stand' in trees, to have a good look round and fix their gaze on any form of movement from which they might benefit. Unlike goshawks and Harris hawks they will not throw themselves into the thickets on the off chance that they can execute a good rugby tackle, but will wait until the quarry is in a more committed position.

As they decide to attack, they launch themselves rapidly and determinedly, accelerating into a flat glide. They can close the distance with very few wing-beats and will certainly take on very long slips. They have a very supple feather which accommodates high impact. Once they are within range to strike they simply pile in with considerable force. With large ground quarry they will often twist and turn, fighting to get the best hold. Their feathers are quite capable of resisting collision of this kind.

Having caught its quarry the red-tail begins to resemble a small golden eagle. Its grip is fatal because of sheer pressure. Rearing back on its tail with wings spread and crest fanned and erect, it is to be respected and left to allow the adrenalin levels to subdue before you attempt to release it from the food source. This posturing is purely so that the red-tail can concentrate all her energies into ensuring her quarry is completely lifeless.

If on the other hand it is unlucky and misses its quarry by poor footing or mistiming, the red-tail, unlike goshawks and Harris hawks seems unable or unwilling to get up and take up the pursuit again. Sometimes a near miss will cause it to switch off and sit in the nearest tree to 'ponder the situation'!

In the wild red-tails are highly visible. They spend much of their time soaring and indeed are extremely vocal in each others company, often drawing attention to themselves.

All red-tails are shades of brown throughout their lives, but as their name implies their tail after their first moult develops a magnificent brick-red colour. In the USA there are several different colour phases which span fourteen different races or sub-species. Perhaps the two most spectacular are the Harlan's red-tail (*Harlani*), almost black in colour, and Krider's hawk (*Kriderii*), with an almost white tail.

In the wild the red-tail has a varied diet that consists of lizards, snakes and rabbit, but it has also been described as taking meadow mice in winter and medium or fairly large birds such as quail and meadowlarks, mainly caught on the ground. It makes particularly good use of telephone poles and other suitable look-outs from which it has a much better than average success rate in striking at prey.

The key to its aggression lies in its adaptability. Capable of maximising on all available food resources it is a competent hunter in the field.

The red-tail is too strong and powerful to be a beginner's bird. In addition, an imprinted individual can prove quite a handful. Robust and rugged they are long-lived and appear to have a strong resistance to disease.

Ferruginous Hawk *(Buteo regalis)*

Range: Dry, open country in south-western Canada and the west-central USA. Winters in the south-western United States and northern Mexico, including Baja California.
Flying Weight: (F) 3 lb 8 oz–3 lb 12 oz. (M) 2 lb 3 oz–2 lb 5oz.

In the wild this species of hawk inhabits open country, utilising mounds or hillocks when trees or posts are not available. It feeds chiefly on small to medium-sized mammals such as prairie dogs and ground squirrels. The males have been seen taking mice, rabbits and birds such as meadowlarks. When locusts are swarming they take large numbers. Because of their predilection for ground squirrels they will often build their nests near a colony of this species, feeding their young exclusively on this diet. However ground squirrels are prone to long periods of hibernation (five to seven months) and consequently ferruginous hawks have to be highly adapable. When the ground squirrels are not available they will seek out much large quarry such as desert hares, often tackling them with long distance pursuits, in a similar fashion to eagles.

Indeed their eagle-like quality is their greatest attribute. Between the sexes there is much greater dimorphism than with red-tails and generally speaking the females that are falconers' hawks in this country are more successful than the males, probably because males are too often faced at unsuitable quarry. The ferruginous has surprisingly small feet by comparison to its size. This feature can be related to the variable species of quarry taken and a foot designed to hold small or large mammals, very similar to that of the common buzzard.

Having said that, the ferruginous uses the strength of this smaller foot with great skill. Both females and males are at their best in soaring reconnaissance flights. As birds of open country they excel at stooping, particularly if there is assistance below and someone is helping to flush quarry for them. They can descend with incredible speed and a female on the attack at rabbit or hare in this manner packs a mighty punch.

Similarly, like eagles, they take on distance slips and tend to want to achieve high pitch to help them in the hunt. Perhaps one of their disadvantages is their huge gape: they can devour smaller quarry literally in one mouthful unless you get to them immediately. In the wild this could well be an essential adaptation which allows them to swallow squirrels, gophers etc rapidly, in order to evade predation by larger raptors such as golden eagles. Although they are not remotely keen on entering woods or dense cover, in open, hilly country they are exciting and challenging hawks to fly.

One other way in which they resemble eagles is in their loss of flying ability if their primaries get wet. The configuration of their primaries is indeed very similar to that of eagles with extended emarginated feathers. These are too narrow to shed water rapidly, which makes the feather look like a knife edge. Designed for deserts and arid savannah, these feathers mean that high rainfall climates can have an adverse effect on the ferruginous's flying.

However, they can counter this with their power of flight in the most windy of weather which would buffet Harris hawks or red-tails about; in fact they have been equated to gyrfalcons in their power and style. The speed with which these hawks stoop after quarry makes them one of the most spectacular of all buteos.

Harris Hawk *(Parabuteo unicinctus)*

Range: South-western Louisiana to Kansas, south-eastern California and southern Texas. South through Chile, central Argentina, Paraguay and east into Venezuela. Also found in Brazil.
Flying weight: (F) 2 lb– 2 lb 6 oz. (M) 1 lb 4 oz–1 lb 9 oz.

In the wild these can be found in semi-desert and arid savannah and occasionally in sparse woodland. They are often seen perched on tall cactus or telephone poles, quite often sitting beside another of the same species. The Harris hawk has been seen to take teal, rails (corncrake, landrail etc), gallinules (birds of the moorhen family) and small birds the size of thrushes. In addition it predates on rodents, full-grown rabbits and even jack rabbits.

This hawk has had a more dramatic effect than any other on modern falconry. Not particularly memorable for its size or plumage, its behaviour and adaptive qualities put it in a league of its own.

There is a huge weight range for this species in falconry, the sub-species *p u superior* is known to be larger and heavier. Many of the early imports to the UK were of this calibre. This sub-species is found in California, Arizona and Mexico. However the weight differential does not have any influence whatsoever on the bird's flying abilities – small or large they are outstanding performers.

Most known raptors hunt singly and perform outstandingly as individuals. Occasionally in falconry a cast of tiercel peregrines will excel at a certain quarry, but by nature they prefer to execute the whole hunt single-handed. Harris hawks actively engage in co-operative hunting. In the field, when flown as casts or social groups they hunt the same quarry without fear of reprisal or conflict in a form of avian mutualism.

This idiosyncratic behaviour makes the Harris one of the easiest of hawks to fly. It is gregarious by nature, which makes it a difficult hawk to lose in the field. No matter where the hunt has taken it, it needs to know where you are and will actively come looking for you. It can be flown direct from the fist at ground game (it makes an excellent rabbit hawk) and can be flown in a wide variety of terrain, be it woodland or fellside.

They are highly efficient still hunters. Their ability to see opportunities from which they can benefit enables them to make quite dramatic stoops into the densest of cover with the speed and determination of a goshawk. With their longer tarsi and span of foot similar to a goshawk's they can hold tricky quarry such as large rabbits in dense undergrowth.

Like all buzzard forms, Harris hawks can soar effortlessly over hilly terrain if they are physically fit. They enjoy this high-altitude flying and seem particularly adaptive if opportunities present themselves. Typically, they will simply crank over and descend at speed, wings held tight to their body, towards the cover below, throwing themselves into the heart of it to seize the quarry. They prefer to negotiate quarry in this style because they do not have the closing speed and acceleration of accipiters in level pursuit. Using height combined with stooping tactics, they can dramatically stop a bolting rabbit. They can equally perform this feat from the fist on quarry that is jinking and stopping, using cover to evade the hawk. In a straight line chase Harrises can stop and hold position briefly above the undergrowth. They check the movement below and if the quarry is there they 'wing over' and hurl themselves into the cover to secure it.

Male Harris hawks are just as versatile as the females. From an early age they seem to have a greater urge to hunt feather than fur. The majority of males are competent at rabbit and courageous in attempting larger quarry, but they prefer pheasants and smaller game birds, which they tackle with skill. Although not equipped with the sprinting powers of the tiercel goshawk they can accurately mark down a game bird that has gone into cover and by taking stand over it in a tree or bush will, upon the slightest movement within, hurl themselves after their quarry. Generally speaking they are successful in this method, but cannot compare to the more positive, spectacular techniques of the tiercel goshawks, who can take such quarry in flight.

Harris hawks seem particularly quick at interpreting the movement of falconers when a hunt is in progress. Where rabbits are in heavy cover such as bracken, or dense undergrowth in woods and copses, and the quickened pace of the falconer and dog indicate that a rabbit is running around in the cover, Harrises will leave their vantage point to cruise over the area being worked. Then, should the quarry move below, they are in an extremely good position to see it from above and take action. They will also use this method to hunt for themselves and this cruising, ad-lib style of hunting may well pay dividends, as it means they can check out a much larger area. Anything that they can see moving can be approached by stealth and of course the hawk already has momentum.

Lighter and less robust than their cousins the red-tail and the ferruginous, both male and female Harrises are more like the goshawk in their span of foot and approach to hunting. Like the gos the Harris can pick itself up from a standing start if it has missed the quarry to have one or more further attempts at it.

With a profound interest in a wide variety of quarry species, this versatile all-rounder has fast become the beginner's bird and advanced hawk in one; for most falconers it is all they will ever require.

Chapter 4
Falcons – The New Wave

The Prairie Falcon *(Falco mexicanus)*
Range: North America. Arid plains and steppes of the western United States, British Columbia, northern Alberta, Saskatchewan and western North Dakota. From California and Mexico across to southern Arizona, New Mexico and northern Texas. Common where it occurs.
Flying weight: (F) 1 lb 10 oz–2 lb. (M) 1 lb 2 oz–1 lb 4oz.

Probably the least known and least flown of the desert falcons in UK falconry terms. A fast, agile hunter similar to the peregrine but of a slighter build. In the wild it will perch on telephone poles and cliffs or even grassy hillocks. A bird of treeless, arid and semi-arid deserts, it is capable of taking a variety of mammals, lizards, insects and birds, but seems to prefer the smaller species of ground squirrel. Their ability to tackle formidable quarry is evident in the fact that a Californian ground squirrel can weigh 2 lb 3 oz and they also prey on the prairie dog, which weight up to 3 lb 3 oz. Their feathered diet usually consists of ground-nesting species such as quail, grouse, meadowlarks, doves etc; and these are caught by fast, low-flying attacks which take the prey entirely by surprise. During the breeding season the prairie tends to specialise, with a high proportion of birds featuring in their diet. This is also noticeable when squirrels have become dormant after the prairie's breeding season. During the winter months prairie falcons tend to congregate wherever large flocks of wintering birds are to be found.

By virtue of its adaptability and courage in the hunting field the prairie is a falcon of changeable personality invariably described as an irascible, excitable bird capable in the wild of merciless attacks on larger and slower hawks and eagles. Its temperament is certainly fiery – no doubt a genetic trait evolved through environmental influences. Any falcon that spends the greater part of its life in quite inhospitable terrain presumably has to develop the persona to withstand this.

The prairie is distinguishable from the saker falcon by its flatter, squarer head and particularly large eyes. Of all the falcons, the prairie has the largest eyes in comparison to its body. Quite how this is significant is not known.

Falconers can put the prairie's spirit and courage to good use. With a lighter wing-loading than peregrines it is capable of attaining a pitch quickly, but with a heavier wing-loading than either lugger or lanner, it is in fact very close to the saker in this respect. It would in fact be a perfect match for peregrines in aerial performance, were it not for the gale-force winds and damp climate in the UK.

The prairie's sheer aggression means it can be flown at quarry that peregrines might otherwise refuse. It can switch on to available species with alacrity in any variety of terrains. Of all the flacons it is the most capable of hurling itself into trees and bushes in pursuit of its prey and is a particularly excellent marker if the quarry has 'gone to ground' while it is still giving chase; it will throw itself into the exact spot the quarry entered in the hope of catching it.

The females can be flown at all lowland game. We have found that they make excellent pheasant hawks. Tiercels have been flown at grey partridge and red-legged partridge with a great deal of success. They are particularly good at waiting on flights, being less inclined to 'check' at other quarry. Little work has been done with upland game birds such as red grouse, as one of the main problems has been extremes of weather (high winds and rain) affecting the prairie's abilities in the air. Duck have also featured in their flying: they will commit themselves to this quarry with the same enthusiasm they apply to everything else; at times we have seen them to be quite devastating.

Several of our tiercels have also been used at magpie. They have been as productive as any male peregrine, perhaps more so, in that they are not afraid to enter cover while in pursuit. They capitalise on difficult terrain with waiting on flights combined with sleuth flying tactics similar to those used by sparrowhawks. In many ways more manoeuvrable than a peregrine, the prairie can be flown successfully in small fields. Its feathers are better equipped for 'smash and grab' attacks and are noticeably more supple. With an even lighter wing-loading than a female, the male can dramatically change his flight path and from the bottom of a stoop we have had a magnificent display of 'loop-the-loop' (as if on some giant roller-coaster) while in pursuit. Their dexterity with their feet means they are very accurate in snatching and binding.

These highly individual falcons are capable of taking a wide variety of quarry. They are not for novice falconers. It is highly responsive when trained. It is also courageous and daring. These stylish fliers are very capable in the field and not to be underestimated.

The Saker Falcon *(Falco cherrug)*

Range: Eastern Europe, on the edge of the Steppes: Czechoslovakia, Hungary, Bulgaria, Turkey, Yugoslavia and the Soviet Union. Also parts of Asia. From lower Austria east to Tibet and Mongolia. It migrates in winter to southern parts of the Soviet Union, China, Pakistan, the Middle East and areas of Mediterranean Europe (Tunisia, Italy). Has also been recorded in Sudan, Ethiopia and Kenya.
Flying Weight: (F) 2 lb–2 lb 3 oz. (M) 1 lb 7 oz– 1 lb 10 oz.

Probably no falcon has as many colour variations as the saker. In the nominate race the upper parts are sepia-brown with broad rufous feather edges producing a red tinge. Alternative colours range from a blend of white and tawny-red to gold and brown-black with a variety of one or all of these tones in any individual. Sakers present a stunning array of plumage. In the wild they can be confused with lanner and lugger when they winter together; in flight it is often difficult at a distance to tell them from these two and/or gyrfalcons. They are the favourite hunting bird in Arabia and like their cousins the prairie falcons they have considerable powers.

They still invite controversy through their colour from those to be found in the mountains of central Asia, which more than resembles the gyrfalcon. These Altai falcons are darker and larger than most other sakers and many people have long considered them a subdivision of the gyrfalcon. In evolutionary terms the saker is obviously very close to the gyrfalcon. Its vocalising, behaviour and ecological niche are very, very similar, far more so than any other corresponding desert falcon. The debate continues, montane race or separate species? For the moment the Altai falcon is included among the races of saker falcon.

This large desert falcon, like the prairie, is capable of taking a wide variety of ground game. Essentially a bird of open plain or steppe, it can be found on mountain plateau, but rarely on coasts. It shows a marked preference for small mammals, although birds are also an important part of its diet. When searching for ground quarry it flies in low, using 'snatch and grab' tactics. Occasionally it will fly overhead or go and still hunt by sitting on a perch and scanning for prey. With birds it makes aerial attacks by stooping and trying to catch it unawares. Its most important prey are rodents, susliks (European ground squirrels) making a very high percentage of the intake, with jerboas, gerbils, lemmings, voles, marmots and hamsters adding to the variety. It takes a wide range of birds, from larks to birds as large as herons and bustards. Pigeons, partridge, sand grouse and corvids feature strongly as prey items. Lizards and frogs have been recorded and are thought to comprise an important part of its diet in wintering quarters in India.

Solitary and territorial, it will frequent traditional eyries which may have been occupied for long periods by a succession of pairs. It also uses tree nests and will compete directly and aggressively for nests with larger species, particularly white-tailed sea eagle, imperial eagle and white stork. It will attack other species near an eyrie, but once it establishes superiority it has a reputation for tolerating other birds of prey, large or small in the same area.

Females have been successfully entered at pheasant, partridge, red-grouse, corvids and gulls. They are highly adaptive and have shown they can be successful at all of these quarry species, especially corvids. With their longer reach of leg and heavier wing-loading, they are less buoyant than the prairie and inclined to spend more time flying rather than floating up into position, in order to achieve optimum advantage in flight. Their larger body mass facilitates long chases combined with sustained aerial attacks, particularly when rooks are on passage. Because they have a greater bulk they prefer to fly when there is a degree of wind. A fit saker will cope very well with fairly strong winds. Utilising wind currents she can rise above ground level turbulence, attaining pitch very rapidly. From this vantage point she can put in power-driven stoops. If game birds are being flushed she can easily be called into position above to take advantage of pointers or flushing dogs below her.

She is equally well equipped for straight-line flying out of the hood. This may be on corvids or, in Arabia, at bustard. From this standpoint she is like a long-distance runner: her physical power is her secret. With her smaller footspan designed to catch and keep hold of small mammals, she will nevertheless take a fierce grip on any bird quarry. Because of their size males can tackle a wide variety of quarry from partridge and hen pheasant to corvids and small gulls. They are capable of low-level pursuit or waiting on flights.

Both male and female need plenty of space to fly in. They have a large wing area, very similar to that of the gyrfalcon, so that tight manoeuvrability is not as important as long distance, endurance flying, and in this they excel. Sakers have a tendency to be aloof and independent but will form strong bonds with their falconers. They are also by nature migratory and this may partly explain why in spring and autumn their attitude seems to change: there is a definite air of tension about them. During these periods they may often sit on their blocks, looking into the distance and making slow, deliberate wing beats. Their demeanour is more erratic and they seem to object to you being with them. Flying sakers that exhibit a marked mood swing will most likely end up with the falcon raking off away from you even if quarry is available. It is far better to stop flying the saker for at least three weeks during these seasonal activities and resume at a later date, when their instinctive desire to relocate has passed.

Gyrfalcon *(Falco Rusticolus)*
Range: Asia, Canadian Arctic, Arctic Europe, Greenland and Iceland. Mainly resident in the Arctic and subArctic above the treeline. Frequently found on sea cliffs and islands using overhanging cliffs commonly near sea-bird colonies.
Flying weight: Highly variable, given that within the species there is a very wide weight range.
(F) 2 lb 14 oz–3 lb 10 oz.   (M) 2 lb–2 lb 10 oz.

This magnificent bird, the largest of all falcons, has a wide variety of colour phases. The white phase is more often found in Greenland and the Canadian Arctic islands, with the black gyr occuring in northern Quebec and Labrador, and the grey through Scandinavia and the Russian Arctic. This plumage range is not limited geographically: any conceivable variation or intermediate colours may occur in any one individual.

The gyrfalcon feeds mainly on medium-sized birds and sometimes on mammals. Near coastal nesting sites it takes birds such as auks, kittiwakes and marine ducks; on inland sites ptarmigan, willow grouse and surface-feeding ducks, with ptarmigan far and away the main prey species. Other species include waders, passerines and black grouse. Capercaillie and Barnacle goose have been recorded as prey species, while lemmings, voles, ground squirrels and Arctic hares are taken, particularly when they are in abundance.

Gyrs use low-level flight attack, which is usually direct and rapid. They are capable of accelerating as the prey is flushed and can climb above it, gaining altitude for a final stoop. If this fails they can maintain the pursuit. They prefer to fly into the wind to catch prey and most of this is mainly taken from the ground or water rather than in direct flight. The gyr kills be sheer force of the strike and it is not necessary for it to kill every day. It may consume as much as 10.5 oz of meat in a day in the wild, but then may not need to kill again for up to a week.

Its power of direct, low-level flying is one of the reasons it is difficult to fly in falconry terms. However, much as it may choose to utilise this mode of attack when being flown, it is also receptive to being trained for 'waiting on' flights. One of the problems with the gyr is the amount of time that is required to get it fit. A half-fit gyrfalcon is more likely to try for straight and level flights at quarry than attempt to mount up for a good pitch. It excels in fierce winds and the variable climate in the north of the UK often provides it with ideal conditions. Jerkins (males) are easier to keep fit because of their smaller size. They are capable of tackling all quarry species available in this country and have also shown great style on red-grouse.

Their size often invites comments that they are too powerful for the quarry species available in the UK. Not so: in their natural habitat they would spend a great deal of time pursuing birds parallel to the requirements of a female peregrine. As ptarmigan can form a staple diet in the habitat the gyr may be frequenting, these equate to red-grouse as a suitable quarry. Pheasants are well within the remit of the male but would ideally suit the female, as a cock pheasant can attain a weight of 3 lb 8oz.

With their power of flight, boredom levels can quickly set in if they cannot see the point of the hunt. More than most birds of prey, they need to be in a situation that affords them the opportunity to be successful virtually every time they are flown. This not only maintains the element of fitness that is very important, it helps them develop an understanding of what is possible for them.

In wild populations it has been noted that they stay with their parents well after fledging. This may well be in direct relation to undeveloped skills in hunting and so a greater dependency on parental care. It is noticeable that young captive-bred gyrs seem to need a lot of motivation in their formative hunting lessons: they lack spontaneity and are far more inclined to want to sit on handy fences and walls. They may also simply go on a high-powered flight, then come and land next to you and start playing with tufts of grass! What does bring a change in attitude is the weather getting colder. This, coupled with windy days, excites them and makes them keener to use their obvious hunting potential.

In comparison to other raptors, gyrs often appear remarkably tame when being handled for the first time. This may well be because their natural habitat is such that it precludes human habitation and means they have not evolved a fear of man. However, although they may appear to be dealing with the closeness of the falconer and with their immediate surroundings with consummate ease, they may in reality be highly stressed but not conveying this as other raptors would. In the initial stages a gyr needs to be handled as if it were a wild bird, with plenty of time spent in acclimatising it slowly to its surroundings. Hooding is very important, as this helps to keep stress levels to a minimum and should not be overlooked just because the falcon appears to be sitting nice and quietly. Stress in gyrs can provoke a pathological reaction and they are particularly prone to aspergillosis.

However once they are fully conversant with their situation (in falconry terms) they are remarkably steady. Their playfulness and inquisitiveness never really leaves them and perhaps this characteristic sets them apart from other falcons. They retain their air of unpredictability in flying, but more than compensate by their power and ability in the chase. In the wild they are extremely good at chasing their quarry up into the air. This is not done like a ringing flight, but the gyr can literally stand on its tail and climb at a steep angle until it gets above its prey. In times past this method of hunting was adapted to flying out of the hood at herons, kites and cranes.

It would be interesting to see whether this technique could be used with gyrs at corvids and surface-feeding ducks on rivers and streams in this country and achieve the style of flight that best suits this falcon.

Lanner Falcon *(Falco Biarmicus)*
Range: The whole of Africa; southern Italy, Greece, Yugoslavia and east to Turkey; Libya and east to Jordan.
Flying Weight: (F) 1 lb 4 oz–1 lb 10 oz.   (M) 14 oz–1 lb 2 oz.

Despite the fact that there is a wide variation in weights for lanners the majority will be in the lower weight bracket. The larger body weights refer to the variety found in south-eastern Europe and Turkey *(f. b. feldeggii)*.

This falcon feeds chiefly on small to medium-sized birds but is also capable of taking a wide variety of vertebrates and large insects. Frequently seen stooping on quarry from above, it will also take prey on the ground in low-level attack. Bonded pairs will hunt co-operatively, although the lanner is generally solitary.

It takes birds from passerine size to pigeons and francolins, and small mammals such as rats, rabbits and bats. In desert areas it also takes reptiles and insects. Where waterholes occur congregations of twenty or more falcons may be seen. In parts of the Sahara, the sand grouse is a major source of food.

The lanner is one of the best known exotics in the UK. During the early 1970s it was the most commonly imported falcon and was flown at a wide variety of quarry. The experience many falconers gained with lanners at this time was as a direct result of the lack of peregrines available under licence. Females from the large European subspecies were the obvious choice but not many of these were available, the most commonly flow being Nigerian passage and eyas. Both males and females are talented and courageous. However, in the changeable climate of the UK, they are inconsistent in their desire to hunt. They are extremely buoyant and this ability is utilised very well in order to get up to a pitch that gives them a distinct advantage over their quarry. In Africa they will take a wide variety of birds of very different sizes. The UK does not have the range of prey, particularly in the doves which would suit the lanner, or the weather; it is consequently an indifferent game hawk and success with these falcons has been limited.

When they do decide to strike they are quite deadly. One of our imports successfully took red-grouse and indeed was quite wedded to them as a juvenile, but her slight frame of 1 lb 4 oz meant she just did not have the weight and potential finishing power of the prairie or saker falcon. She was far better suited to partridge, which she took with ease. As an intermewed hawk she was less consistent and generally less interested than she had been the previous year. With many of our lanners we found the same idiosyncratic behaviour. Our most recent female was a perfect example. She was domestic-bred in France and on her first outing decided to tackle hooded crows. This was almost her undoing. Once she had bound to one crow it was quickly joined by others which put her at risk. Her courage was unremitting, and several days later she repeated the contest. The lanneret, which was being flown in a cast with her, was just as bold and also attempted to take a difficult adversary, which proved far too much for either of them. However, their keenness in their first year was not carried through to subsequent years.

They can be productive falcons given opportunities to diversify. Small quarry of dove and pigeon size and partridge can suit them well. In addition they will 'check' at a wide variety of small birds from a waiting on position. In their rapport with their falconers they are faultless. Their ability to respond to discipline, with high mounting and waiting on flights, makes them excellent tutors for any degree of advanced work with their larger desert falcon cousins.

The lugger falcon *(Falco jugger)* of India is very similar to the lanner. It is an excellent flier and again is capable of high mounting flights with females acquitting themselves very well on quarry such as partridge. Although never as common as lanners in this country our experience of them is that they are marginally faster fliers and females once wedded to quarry do not appear to 'switch off' in the same way as lanners do once they have been through their first moult.

Hybrids

Cross-breeding of peregrine-type falcons came into prominence when it became impossible to obtain a peregrine from the wild under licence. Captive breeding was becoming successful worldwide and the pressure to produce this species was of paramount importance in all falcon projects. Hence peregrines were paired up in aviaries and there were just not the numbers available to fly. Hybrids were produced by artifical insemination and were quite simply a means to an end, yet they became accomplished falcons in their own right, inducing a whole new way of looking at the art of flying and at the prey base that might best suit them.

Hybrids exist in many other well-known forms such as cattle, dogs, pigs, horses, sheep, poultry and cage birds. In meat-producing animals heterosis (hybrid vigour) usually demonstrates an increase in size with better live weight gains and a greater resistance to disease. Obviously there is much to be gained from such matings and they too are a means to an end. Dogs, horses and cage birds are hybridised for any combination of factors such as beauty, ability, conformity, stamina. Whatever the motivation, because of its composition of diverse elements the end product will invariably contain many of the desirable factors.

In hybrid falcons the desirable factors are ease of training, size of falcon and aggression, i.e. aptitude for pursuit and capture of quarry. They are not intended for further breeding which cannot produce more desirable characteristics: as with any hybrid interbreeding, the offspring would be unlikely to exhibit the original hybrid vigour of the parents. These hybrids, too, are a means to an end, that of looking at alternative approaches to excellence of performance in falcon types.

Generally speaking when a hybrid is named the species of the tiercel is given first; hence peregrine x prairie means the peregrine is the male parent and the prairie the female parent. This is how they are recorded on registration documents in this country.

The Peregrine x Prairie Falcon
Flying weight: (F) 1 lb 10 oz–1 lb 14 oz. (M) 1 lb 2 oz–1 lb 5 oz.

First bred and flown in the USA, its field trials in the UK in the early '80s showed a falcon that was heavier than a prairie and at the lower weight range of a female peregrine, but was talented in a wide variety of quarry. The peregrine x prairie is highly aggressive, buoyant and courageous. The saying 'there's never been a bad one yet' is true to this day.

Females are very successful at pheasant, partridge, red-grouse and duck. They are highly adaptable to upland and low-ground hawking. With their lighter wing-loading and longer tails than peregrines they are far more buoyant and can acquire an impressive pitch readily and rapidly. Their combination breeding provides two falcon types that are capable of taking quarry from high position aerial attacks and here this hybrid excels. Positive and hard-hitting stoops are typical, with a courage that is reminiscent of prairies. Like the latter they are highly manoeuvrable and can perform spectacular loop-the-loops, stunning game birds at the bottom of a high stoop and with typical prairie adroitness bind to the quarry before it hits the ground.

Temperamentally they are more fiery than a peregrine but less so than a true prairie. They most certainly do not want to be imprints as the sheer aggression and temper of both types of falcons comes through, making it too difficult to handle.

They are adaptable within normal wind conditions in the UK, but because of their lighter wing-loading, very strong winds that are often encountered on high moorland or mountainous ground can interfere with their ability to get up to a commanding pitch. They may then either retreat to a calm vantage point or will expend too much energy trying to get above the buffeting winds. In these weather conditions a gyr x peregrine hybrid or peregrine would fair much better and be more consistent.

Males are equally very talented, they have taken every conceivable species of lowland game, including the upland red-grouse. Magpies have also been featured as potential quarry and, like the prairie and the peregrine, they are successful due to persistence. They are extremely agile – a trait inherited from the prairie side – and capable of throwing themselves into cover to secure their quarry.

Gyr x Peregrine Falcon
Flying Weight: (F) 2 lb 7 oz–2 lb 9 oz.   (M) 1 lb 8 oz–1 lb 10 oz.

These weights are purely for hybrids of gyr x *peregrinus peregrinus* and not of smaller subspecies, or of Peales hybrids.

These hybrids are large and powerful. The females are capable of taking all lowland and upland game birds. Their presence has only just been felt in the UK, but the small number that have been flown here have shown that they are very similar to the gyrs in their attitude and slowness to mature. Like the gyr they have the ability to accelerate with power and low-level pursuit is as likely a mode of attack as waiting on.

Their advantage over pure gyrs is that they are far more willing to co-operate in waiting-on flights (very much the peregrine aspect of their breeding) and from this vantage point can make dazzling stoops. Unlike peregrines they are less likely to make spectacular throw-ups from a miss on a high stoop but will make a shallower attempt in order revert to gyr tactics and level out for direct pursuit.

Like the gyrs they take a great deal of effort to keep fit (particularly females) because of their larger body mass compared to peregrines. However these females are far better equipped for flying in the strongest of winds, in which peregrines would be blown about. Their impressive handling of strong winds and their ability to 'tack into' the teeth of such weather makes them very much like the gyr. Equally in such wind they are also capable of hard-driving power chases that are persistent and in which they clearly have an advantage of speed and acceleration.

They need open country in order to fly well. With the driving power of the gyr in them they can navigate over large areas of ground so that pheasant, duck and red-grouse are ideally suited to them as all of these game birds utilise speed and distance as their method of evasion. Any of these require formidable fliers to catch them and this hybrid is well suited to the job.

They have been entered successfully at red grouse, corvids, duck, partridge and pheasant.

Gyr x Saker Falcon

Flying weight: (F) 2 lb 10 oz–2 lb 12 oz.   (M) 1 lb 14 oz–2 lb 2 oz.

Of all the gyr hybrids this is most like the gyrfalcon. Sakers and gyrs are in many ways physically and mentally akin, and the combination produces a lighter, more buoyant gyr type. Females are capable of tackling large quarry and their turn of speed is seen at its best in straight, level pursuit. They are very powerful and will take and handle a full grown cock pheasant, mallard duck and hare competently. Like the gyr they need windy days really to perform well and they put their larger wing area (compared to a saker) to very good use in gusty, stormy weather. Unlike the saker, who would find these weather conditions too squally for her liking, this hybrid is eminently suited to them.

Both male and female have been flown successfully, at low-ground quarry.

Chapter 5
Veterinary Advice on Raptor Keeping
Brian Heal, B.Vet.Med., MRCVS

CHECKING FOR SIGNS OF ILL HEALTH

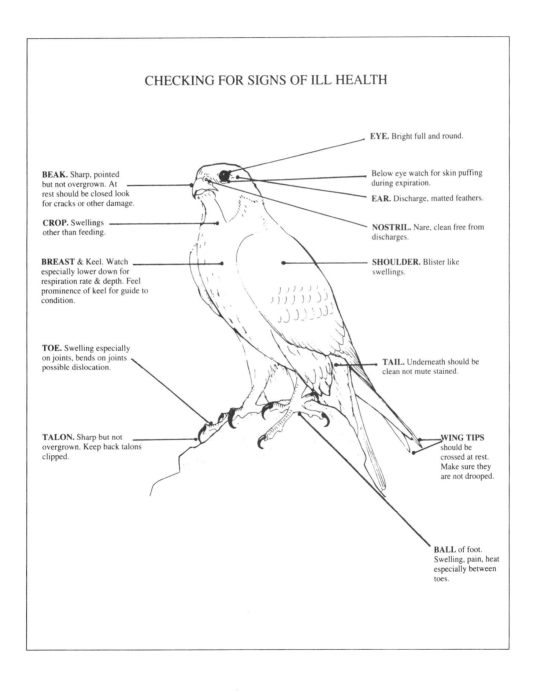

EYE. Bright full and round.

Below eye watch for skin puffing during expiration.

EAR. Discharge, matted feathers.

BEAK. Sharp, pointed but not overgrown. At rest should be closed look for cracks or other damage.

NOSTRIL. Nare, clean free from discharges.

CROP. Swellings other than feeding.

SHOULDER. Blister like swellings.

BREAST & Keel. Watch especially lower down for respiration rate & depth. Feel prominence of keel for guide to condition.

TOE. Swelling especially on joints, bends on joints possible dislocation.

TAIL. Underneath should be clean not mute stained.

TALON. Sharp but not overgrown. Keep back talons clipped.

WING TIPS should be crossed at rest. Make sure they are not drooped.

BALL of foot. Swelling, pain, heat especially between toes.

Many books and articles have been written on diseases of raptors, most assuming the reader already has a degree of veterinary knowledge or a wealth of experience in bird keeping. Very few seem to approach the subject from a point of view of recognising 'health' as opposed to recognising the symptoms of disease. What I hope to achieve in this chapter is to encourage the reader to study his or her birds in health and therefore be able to spot deviations from this state. To this end I think it is important that we have some knowledge and understanding of the functions of the various body systems so that we can better assess which area of the body is at fault when something goes wrong.

Like everything in nature our birds bodies are in a state of equilibrium, constantly being attacked by pathogens (harmful bacteria and viruses) and chemical substances which are being fought off by the body's defence mechanisms. Anything that happens to that body which weakens its defences increases the chances of one or more pathogens breaking into the body and causing a disease. So in our management of birds we must reduce change and stress to a minimum to give them every chance of winning the battle to maintain health.

Let us divide our examination for health into three parts:
  i. External appearance and muscular skeletal system
 ii. Respiratory system
iii Alimentary or digestive system, although in practice these will overlap.

External Appearance and Muscular Skeletal System
Watch the bird at rest and note its general demeanour: it should be alert and upright. The eyes should be bright, full and round, no sign of the third eyelid or any discharges (look for feathers stuck together). The beak should be closed, the nares should be clean and free from discharge. Check around the ears, especially for feathers stuck together. The feathers over the rest of the body should be sleek and laid flat. Any ruffling of the body feathers should be quickly repaired. If the bird is sitting with its feathers ruffled then it is ill and trying to conserve heat. It is normal for birds to stand on one leg for long periods when at rest, but if they consistently rest the same leg, there may be something wrong with the rested leg or foot.

The wings should be held close to the body and well up; if the tips are hanging down then all is not well. The wings will normally be held out if the bird has just bathed or is 'sunbathing'.

Watch its general behaviour, especially if the bird is loose in an aviary. The rest of the physical examination can only be made if the bird is handled daily. For a breeding bird your observations are going to be vital in assessing its health. Check every day that all food is cleared up in the aviary, especially in the summer. Decaying food can be a very serious source of infection; it can also be an early indicator that the bird's appetite is reduced.

Obviously with a bird that is flown a more detailed examination can be made. Its weight and condition will be checked; its legs and feet can be felt and examined visually. They should be clean and free from heat, swelling and pain. In falcons particularly watch for punctured feet: the hind talon can easily penetrate the 'ball' of the foot and introduce infection. This is particularly important: one of the commonest complaints I see is bumblefoot infection in the feet. The first indication of this is often a tendency to favour one leg, resting the other for as long as possible. Closer examination from above will often show a swelling between two toes or on the side of the foot. The swelling will be hot to touch. If the underside of the foot can be examined the swelling will usually be much more obvious, often with a hard centre or core and a reddened edge. Aviary birds will often be seen lying down for long periods of time especially if both feet are affected. In my opinion all cases should be treated surgically and the earlier in the condition surgery is performed the better the end result. Chronic bumblefoot will often result in the bird having to be destroyed, so spotting it early is imperative.

The wings too should be looked at closely and felt along their length. Pay particular attention to the carpus or wrist joint, as swellings in this region can be caused by repeated injury i.e. when bating or trying to fly off. The leading edge of the wing can strike the ground or any solid object. Obviously the source of the injury should be removed or the bird's situation changed so that it does not bate. This swelling over the carpal joint is often called blain. There is some debate as to whether these should be drained or not; my view is that they should not be. The 'blisters' are to protect the joint from further injury; if we drain them we are removing that protection (unless there is evidence that they are infected, in this case the chances of successful treatment are slim).

With a bird which is handled every day it is much easier to examine the mutes and pellets, especially if the bird is inside and the floor covered in paper. Mutes should have a dark, almost black centre, which can, when the bird's weight is being reduced, have a bright green tinge to it. However if the bird is high in condition and its weight constant then a green tinge should be considered abnormal. The quantity and consistency should be noted; if the dark centre is not formed the bird may be in the early stages of diarrhoea. The converse is also true: if the centre is very hard the bird is constipated, although this is not common. The liquid white outer part comes from the kidneys, so either an increase or decrease in the amount can be caused by kidney disease.

The pellets are formed from undigested remains of the food, fur, feather and bones, so the colour will vary depending on the type of food. Again if the bird is being dieted to bring its weight down they may become tinged with bright green – normal under these conditions, abnormal if the weight is constant. The pellets should not smell and should not be slimy; either could mean the start of 'sour crop'. Feel the area of the neck over the crop: if it feels spongy or the bird resents it, smell its breath. Once you have smelt sour crop you will not forget the fetid, sickly, rotting smell. Seek help immediately – this is not a condition which can be left until a more convenient time! If there is a considerable amount of food left in the crop it may be necessary to remove it surgically, otherwise irrigation with a crop/stomach tube followed by antibiotics should be sufficient.

Once your daily assessment of the bird is complete you must decide whether the information you have gathered means the bird is healthy or unhealthy and proceed accordingly. There is, however, one condition which you may suspect because something in your examination does not 'fit'. The feathers may be a bit dirty, the surroundings may be more disturbed than normal, the bird may appear a little 'vacant'. The possibility here is that the bird may have had a fit or seizure. They are quite common in accipiters and Harris hawks. Unless you actually see the bird in a fit it can be very difficult to diagnose. The two commonest causes are hypoglycaemia (too little sugar in the blood) and hypocalcaemia (too little calcium in the blood). Both are treatable, the former though you should be particularly careful with because it is effectively starvation. If you suspect a fit, weigh the bird, is it too light? – the answer has to be yes if the diagnosis is correct. Don't use starvation as a substitute for manning! There are of course many other causes but these are better left for the expert to distinguish.

Respiratory System

The respiratory system is perhaps even more important in birds than it is in humans. It has to be extremely efficient – it takes a lot of energy to fly and the only way this energy can be produced is by burning calories. This process is rather along the same lines as a car burning petrol to make it move: the burning can only take place when both petrol and oxygen are present, so as the engine's speed increases, so does its requirement for both petrol and oxygen. Exactly the same applies to birds: the faster they fly the greater the requirement for calories and oxygen. There is also another complicating factor limiting the lung capacity of birds, that is the development of the powerful flight muscles. To work effectively they need a rigid anchor to pull against. Unfortunately this 'anchor' is the ribs and rib cage. So we have the requirement for great lung capacity which must nevertheless be in a rigid framework – not an ideal combination. Imagine trying to run around with a belt tied tightly around your chest!

Nature has overcome these problems very effectively, though in a rather complicated way. The bird's lungs are effectively fixed, but by a system of air sacs, fresh (i.e. high in oxygen) air is passed through the lungs when the bird is breathing both in *and* out. The bird therefore gets twice the amount of oxygen out of each breath.

As the bird breathes in, some air will pass through the lungs (having much of the oxygen removed from it) and into the anterior air sacs. The remainder of the air will bypass the lungs and arrive in the posterior air sacs (so it will still have a high level of oxygen in it). As the bird breathes out, the air from the posterior sacs passes through the lungs and that from the anterior sacs passes straight back into the bronchi. Very clever and very effective!

However, this system can have its drawbacks. From a veterinary point of view, we have not only the lungs, which are susceptible to disease in the same way ours are, i.e. bronchitis, pneumonia and so on; but we also have vast areas of very thin-walled sacs spread throughout the body, many of them in places which are very vulnerable to injury. Once an air sac is punctured air can be drawn in through the puncture, avoiding all the body's normal filters and defence mechanisms which remove most harmful particles from the air.

So, how can our examination help to distinguish which part of the respiratory system is under attack?

First of all look for behaviour changes. Is the bird flicking food away, sneezing, coughing, are there any nasal discharges? If it is showing any of these signs, does it look 'ill', are its feathers ruffled: if not then the chances are the infection is limited to the upper respiratory tract or pathway, i.e. the nares, sinuses or trachea. Unless the condition has been present for a long time this is little more than a minor nuisance to the bird and it will eat and behave relatively normally. However, if the condition has been present a while and has progressed into the sinuses, then the bird will become more miserable. You may see the area of the face just below the eye puffing out as the bird breathes: this indicates that the sinuses are becoming blocked. It may also start to 'mouth breathe', especially when exerted. This makes eating quite difficult although the appetite may still be good. So when it is fed, the bird seems keen but will flick food about because it is difficult to swallow. The actual respiratory rate (breaths per minute) may not be affected unless the infection has progressed lower down the respiratory tract.

Once there is an infection in the lungs we can expect the bird to look 'ill', appetite reduced, respiratory rate increased and increased effort in breathing (watch the tail when the bird is at rest, it will go up and down with the respiration – the greater the movement, the more the respiratory effort). If a bird is showing these sort of symptoms, professional help should be sought immediately.

Infections in the air sacs may occur on their own or together with either or both the previous conditions. The signs will vary with the severity and extent of infection. Some cases actually go unnoticed until the bird is post mortemed for other reasons.

So, like humans, our birds can suffer the full range of respiratory conditions from mild inconvenience to death. There are various reports concerning the incidence of death by respiratory disorders: in all of them it came high on the list and in one case top of the list. So the moral is – ignore respiratory signs at your (or your bird's) peril!

There is perhaps one respiratory infection that I should mention specifically, partly because it can show any or all of the above signs, and partly because it is probably the most commonly diagnosed respiratory infection. That is aspergillosis.

It is a disease or syndrome caused by the fungus *Aspergillus fumigatus* (and possibly one or two other fungi). It is quite peculiar in that spores of the fungus are found almost everywhere, but most birds do not suffer from the disease; some factors are involved which prevent the bird reacting to the inhaled spores. One of these factors is genetic: certain types of bird are known to be more susceptible than others. The gyrfalcon, golden eagle, goshawk and red-tailed hawks can be considered most at risk: whether this susceptibility is related to their temperament making them more prone to 'stress' remains a matter for conjecture!

The symptoms vary enormously from asymptomatic, 'diagnosed post mortem as incidental to another cause of death', through mild to severe respiratory distress, with or without loss of appetite, vomiting, diarrhoea – in fact almost anything abnormal.

Diagnosis in the living bird can be very difficult. There is no single accurate test available. So it is normally diagnosed by building up a picture from clinical history, test results, radiography and possibly endoscopy. Treatment again is very difficult, few of the antifungal drugs seem to have a potent effect against *Aspergillus fumigatus* in the bird's body. Often combinations of drugs are used, some even washed directly into the lungs. The prognosis or outcome varies with the severity of symptoms; sometimes it is fairly localised in the treachea or perhaps in an air sac, which may be removable. If, however, the condition is widespread the prognosis must always be very poor.

Avoidance of the disease comes back to reducing stress, especially in the more susceptible species. it is important to keep aviaries clean, using coarse material on nest ledges, i.e.: not fine peat which can be dusty. Regular spraying around nest ledges and perches with a 'safe' disinfectant such as Virkon when the bird is not there will also help to reduce the level of infection in the aviary.

The Alimentary or Digestive System

The vast majority of problems associated with the digestive system are human induced, so this is one area where meticulous management can reap large benefits. Make sure your bird is not overfed, so that decomposing food is left around, or underfed, so that it becomes stressed and therefore susceptible to all sorts of disease. Pay particular attention to the *quality* of food given to your birds. I know in the wild raptors will often make use of road casualties and other carrion, but many wild raptors do not live to grand ages either, so *do not use* road casualties, animals or birds found dead in a field, or even shot birds or animals unless you are one hundred per cent certain they contain no lead, i.e. they are rifle shot. Also, if possible, take notice of what type of food your bird would eat in the wild: falcons tend to take flying prey, so it would make sense to give them a high proportion of birds in their diet. Similarly buzzards and red-tails tend to take ground game, so rabbits (be careful with the source) or rats would be better to give them.

Day-old chicks are probably the most widely available food source and are usually of reasonable quality; however, if you buy them fresh, make sure you have the freezer capacity to get them frozen quickly, especially in the summer. They are also not the most balanced of diets, so either do not feed them as the sole food source or use a supplement to balance their nutritional value.

A further comment on supplements: try and make sure the one you use is actually suitable for the purpose. A bird's requirement is generally 1.5 : 1, calcium:phosphorus but many supplements are based on bone meal, which only approximates to the correct balance of calcium to phosphorus (1.2:1). If you are feeding chicks, which have a low calcium-to-phosphorus ration (1:4), then this will not restore the balance; you need something with a high calcium level, such as Nutrobal by Vetark 40:1. Remember also that all supplements are designed to be fed at very low levels: giving more than the recommended level is not better, and in some cases can be harmful. Enough is enough!

If you are feeding a good balanced diet, supplements are not really necessary at all except during periods of stress – during the breeding period for example.

Probably the best food source for falcons is quail, generally in good supply (but may be short at certain times of the year), and fairly reliable in quality – although I have bought frozen ones which were black inside and covered in fly eggs, so shop around! Pigeons, too, are a very good source; availability is the problem here. One word of caution: many pigeons carry trichomoniasis (often known as 'frounce' in raptors), so be very careful and always remove the head, neck and crop. Gut them thoroughly, including the liver and then freeze them for three months; after that they should be pretty safe.

So after being meticulous in what we feed and how much, what do we look for to see if all is not well?

Much of the evidence we can gather about imbalances of the digestive system comes not from the bird but from its surroundings, which will contain its mutes and pellets. Again I will stress the importance of knowing what is normal for your bird: you must look at these signs daily – if you don't, how do you know whether they are normal or abnormal? By the same token, you cannot expect a virtual stranger (i.e. your vet) to know instantly that they are abnormal unless you can tell him or her what they are normally like.

The other obvious sign of digestive upset is a change in appetite. Change usually means reduction with most problems, but there are times when an increase in appetite, especially if the bird's weight is reducing or constant, can be a sign of trouble.

From the outside the only parts of the system which are visible are the mouth, the position of the crop and the cloaca. All of these can reveal small pieces of the jigsaw puzzle. The beak and the area immediately surrounding it are normally quite clean. If the bird has been vomiting it will probably be rather sticky and messy: opening the beak may show an excess of sticky saliva or small pieces of part-digested food which may be very smelly, all good indicators that the bird has vomited.

Obviously you cannot see into the crop (without an endoscope) but you can see whether it is swollen or not – if the bird has recently fed then it should be large, otherwise any swelling is abnormal. If you can feel the swelling and it is gassy or spongy, especially if the bird resents it, then it may have 'sour crop', where food is fermenting rather than being passed on into the proventriculous for digestion to continue (it smells very much like rotting food). If the swelling is hard or sharp, think whether the bird has had bones recently – it could be that some bone is still in the crop. The bird should be able to cope with this so leave things alone for 6-8 hours but watch carefully. The swelling may not be in the crop itself – if a piece of bone has penetrated the crop wall, there may well be an abscess forming. All of these conditions require veterinary attention.

At the other end of the system the cloaca can be examined visually and, by a vet, internally. Any matting of feathers around the cloaca should be carefully examined. If the matter is largely dark, then the problem is most likely diarrhoea; if it is predominantly white, then a kidney problem should be suspected.

If in the latter case there is also an apparent constipation then it is worth gently feeling the cloaca to find out if there is any obstruction: urates can crystallise in the cloaca causing a blockage. 'True' constipation is quite rare in raptors, so if there is no blockage, reduction in the amount of mutes passed will usually be due to reduction of food intake. (In aviary-kept birds look around for food 'caches' – food may be being stored, not consumed!)

Sometimes problems within the abdomen can be detected by gently feeling as tumours or a swollen liver can *sometimes* be felt. However, they can more easily be seen by a technique called laparoscopy. A small tube and light source is introduced into the abdomen via a small incision (usually under general anaesthetic). Most of the abdominal organs and some of the thoracic ones can then be seen – a very useful diagnostic tool.

Finally a word on veterinary care for your birds. Not all vets are familiar with raptors, and some may have definite aversion to creatures with sharp beaks and even sharper talons! So it is worthwhile ringing around vets in your area *before* your bird is ill or needs attention. Most practices will be able to provide emergency treatment, but it helps if you know who to ring before the emergency arises. If you are a member of a club, ask around and find out which practice the majority of people are using, on the basis that the more birds the vet sees, the more practised he will be at examining them and diagnosing problems.

Chapter 6
Game Hawking

Red grouse, partridge, pheasant and duck are the basic quarry of game hawks. They can be taken by a wide variety of hawks and falcons, but for sheer style and accomplishment the group of 'power' falcons and their respective hybrids which have the ability to wait on provide the supreme attraction of game hawking. Peregrines, prairies, peregrine x prairies, saker x peregrines, gyrfalcons, gyr x peregrines, gyr x sakes and gyr x prairies are all power birds that are superbly well adapted to the demands of energy levels needed to sustain precision flying and chasing of difficult, testing quarry.

To get them to this peak performance requires skill and essential training methods from the falconer, an accomplished and steady pointing dog, plus time and access to the habitat which best suits the particular game bird.

Training the Falcon
A falcon of the year taken from her aviary after she is hard penned will be like a wild bird, with little concept of people and their surroundings and a certain degree of temper. She will need to be coaxed into a strong, bonded relationship that will become a hunting partnership between herself, her falconer and the dog.

We start by kitting out our young 'trainees' with a good-fitting hood. They are then brought into the house firmly and expertly held in gloved hands. At this stage they are persistent biters and although they are hooded, if they find a purchase on any bare skin the fitting of their falconry equipment can become extremely painful!

Aylmeri anklets are fitted with mews jesses, a stainless steel swivel and round braid nylon leash. Bells are also put on at this point. In the next few weeks of her training the sound of her bells, even when she is sitting on her block, will indicate whether she is still, scratching an itch, or bating. These sounds are very useful indicators to you if she is not actually in sight. However, you may well need to repeat the performance of putting them on at regular intervals, as the falcon will attempt to remove them at her earliest convenience.

She remains with her hood on and will be shown how to stand on the glove. For her this is usually a difficult affair as she cannot see her perch and she knows you are somewhere close to her. She will quite naturally throw herself off, usually with a great degree of temper. She will be firmly and patiently put back on the glove, allowing her the opportunity to balance and get the 'feel' of her new perch. She is then walked for some length of time, perhaps as much as an hour. On our return she is taken to the weighing scales and her weight is recorded on the weight charts. At this point she should be steady enough to allow you to position her on to the weighing bar without throwing herself off in a frenzy of uncertainty and temper.

Walking her is part of the manning process and for falcons is one of the very best routines for developing steadiness. Her balance on the glove will improve as the walk progresses. At the end of the walking session she will be more composed than when she started. After weighing she is then gently asked to step back on to her block for the first time. Generally speaking she will do it if she can feel the block with her ankles. With your right hand gently lift her tail so that she can step backwards on to it. She is then put into quiet surroundings away from the noise of people and dogs that might upset her. In the twilight of the evening an attempt is made to feed her.

Pieces of rabbit with no casting are cut up so that she can swallow them easily and we can hold them in a pair of blunt-ended tweezers. In a semi-darkened room she is put back onto the glove and the hood is removed. Her initial reaction will be to open her beak and spread her wings out, because you are so close. The tweezers are slowly lifted to her mouth and the food put onto her tongue. If it is put in far enough she may well swallow immediately. If not she will flick the food away. When she does this I hold the tweezers with a piece of meat on and touch her breast with this hand. She may well then lean forward and strike at it, taking the food as she does so. In these initial sessions she will eat cautiously. As soon as she has finished, the hood is quietly and carefully put back on and she is returned to her perch. We remove their hoods when it is dark, because the birds are in strange surroundings and should they jump off their perch they will able to regain it unhampered. First light next morning they have their hoods replaced. These perches are always blocks on the ground, not more than 12-14 inches high with astroturf tops.

The following morning she will be taken through the same routine of walking, only this time for a longer period. During these carriage sessions the falcon should be stroked gently, either with your hand or with a feather if she's a biter. We stroke on her shoulders, then down her back and right down to the end of her tail. This is very important as we fit our telemetry on to tail mounts and the falcon must get used to having her tail touched and handled. Manning in this way will continue until she is capable of feeding freely from the fist in the evenings. When she will take food readily unhooded at dusk, we start to attempt to feed her during daylight.

Every twenty-four hours her weight is recorded. On a reduced diet it is very important to monitor weight reduction constantly to check that it is not too rapid and that she is receiving proportions of nutrients that will make her tractable but not weaken her.

Once she is feeding freely during daylight hours, she can be taken on her manning sessions unhooded with some tirings. These are usually rabbit backs that have had much of the meat scraped off, or pigeon wings which have very little flesh on and she will enjoy plucking. During these lessons the dog begins to make outings with you so that the bird can get used to it being part of the group. Initially it will need to be on the lead and gradually let off to run around. Rapid movement to begin with would alarm her, she wouldn't eat and she might even start bating. This would put back the valuable time you've spent with her. You can walk with her unhooded in this way until she loses interest in the tirings. You may wish to feed her all her food now or walk her again later on. Once she indicates that she's bored and begins to look around, put her hood back on. If this is not done smartly, then a bating contest will develop. Getting her back on the fist and hooding her while she's in a shrewish mood will only end up convincing her the glove is a far from agreeable place to be.

I often walk sakers and peregrines (once they will co-operate) unhooded on tirings, plus dogs on a lead, for thirty minutes. This advanced carriage makes them bombproof. They do not bate from the block when seeing you or the dog and they are less frightened of strange people.

As she becomes very confident with these lessons, the art of jumping for food is the next step. Exactly the same way as for a hawk, she will be placed onto a fence post or wall and asked to jump a leash length for her food. It doesn't take her very long to grasp the point of that! She will be rewarded with half her full meal so that we can repeat the learning process.

When she is sitting on the block outside unhooded she should be in a quiet part of the garden or in a sheltered weathering. Ideally she should have a wall or fence to her back so that you always approach her from the front. This effectively gives her time to view you and can stop her desire to bate away. Pick her up with a bechin (titbit) and she will come to welcome your visits. A bath should be available, weather permitting, so that she can make full use of her weathering time.

Once she is *au fait* with walking, feeding and basic jumping to the glove the next step is to get her to jump to the fist over longer distances. There is a school of thought that suggests this is an unnatural function for a falcon and that hawks are better trained in this way. I feel that any raptor that is expected to bond with a falconer and to associate the gauntlet with security and feeding should be capable of demonstrating this degree of training over a distance. If a falcon will not fly to you onto the glove over 30-40 yards and land on it for a reward simply because it has no fear of you, what chance have you when you lose it of going to pick it up, without having to resort to complicated techniques of getting it back? No amount of lure swinging will bring back a touchy falcon that is slightly high in weight and is shying *away from you*. In other words a breakdown in communication between the two of you is a direct result of inadequate manning. The process of extended glove feeding is an advanced form of manning that will produce a very steady and reliable falcon.

Now that she is going to fly to the glove on the creance, a whistle is used to signal to her that food is being presented. I use a thunderer or referee's whistle which is loud enough for her to hear at considerable distances. From now on the whistle will be used at all times when food or bechins are involved. Two people are needed to do this correctly. While one holds the hooded falcon, her falconer walks 6-8 feet away with a good portion of her meal on the glove. The bird is unhooded, the whistle is blown loudly and she should jump the distance to the food on the gauntlet. As she becomes more successful the distances are increased.

In mode of approach the falcon is unlike a hawk, which is more positive and will want to settle neatly on to the fist. The falcon is much more inclined to overshoot the glove, having attempted to snatch the food as she is going through. This is purely because she is a sky hunter and not familiar with landing into or onto objects with 'quarry', as hawks are. However, the force of her arrival is absorbed by moving forwards with her and getting her to correct herself on the glove. She will soon grasp that it is easier to feather down onto the gauntlet than to attempt to hit it hard and try vertical take-offs at the same time.

Only when she is capable of co-operating over the 40 yards to the glove will she begin her lure work. She may well show a degree of confusion here in the initial transition lesson. Having learned to come over a distance to the fist she will be looking for that method of feeding and not looking at the lure.

Lure work should be done as carefully as the previous lessons. Her introduction will be from a short distance, 3-6 feet. The lure, well garnished with the food *very tightly* tied down (so that she cannot steal the food and make off with it), will be dropped on to the floor for her. The person holding her should kneel down so that she has the shortest route to take to jump onto the lure. Whether she jumps to the floor and cautiously walks up to it or leaps onto it with determination doesn't matter. Her food must be on both sides so that if she should turn it over she is not disappointed. Allowing her to eat large rewards will get her to focus her attentions on the lure over longer distances. When she has finished her meal, bend down and with food in your glove blow the whistle so that she steps up on to your hand. Now the previous lessons to the fist will pay dividends. She will be very willing to jump up to you. If she is still busy examining the lure, wait until she looks up at you, then put the food under her breast, blow the whistle and get her to step up. On no account should she have one foot on the lure and another on the glove while you are trying to hoist her up off the ground. At all times she should be composed and she should step up onto you with minimal effort.

She will graduate to longer call-offs as she learns her early lessons. Now when she is on the lure it should be firmly pegged down and you should walk around and over her so that she continues to eat her food without concern. This gets her into the frame of mind that when you approach her, perhaps on quarry, she has no need to feel apprehensive, or worse still carry her quarry off. In my experience the use of heavily weighted lures does not prevent a falcon or hawk from carrying prey away. A bird certainly won't attempt to carry a heavy lure, but it will still carry quarry. What does have a more powerful impact on this aspect of behaviour is good initial training and manning.

While these lessons are being taught the dog should accompany you in the field at all times. It should be in the down position while the falcon is flying to the fist or the lure and the falcon should feel relaxed and composed in the dog's presence.

One further aspect of her training that will give her poise and allow her to concentrate on a sequence is the removal of the hood. This involves two people. If her handler shields her from the falconer with the lure, she will invariably rouse before take-off. If she is then held on the outstretched arm she will be in a more composed state of mind. She will be far less likely to bind to the glove and attempt to take-off still clutching at your fingers; this is a form of lure anxiety, in which she anticipates what she will do with the lure when she arrives. Far better that she has the sequence in its right order to start with, as this trains her mind to think in positive steps when out hunting.

Once she is prompt over 50-60 yards on the creance three or four times each day, the time is rapidly approaching for her maiden free flight.

Our falcons benefit from the well-contoured ground of the Border countryside which invariably has favourable winds blowing into them. Consequently maiden flights can be quite dramatic affairs. The novice falcon is called to her lure exactly as she has been in the past, and duly rewarded. On the second flight the lure is swung then hidden in the bag and for a brief moment you turn your back to her. As she wonders where her lure is, she takes the opportunity to swing past for a better look and will find herself flying into the prevailing wind. She invariably decides to explore and will drive out in front and upwind. Some of the novices, notably sakers and gyr x saker hybrids, prairies and prairie x peregrine hybrids, power their way into the saky as if they had always done this. At this stage in their training they are not very fit, so you should not allow them to remain aloft to the point where they become too tired and go and sit down. This is a habit they can quickly get into and it should be avoided. It takes an experienced eye to judge the right moment, but when she is at her highest point and still looking strong, blow the whistle and throw down the well-garnished lure for her so that she has to side slip through the airstream to land on it. Her return should be immediate. The falconer must not attempt to let go of the lure stick as in her enthusiasm she may well pick the whole item up and make off with it.

From this point on she is slowly going to build up muscle and stamina. She needs to work at this and yet without something to motivate her she will become lazy and be quite prepared to sit for long periods of time.

If she is to be flown at red grouse, then she should be ready to take up onto the hill for the start of the season. She will be keen to explore the sky and use her new-found flying skills; the instinctive desire to chase is of course, already there. We have noticed that if our falcons show a marked desire to hunt corvids and are successful, then without fail they prove to be excellent at grouse. In the summer months many of the fields near us are full of rooks and crows. Stubble fields are usually excellent areas to find them, as is marginal ground where they will be busy looking for leatherjackets, grubs and worms. Many of the adults will still be in the moult; these and young novice rooks provide the potential for the young falcon to learn her hunting skills. We normally fly our game hawks at corvids for some time, providing them with very necessary lessons in power flying, footing and stooping.

Flying in horizontal planes may seem a complete paradox to waiting-on training. However, the latter can only be achieved if the falcon is fit and has the energy to wait above you and in contact with you, in a form of opportunistic flying. In other words, once she is airborne and upwind of you, the activity of dogs and people below focus her attention. Should movement suddenly occur, say if grouse are flushed, she will immediately take the opportunity to chase. Whether she was in a good position is immaterial at this stage. She will begin the learning curve of precise positioning when she sees that her falconer will provide quarry for her. From this point on, particularly if she has become proficient on corvids, she will pay particular attention to detail and because of the bonding process that has taken place between her and the falconer she will quickly respond to her falconer's calls and signals to come into a commanding position in the sky.

Grouse are far more difficult for her to catch in any straight, level flying. It isn't long before she realises this and seeks a suitable alternative in order to try to secure them. With the opportunity on good grouse moors of repeating her lessons frequently, she is able to grasp the refinements of waiting-on very quickly.

The one factor that initiates her so well is that invariably there is nothing to check at on the moor. Were she able to fly after anything other than her chosen quarry, the intended lesson would be too difficult to execute.

Waiting-on flights are not easy to engineer if the ground is flat. It needs to be contoured, preferably quite hilly, with the wind blowing into the face of the hill you are flying from. Secondly, the falcon will require the ground to have some element of interest for her — preferably quarry species. Naturally quarry isn't going to be there every time you want the falcon to chase something, so alternative venues need to be found that have the options that she requires.

Once a bird begins to show the element of fitness and strength that will keep them airborne so that they can experiment with pitch above you, it is time to enter them on to your chosen quarry species. For a novice falcon this should always be as soon as that particular game season begins. Both falcon and food source are beginners. The falcon should be in a position to face young birds that will provide her with the confidence to improve her latent hunting skills, otherwise she may decide this is all too hard for her. This is exactly as her cousins in the wild would attempt to develop. If she learns quickly, then her prospects of survival are good if she is ever lost while flying and has to spend a night out. At least you know that she can fend for herself.

Once these lessons are mastered then it is not necessary to use a more experienced falcon on 'easy' quarry. That is the time to be selective and for you to fly her when everything is well on the wing, so that it can really test her skills. Normally this would be in her second season.

Training the Hawk

The training procedure for falcon and hawk is obviously very similar in the early stages. Goshawks will take considerably more time to 'man' than the more docile Harris hawks and as hawks invariably spend more time unhooded than falcons, great care needs to be spent when carrying them: what they see of their surrounding areas will influence their view of you and their immediate world.

When hawks are taken from their aviary for the first time as raw recruits, we hood them. The degree of stress a young hawk suffers when handled for the first time cannot be measured. In these early days of association hooding is vital. This is equally applicable to Harris hawks who if they are parent-reared, like goshawks, can be subject to stress-related fits, which are in direct response to environmental changes coupled with handling and controlled dieting.

They need to be kept in a mews free from interference from people and dogs. Like the falcons, weighing them and careful daily manning will bring them slowly towards accepting you.

Hooding may be comparitively easy to start with as the hawk is infinitely more frightened of you at this point and shutting out the harmful external stimuli is preferable to seeing you and having you too close to it. However, Harris hawks are capable of overcoming their initial fears in a much shorter time than goshawks and once they have done so are much more difficult to hood on a daily basis. They will simply not be hooded. For many falconers this becomes a trial of patience and in the end the Harris hawk remains unhooded. Although they are generally easy-going characters there are many occasions when it is much easier to hood the hawk – when hunting with other hawks, travelling in the car, etc.

A good-fitting hood is essential. During the lessons for hooding the hawk may continuously bate and or snake its head into its shoulders. Either way this becomes fraught with difficulty. In order to get the operation completed, first pull the braces slightly so that the neck opening is not quite as large. A hawk that bates when it sees you are going to hood it will eventually sit still long enough on the fist to fit the slightly closed hood. Bating will take more energy out of the hawk than out of you, so when it has had enough you will find that it hoods comparatively easily.

Hooding a snake-necked hawk is more complex. It simply doesn't allow any space for the hood to sit properly. Place the slightly closed hood onto its head, even though it does not fit properly. Because you are effectively blocking out the light, the hawk will move backwards, away from the hood. As it does so it will be leaning off the fist which will give you the chance to push the hood on properly, as it will have arched its neck into a better position. It does require a deft turn of hand, but when you put your mind to it, this is not too hard. As the hood slips neatly onto the head, either get an assistant to tighten the braces or quickly do so with your teeth.

Alternatively, if the hawk is capable of eating off the glove, put small titbits of meat into the hood. Hold the hood on the glove so that the hawk leans forwards and takes the piece of meat. Allow the hawk to do this over the course of several days and then try slipping the hood onto the hawk as it bends down to eat from inside it. Quickly take it off again. As you practise this routine, you can begin to leave the hood on for longer periods.

Hooding of difficult hawks becomes easier when this is practised each day and they begin to associate it with going out hunting. Goshawks and Harris hawks that have had time spent on this and have been preservered with do become good hooders.

As the basic training follows the same pattern to that of falcons, the hawk will begin to accept the closeness of a dog in your company. For hawks this is very important if you seriously intend to game hawk with them. If they cannot tolerate a pointing dog working with them, you are going to be relegated to random walking through fields and woods, hoping to spring some quarry species yourself. This is good for recreational walking, but not constructive to any form of advanced hawking. As hawks have a natural reluctance to work closely with what to them is another predator, you should be sensitive to the hawk's wariness when introducing it to your dog. Our own Harris hawks work particularly well out in the field with the wire-hairs, but if we attempt to walk the birds past the kennels, or have the dogs jump into the hawking vehicles, they simply revert to frenzied bird maniacs trying to get away from them. Their tolerance levels are only on a higher plane where the partnership has obvious benefits to the hawk. So that we don't have too fraught a journey with them, the dog is usually sitting in the front of the vehicle while they are in the back, or the hawks travel hooded or in hawking transit boxes, with their *bête noire* well out of sight.

Goshawks for some reason are not quite so insistent on this love-hate relationship with the dog. They are more composed when they are familiar with their hunting companion, although just to be contrary they are least likely to hunt when any other type of dog is in the same field as them. However for pheasant and partridge hunting a pointing dog is without question a vital part of goshawking. The gos doesn't take very long to realise that the dog on point will have immense benefit to its opportunity to catch these game birds.

To get them into this frame of mind, training in their early days is carefully monitored so that they are quite prepared to complete their lessons with the dog always in their presence. While we are practising calling to the fist on the creance, distance work and chasing the dragged lure, we will always have the dog lying down in the training paddocks so that the hawk can see it. When the bird is eating from the lure, the dog is brought steadily closer each day until it can lie almost with its nose against the hawk.

As the lessons progress and the hawk is taken off the creance, call-offs to the glove for bechins will initially still be with the dog lying still. Later as the hawk becomes more confident with flying freely to us, we allow the dog to run around. Sometimes young hawks that get themselves into tall trees for the first time show a marked reluctance to come down. This is not necessarily because they are a little heavy, or high in weight but often because they haven't learned how to approach your glove from a height. In this dilemma they can remain up there for some time and other factors which were normally quite acceptable before – such as the dog running around – add to their nervousness. They must be taught how to approach you from early free-flight training by using small trees (dead ones are the best); as you walk a short distance away, call the hawk to you. You can then graduate the height and distance from which the hawk will come to you. Fit hawks that leave the fist and can power their way right up into the top canopy of oaks and beeches are quite spectacular to watch. This is very good training for vertical flying, particularly for flying at pheasant.

Goshawks are much more inclined to make their first kill rapidly after training than are falcons. They are instantly activated and triggered to respond to movement which, combined with their natural reflex action, means they may well be onto a rabbit or game bird without knowing quite what all the fuss was about.

Harris hawks develop at a slower pace and are by comparison very immature for a longer period. By this I mean that young Harris hawks often are singularly uninterested in what might well have been easy quarry to the gos. They tend still to look to their falconer for food and seem unable to relate rabbit lure training to hunting in the field. Again this is very much tied in with fitness of the hawk, but the will to chase moving quarry seems to be linked to their interest in exploring their immediate surroundings. Once they understand that they are free to fly into trees other than the one they're sitting in, they may well begin to look with greater interest in the undergrowth below. During these periods of self learning they most often take the initiative for the first time by pursuing rabbit in cover. Although ferreting is a good way of producing many opportunities to hunt this quarry, it still has the drawback that the Harris hawk may not be mature enough to want to tackle rabbit.

When using goshawks at gamebirds I prefer to have them in a tree wherever possible: there they have the advantage of height, which will also give them speed. In close, dense woodland, it may be that it will be of greater benefit for the hawk to remain on the fist. In tight woods the hawks often go and sit in the trees that offer the least opportunity to get to grips with their quarry. They're just too far away from the action. Once the dog has a point, then walking over and standing to one side of the dog will give the hawk the opportunity to sprint and rise with pheasants over a short distance and to manoeuvre rapidly between the trunks of the trees.

Hawks flown in conjunction with pointing dogs soon become very fit indeed and, with opportunities to tackle a variety of quarry, will learn to identify strongly with them. To this end they will soon begin to follow the dog through the woods in order to be in the right place at the right time.

Although Harris hawks and goshawks won't travel too far out of range on a hunting day, we use telemetry on them at all times. Often if they've made a kill they will attempt to drag it into cover and you might spend the next few hours looking all over the place for them. Instinctively they remain silent when you're close to them and if you cannot actually see them they may well have eaten all their kill before you'd find them. Telemetry takes the agony out of searching tediously for the 'lost' hawk and certainly makes the flying of them more fun as they can become more adventurous without causing the falconer to panic.

The sound of bells can often be muffled by undergrowth or quarry feathers, or the hawk remaining still. We use the dogs on these occasions to locate before we resort to the use of telemetry. By going into the undergrowth in an area where we think the hawk is, the dog can hear even the slightest 'chick' of a hawk's bell. If it has quarry with it, the dog will be particularly slow in coming out. It usually likes to get up close to see what the bird has caught. In addition if it has found the hawk the dog will be quite willing to go back into the cover to relocate it. This is merely because the hawk has got an item of quarry and the dog is ever hopeful that it may give up its prize so that it can retrieve it to you! A little bit of rivalry, but nevertheless another way of helping you.

Telemetry

For many years I never used telemetry. Good, resonant bells were always the way of locating the goshawks. However flying falcons was a different matter. Unless you were flying in vast open spaces, which for the most part we weren't, then it could be hazardous if you had the hawk's weight wrong – you might well have to spend much of the day (and the following days) looking for it. We have used telemetry for the last fifiteen years. It does allow a much greater freedom in the flying of both long-wing and short-wing when fully trained. It was never designed to short-cut the manning process, but it does allow the hawks to carry a bit more weight, which allows them greater powers of flight over greater distances. The major change it has ultimately made is in enabling us to fly falcons in enclosed country.

The transmitter can be mounted on the hawk in three ways: leg mount, tail mount or neck mount. I prefer the tail mount in all cases, although from time-to-time it becomes vulnerable if it stands too proud on the deck feathers. In this case a hawk or falcon going into or low over some obstacle such as a fence or a bush can wrench the decks clean out. Leg mounts have always got the problem of being knocked about if the hawk lands hard onto dry stone walls or buildings and is very easily pulled and twisted by the hawk. Neck mounts I do not use. With the amount of wire we have here, they are a recipe for instant garrotting. Sadly a fine falcon of Ron Hartley's in Zimbabwe was lost this way. She had picked the only piece of fence for miles around to fly over and it happened to have a strand of wire on top. Her antennae caught round it like a whip. The result was a fatal accident.

Good transmitters can be purchased from the USA or in this country for use with both falcons and hawks. The receiver and hand-held directional aerial should be robust and well made so that they can withstand the knocks they will get out in the field.

When flying hawks at field meetings or social groups at weekends it is most likely that all the flying hawks will be wearing transmitters. We usually have our frequency

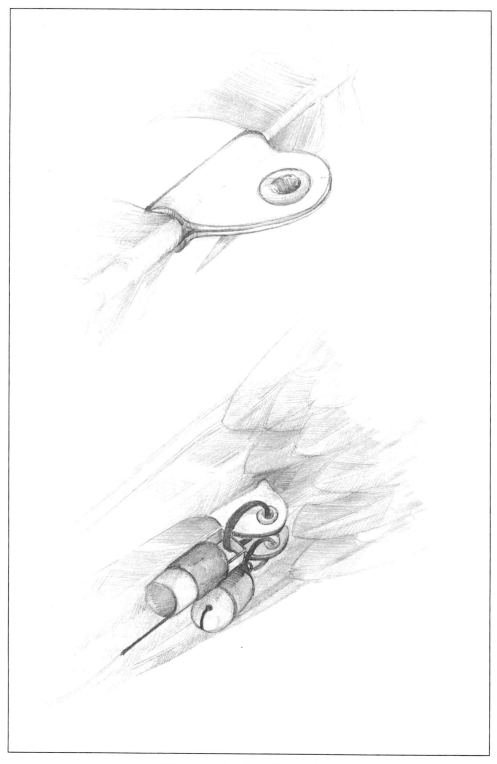

Telemetry. I prefer tail mounting.

written in indelible ink on the side or in the lid of the receiver box. It is a good idea to put a piece of sticky paper on the side of your box with all the other hawk's frequencies written on it. In the event of you having to join in the search for a friend's lost hawk you can switch instantly onto the right frequency.

Knowing your system is functional is vitally important before you ever lose a bird. When you cannot see where it has gone you have only the machine to guide you and you will need to trust it. You can rely on it in this way if you have already learned how to use it properly.

We live surrounded by vast tracts of conifer forest, in fact part of the largest man-made forest in Europe. We have found that trees absorb the signals of a lost hawk, making you believe that the bird may well be in the heart of the forest. Standing with your back to such natural obstructions and panning the hand-held aerial away from the trees will often give a much more precise and booming indication of where the hawk is.

Getting to the highest point on the immediate landscape is one of the best ways of receiving a signal. Very often the hawk will be down in the low ground, either on a kill or just flying around. Once you leave the high ground the signal may become very faint or disappear. Buildings, woods and forests, mountains and steep contours all act as a barrier to your hearing the signal. The use of a car roof-mounted aerial helps in these situations. Driving into the area where you anticipate the hawk to be will, if it is there, give a strong pulse on the receiver. Once this has been pinpointed, then it's out with the hand-held equipment to get an exact location mark. The equipment can be kept in a neat quiver or carrying bag (usually green in colour). I prefer to carry ours in a rucksack of a luminous colour. Then if I put the rucksack down on heather or deep cover I won't lose sight of it if I happen to walk away from it.

Not all hawks like or will tolerate having transmitters attached to their person. If your hawk is one of these then it is better to train it to wear a dummy transmitter at all times until it learns to leave it alone. Otherwise it will most certainly attempt to pull the real one to bits once it is out on the loose. I have known of cases where the hawk has taken the transmitter off and never been seen again.

Batteries which power the transmitters have a limited life-span. How long that is if you only have the system on for a couple of hours a day is unknown. However, they need to be tested individually each time you use them with a battery tester. If one is starting to show decline of power, replace it – or both if it's a double system. Generally speaking if they have had twenty days' continuous use, even of a short duration per day, then they should be discarded as a matter of routine. The cost of two replacement batteries is nothing to the cost of trying to replace a lost hawk.

Occasionally transmitters fail through no fault of yours. It is not common, but it does happen. If this occurs while your hawk is on the loose, there will be little you can do about it. More constructively, try not to panic. Go back to the area you last saw the hawk and begin luring. Falcons will often return to the area, even though they have never flown there before. Their locational ability is excellent. Flying another falcon in the same area will also attract her attention. Even if she's out all night, if you return to the place where you lost her early next morning, you may find her. In my experience a lost hawk does not travel very far away. High winds and abrupt changes in weather may alter the prospect of finding her, though. In these circumstances make it known in the area that you have a lost falcon: tell the police, the RSPCA, local licenced rehabilitation keepers and anyone else to whom a lost bird might be handed in. Also phone your case officer at the Department of the Environment: they will be able to inform you immediately if anybody has reported finding a falcon.

Chapter 7
Tame Hacking

Fitness is the key to a falcon's success, but there are different ways of achieving this. Hacking in its traditional sense is a very good way to allow falcons to become fit, as well as beginning to develop the flying skills necessary for hunting. The experience needed to monitor traditional hack and the correct terrain to have the falcons out and about means that not everyone can practise this. However, a possible alternative is tame hacking. This has been brought to a fine art by American falconers and we have found that it is a very useful element in the flying education of young falcons.

It requires a reliable system of telemetry with which you have experience. We use this method of hacking only on imprints. This is purely because they are already highly motivated to us and their desire to return to familiar surroundings is very strong.

Once the young falcon is capable of standing upright, at about five to six weeks, it is taken out on to some elevated position, preferably a hill, to become familiar with its immediate external environment. This is very similar to hacking as the young bird will need to identify its surroundings with landmarks and geography. However, from now on the process differs greatly. Tame hacking requires that you stay in the vicinity with the hawk; it can be also achieved with one youngster, while traditional hacking requires a group or crèche for success.

Weather permitting, the youngster is taken each day, and the dog will also accompany us on each outing. At these times it is encouraged to feed from the lure. Sometimes it will play with the food, at other times will want to eat. When it begins to see the lure as a reliable source of food and will jump on to it readily, it's time to start the tame hack. Now hard penned, the tail mount that we use can be fitted. In preparation the youngster will also have been equipped with aylmeri, jesses and bells, and will have learned to take the hood.

It can now begin to explore the immediate vicinity. This may mean hopping along the convenient dry-stone walls or taking a short flight around the field. It will find both you and the dog an attraction so it will want to keep you in sight. The dog may well be hunting round putting up small birds, which the falcon will often decide to chase. Finally when it looks as if the falcon doesn't want any more recreational work, drop the lure on the ground and it will come in for feeding. When it has eaten as much as you've tied on (about half its daily consumption) encourage it to leave the lure for the rest of the food in your gloved hand. This training session will probably last about an hour and concludes the day's hack.

At this point in the learning curve, the youngster does not require any weight reduction. Its enjoyment of flying and the knowledge that it will be fed are a positive form of control at this stage.

Imprints are quite unconcerned by the immediate world of humans. They will go and sit on anyone's barn or house and in fact allow strange people to approach very close. In many ways this is not a bad thing but it does have inherent dangers, so such birds always require watching.

Flying time is nearly always sometime during the afternoon and we begin to get the birds used to this timetable. They will also begin to start to work up an appetite around this time each day, which makes their interest in the lure more positive and they are slightly less inclined to want to stray too far. If they do go some distance, we find that if you go and sit out of sight it isn't long before they come back looking for you. This is because they view you as their parent and as such they still need you to feed them.

However, given good weather conditions during the tame hack they not only begin to develop their power of flight, they also start to explore their terrain. Any pigeons or crows in the immediate vicinity are destined to become target practice in the art of stooping and chasing! Young falcons can't help themselves – they are drawn like magnets to potential quarry, which naturally very quickly evades such 'childish' attempts at capture. If these larger species aren't in evidence, small birds such as pipits, finches, the thrush family, etc all get equal attention for chasing. The young falcon seems to relish these moments and can be seen putting in some stern chases with practice at 'throw ups' when possible.

Eventually the time arrives when the falcon will venture out in hunt mode and you can see by the speed and attitude that she is very determined. Sometimes with our falcons a local rookery is the prime target. Your falcon may well be harassing a quarry with intent and it is to be hoped that she doesn't actually make a kill at this point. Telemetry is important for keeping in touch with her, but very often if the foray is unsuccessful she will return home for her usual feed on the lure. Now is the time to bring her recreational flying under some degree of control.

Reducing the amount of food she is getting on the lure means that her appetite will be sharper the following day and her responses to the lure will subsequently be quicker and smarter. What is very important now is that the bird has the opportunity to hunt, with the falconer calling the tune. She has the power of flight, she can and will return willingly to the lure, and she is already beginning to show a desire to fly high, which is the introduction she will need for waiting-on flights.

Imprints

For many falconers these are a no-go zone. Their personalities are very different from those of parent-reared siblings and for many people they are anathema.

We have had our greatest successes with social imprints. They are paradoxically the easiest kind of falcon to work with in that they enjoy being with you. When they are being flown they may make long distance flights in pursuit of quarry but they are infinitely more inclined to turn back once they lose sight of you. They can also be flown in condition that does not require strict dieting.

The process of training begins virtually as soon as they can fly. Not only are they very familiar with you, but like the tame hack falcon they can be taken into their immediate flying grounds as downy young and from a very early age can identify with the area. Additionally they are always accompanied by one of the dogs and as the dog busies itself through bushes and undergrowth flushing small birds, the young falcon will instinctively begin chasing these – a prelude of things to come. All this preparatory work saves months of training in the formal way.

Because of these factors they are in contention with game at an early age and as a consequence are highly successful. The extreme aggression which they all display is what makes them quite spectacular in the field. They show much more courage and fortitude in their early days of game-hawking than do parent-reared falcons.

Non-Imprints

Parent-and/or foster-reared young suit the majority of falconers. They are unlikely to vocalise, they have very good manners, and they do not require the time-consuming work of the tame hack. Their training is done by orthodox methods and requires considerable time spent in the manning process. These birds are likely to be more reserved than imprints, and forming a bond with them must be done thoroughly. Because of the nature of their training they may well be introduced to quarry at a later stage than imprints. They must have plenty of opportunity to be amongst the species that you wish to fly them at because they will not have had the prior practice at chasing and footing which the tame hack bird or imprint has received. At the end of the day there should be no difference in performance: given time and circumstances they too should become excellent falcons in the field.

Chapter 8
Upland Game Hawking

Red Grouse

This has been called the king of game birds. A cousin of the North American and Scandinavian willow ptarmigan, it is exclusive to Britian and Ireland and is found mainly on the heather moors of northern England and Scotland. It is a handsome bird with feathered legs; the cock shows a prominent red eye wattle which is inflated during courtship and territorial disputes. Although it has a wide range of calls during the year, *go-back go-back* is one of the most distinctive sounds of British moorlands.

The red grouse is the only bird that has become adapted to feed predominantly on ling heather all year round. This tough diet of fibrous heather shoots requires a specialised gut; hence the grouse eat particles of quartz grit which are used to grind the heather in the large gizzard.

Adults weigh between 1¼–1½ lb on average, although with the falcons we have taken males up to 1¾ lb.

To hunt these fast-flying, dramatic game birds requires very fit falcons and experienced pointers. Falcons that are already capable of waiting on are far more likely to be successful: in fact, you should ideally use one that will come when you indicate either by glove swinging or whistle and not rake around the sky doing its own thing. Discipline and co-operation are paramount.

Young, inexperienced falcons, even though they are capable of waiting on, need to be brought into a position from which they can hope to benefit. Once the dog has got a rock-solid point, the unhooded falcon is cast into the wind. As she begins to mount upwind of you she should have made at least one cast over her hidden quarry. This will effectively cause the grouse to squat tight in the heather and keep a good watch on her. Providing you make no movement at this point the grouse will remain hidden. When the falcon has gained her pitch, begin to signal her back. At a height of 200–300 ft she would need to be in a very commanding position to catch her quarry when they flush. However, from heights of 500 ft up to 1,000 ft or more her exact position doesn't matter, as from here she will be in total control and can master the grouse's attempts to evade her. At the lower levels if she is out of position the grouse will realise, she has no chance to get to grips with them and may well flush of their own accord.

It is possible to navigate around the pointing dog in a large circle so that you eventually stand with the wind at your back looking towards the pointer. Somewhere between you and the dog are the grouse. You will need to estimate where you think they are; in addition you will need to go as far upwind as is necessary to bring the falcon into position, paying attention to the strength of the wind.

This action takes some experience to perfect, but it comes with knowing the length of your dog's 'nose', i.e. his normal range of drawing onto scent before he stops on point at the grouse. The falcon will need to be upwind far enough in front and a good height (400 ft plus). These tactics work best on windy days, which on moors tend to be most of the time. Bringing the waiting-on falcon directly over you puts her into a very good position for a downwind slip. It also effectively stops her waiting over the dog, which ninety per cent of the time will not be where the grouse are, as they will almost certainly have run on in front for a better exit.

As the command for flush is given, providing you are well in front of the grouse they should leave on a downwind circuit – which for the falcon is the advantage she's been looking for.

Many of the turn-of-the-century manuals wrote of heading the point. When the dog pointed they would walk around in a large circle until they were facing the dog and the falcon was then brought into a commanding position. The *Falconer* would then flush the grouse. In this instance the slips were always attempted downwind as the grouse were capable of flushing at any angle if the falcon moved out of position. This principle evolved mainly because the dogs could not be relied on to flush on command. To assist the falconer a spaniel was also used and was controlled by a dog handler.

Today the method of teaching an eyas about correct positioning is akin to heading the point, but the *dog* must do the flushing. With our young falcons who will literally follow you through the sky, we wait until they have reached their maximum pitch: you can see this when a bird turns into the wind, rests on her wings and fans her tail. The falconer will now begin to move out to the side of the pointer, making a 50–70 yard circle round in front of the dog. The falcon is beckoned to follow. As she does so should she move away in the sky, the falconer then stands still until she is called back once again into position, slightly in front and upwind.

The falcon will cause the grouse to remain still. If she is well disciplined, she will be obediently following her falconer with no loss of pitch. As she comes directly over you and is facing into the wind the call is made for flush. Should she not wait long enough in this position, you will need to bring her quickly back so that the flush is not made when she may well be flying further in front and away from the action. She will invariably be unsighted like this and will turn to meet her grouse at a complete disadvantage.

Success at upwind slips depends very much on circumstances. A young falcon trying these must be fit and have had previous flying experience shepherding and chasing quarry. In other words, she must be an accomplished flier. These slips are the easier of the two for a falcon to perform, as she can steer and navigate far better into the wind than she can downwind. By dropping in behind her quarry out of a high stoop she is aerodynamically in a better position to catch what is front of her.

The other vital ingredient is a dog of experience. For once the call to flush is made and you need to re-adjust the falcon's position the dog must be give the stop signal, to hold temporarily. Not every dog can execute such control to start with, but they should improve as they become more familiar with the job and their confidence grows.

The dog is capable of flushing the grouse right underneath the falcon. In her position over the falconer she is capable of turning either right or left and stooping back down onto them.

The flush should be engineered so that the grouse are pushed away from bracken beds or streams in which they will immediately drop into cover, giving the falcon little or no chance. If the point is on a hill which has the prevailing wind coming into it then flushing is best done along the side, otherwise the falcon will have to make allowances for uphill flights: in the early stages these may be beyond her range of experience in manoeuvrability.

Grouse hawking in August bears no comparison with that of September and early October when the young birds of the year have developed superb flying skills and are more than a match for any falcon. Their flight seems rocket-driven and their skills of outwitting and outmanoeuvring the falcon are equally stunning. They are compact and extemely strong, requiring large, hard-hitting falcons.

A high-mounting falcon will be in control of her grouse and can stoop at them even though they may flush wide of her. Very often, however, this can be something of a disadvantage, as it takes her so long to get down that the grouse have gone to cover in bracken beds or streams. Grouse are capable of expert use of contours, flying between them at incredible speed 1–3 feet above the ground, accelerating and twisting as they power away. They are masterful at outmanoeuvring the falcon. If she should get too close for comfort, they can twist upwards or downwards out of her line of attack, or simply throw themselves into the heather at the vital moment when the falcon simply cannot correct her trajectory. If she attempts to follow her quarry into cover they wait until she has stalled to land, then accelerate up and away.

Although the young falcon has a lot to learn she has few distractions on the moor to check at and can concentrate on getting it right.

Her one great ally is the dog. A well-trained dog that can locate game, be steady on the point, relocate running birds and be equally steady to flush is the very thing that will eventually make her. She will come to recognise that the stillness of the dog on point is worth investigating. In so doing she will pass over her intended quarry and cause them to squat. This will give the falconer time to get into an optimum position for the flush.

An experienced falcon can be spectacular. If she is high pitching, her response to the shouting for flush is dramatic. She simply rolls over into a vertical position, closes her wings and gains speed. From such a height she will resemble a raindrop as she hurtles earthwards to the grouse crossing underneath her. The stoop is breathtaking and this adaptive attack behaviour is taken to perfection when grouse hawking.

At the bottom of the stoop the falcon changes from the vertical to the horizontal position, aligning herself behind the grouse. She may well be reaching speeds of 100–150 mph and will soon close the gap. Her grouse is now very low to the ground as it uses every contour and outcrop of heather in an effort to unsight its pursuer.

At this point the falcon either masters the grouse by shepherding it in front of her, finally binding to it, or the grouse manages to dive into the cover, leaving the falcon travelling at such velocity that she cannot do anything other than sky upwards in an equally spectacular throw-up.

Sometimes the chosen grouse does very little in body swerves or counter moves and simply tries to outfly her. Should she make contact she will use direct impact as a means of stopping it. From a mortal blow such as this the grouse will often drop like a stone onto the heather below, while the falcon will throw up in a shallower arc, then winnow down beside it.

Concentrating on performance levels such as these means that it is always preferable to have someone else working the pointers for you when it is your turn to fly. This leaves you free to position the falcon and to get her into an optimum pitch in the sky without worrying about what the dog is doing. With one or more falconers on the moor, all with competent dogs, this role change works particularly well and is important in training novice grouse hawks.

Black Grouse

Blackcock (male) and greyhen (female) can sometimes be found on the periphery of moorland. To a large extent the availability of birch, the preferred winter food, determines their overall distribution. Pines and alders are also favoured tree species, particularly where the stands are sparse and between 20–60 feet in height.

Females, with their brown vermiculated plumage, resemble hen pheasants in their colouring but are considerably larger. They have a white wing bar and a slightly forked tail, which is really only visible in flight. The males are stunning in their glossy black feathers with a white wing bar, a bright red eye wattle and a unique lyre-shaped tail. In flight they alternate quick wing-beats and prolonged glides. With their dark colours they resemble capercaillies, but they are definitely more agile and have the distinct forked tails.

They are large and heavier than red grouse, but a good deal faster. In flight they resemble the pheasant in that they use straight-line flying as a means of exit, unlike the highly manoeuvrable red grouse.

It takes a hard-hitting falcon to tackle black grouse, particularly the cock, which needs to be taken in the stoop. As they are often seen in and around conifer plantations in the autumn their usual route of escape is into the tree line, which can make flying them rather difficult.

Ptarmigan

The most Arctic-adapted of all the grouse, the rock ptarmigan is more widely distributed in the high Arctic. In Scotland they occur at altitudes of over 2,000 ft and are to be found in mountainous habitat. During summer they resemble red-grouse in their plumage, but in winter both sexes are mostly white with blackish tails. They feed on a variety of low-growing plants, particularly evergreen and berry-producing species. In winter they will seek out those that are easily accessible and have a high sugar content, although those with a high protein content are also eaten when available.

Although the rock ptarmigan is the most northerly breeding of the ptarmigans, it is considerably smaller than the willow ptarmigan (red grouse). This is curious when one consider that Arctic-breeding birds normally have a greater body weight. This could well be in direct relation to the fact that smaller body size is applicable to reduced food supplies.

Flying falcons at these Arctic-Alpine birds is something of a challenge simply because of the climb one has to negotiate to get them, over 2,000 ft above sea level. They are noticeably less nervous than other game birds of seeing human beings, which again is probably a direct result of living in a hostile environment where few humans venture. The few that have been flown by falcons are comparatively easily caught and are nowhere near as testing a quarry as their lower-altitude cousins.

Chapter 9
Lowland Hawking

Partridge

Partridge hawking is rather like grouse hawking in its need for falcons that will wait on and can recognise the role of the pointer in the field. However, falcons flying at partridge do not always require the assistance of a dog and consequently partridge are an easier quarry than grouse.

Falcons that have come direct from upland game hawking onto partridge ground may well have evolved a pitch that is just too high for this exercise. After a few abortive attempts from 400-foot pitches they soon learn to drop down to a height that will give them a chance to be successful. The grey partridge is far and away the more sporting game bird; the red-legged partridge has a tendency to run rather than to fly as a covey.

Partridge are usually marked down in fields of stubble or on the plough, giving the falconer time to decide on a plan of campaign. Over large tracts of ground known to be good partridge-feeding areas, binoculars will be needed to scan and pinpoint them. They are wonderfully adept at disappearing unnoticed into cover, which is generally the time that we use the dogs to relocate them.

These superb little game birds, weighing 13–15 oz, are made up of a large and diverse group of Old World birds of eighty-four species in about seventeen genera. These include bush quail, francolins, spurfowl, snowcocks and pheasant grouse; grey, red-legged, sand, snow, stone, tree, wood and bamboo partridge. In most species they are similar in sex and pattern. They nearly all prefer grassland, scrub and farmland, yet can inhabit desert or Alpine meadows and dense tropical rainforest. Most partridge are monogamous and a pair remain formed throughout the year. They are also highly gregarious and can be found for much of the year in coveys comprising one or more family parties. These vary in number between four and ten or sometimes more. In spring the bonded pair leave the covey and remain dispersed during breeding. Solitary and territorial, they do not defend boundaries, but observe a tolerance of close proximity which is akin to territorialism.

Sadly the grey partridges *(Perdix perdix)* are nowhere near as common as they ought to be throughout the UK and the current decline is largely due to the increased use of pesticides which kills chick food. However, where they do occur they are abundant.

Many varieties of falcons, tiercels and their hybrids are flown at this quarry with great success. One of the early falcons that we flew who got to know her job very well was an imported passage lanner falcon. Lanners are particularly good at waiting-on and this facet of her hunting technique was used in a dual role of search and locate. She would be cast off in an area of a reliable initial sighting of a covey and as she got up to a commanding pitch at 150–200 feet, the wire-haired pointer was quartered-on in front. The airborne falcon would effectively cause the covey to freeze and the pointer could then give an accurate indication of their position. By bringing the falcon round upwind of the point we could usually provide the perfect flush for her, and she became very accomplished in this style of hunting. Interestingly enough this same falcon was taken onto the grouse moor prior to partridge hawking and was one of the very few known lanners to take red grouse.

Tiercel peregrines or relative tiercel hybrids are the ideal size of falcon for these game birds. With their smaller frame they are more highly manoeuvrable and consequently can make adjustments quickly when flying in or around cover. Falcons are generally overpowered for this quarry and are more than capable of carrying grey partridge, which is a vice not to be encouraged.

It is just as possible to fly at coveys without the use of a dog. When they are out on large stubble fields feeding it is quite possible to mark them down and with a small group of helpers beat them up for the falcon. Once they have been spotted the falcon should be cast off so that the covey remains still. As the pitch is reached the line of beaters begins to walk towards the covey until it flushes. By waiting-on over the falconer the falcon should be able to stoop upwind or downwind. As partridge are not such strong fliers as grouse, the necessity of downwind stooping is not quite so critical.

One area they will attempt to fly into with regularity are crop fields. Turnips, oil-seed rape and brassicas all have an immediate attraction for departing coveys as it is much more difficult to reflush them from this dense form of cover. In here they will run around with gay abandon and although the dog will point them they never seem to remain in the immediate area the dog first located them. Attempting to get them out of this cover usually has the waiting-on falcon dropping its pitch or, worse still, going after check. Partridges really need to be in the open for the falcon to be successful.

Pheasants

No game birds can compare to non-domesticated pheasants. Today, through the release scheme of many country estates, large quantities of home-reared birds are to be seen and admired virtually in every field and by-way. It is very tempting to fly these as quarry during the best months of long-wing flying, but these birds never really test the flying skills of long-wings until late in the season, when falconers have normally put their hawks down for the moult as keeping them fit during the short winter days is too much of a problem.

Wild-raised birds are a different kettle of fish. As soon as the season begins these birds are fast and hard on the wing, capable of distance flying and maximum use of cover as escape routes. To take either sex, but particularly the cock birds needs powerful, determined peregrine falcons or any of the power-bird hybrids. Cock pheasants are extremely tough characters and with their power of flight can accelerate and climb with ease, which means the long-wing in pursuit has to be fit.

Most pheasants worldwide inhabit forests. They are heavy birds, with short, round wings, curved and fitting closely to the body. They are capable of powerful, fast flight, offset by the fact that this is not sustained for long. An introduced species it is now well established and can be found in all areas that have mixed woodland, open grassland, rocky hillsides or reed-beds. Pheasants are normally sedentary and remain attached to their locality. The polygamous males defend territories in which one or more females live.

Should the falcon be capable of waiting-on, then the situation can quickly become dramatic. From her pitch she will stoop at the pheasant and most certainly attempt to come in behind for a bind. Pheasant appear to be remarkably easy once they have been caught in this manner and do not in general tax the falcon's agility, merely her staying power.

Dogs are always used to locate pheasants, which can be found and pointed best in cover. The ideal cover is root crop or hedge bottom, as woods or copses generally mean the falcon will be unsighted at crucial times. Providing the game cover is not near woods and there is some distance between the next patch, some excellent flights can be had. Hedge bottoms are a great favourite for pheasants (and partridge). It is far more difficult to execute a flush from these areas as the birds run like blazes along the bottom. The technique of executing the right flush is important if the falcon is to understand what is required of her. However I do find pheasant instructional as quarry for long-wings in one other respect: it teaches them to wait-on in country that has many opportunities for check. Pheasants, because of their size and comparative ease of flushing, allow the falcons to concentrate on what is going on below them and not to be easily distracted.

Ducks

Ideally ducks need to be on small water, that is ponds or pools that they would choose to leave because it doesn't offer enough cover or protection. In the UK these waterfowl are often found on big water – lakes, lochs and rivers, which can be difficult to hawk. Here in the Border country the rivers tend to be narrow, no more than 20 feet from bank to bank, and although mallard will fly hard and strong they will at least get up and follow the contour of the river before plunging back in if a falcon is in close pursuit. Flights with falcons in this situation are very much like flying out of the hood at corvids. The falcon simply powers after the quarry, following them as they depart. For this type of pursuit hawking, the large power-hybrid females, particularly gyr hybrids, are excellent. They can cover air space rapidly and the duck which have been flushed purely by the presence of humans are often unaware of the pursuit falcon, which usually gives her time to get in close to them.

Our rivers are made up of small eddies and pools with overhanging trees, and ducks will invariably be gathered onto them during the day. We try whenever possible to scan the water with binoculars to ascertain whether ducks are in residence. If so, then peregrine or hybrid falcons that will wait-on are best suited to the techniques of flush. With the falcon waiting over the falconer she is taken over the pool. For this one dog and several beaters are required. When the falconer calls for flush the dog handler and second beater surge forwards into the water or to the water's edge. The duck will either dive away from the beaters or rise. If they flush and rise it is because the beaters' approach to the bankside has been quiet and careful; they have not allowed the duck to hear them coming and by keeping a low profile they haven't been seen either. The duck will dive if the beaters have been noisy or careless in their approach. As they then flush, the falcon will immediately enter a stoop towards them. If the dog and beaters can keep them moving she will be successful. If the duck feel the pressure is too great, they will dive immediately and finding them again becomes virtually impossible. Their natural wariness and superb powers of flight make them one of the more exciting of game birds, requiring fit falcons.

Dabbling ducks belong to a large and very varied genus which includes mallard, teal, wigeons, shovelers and pintail (the latter is probably the most numerous species in the world). In winter and spring the males have bright plumage while females remain a rather dull brown. They are all essentially aquatic, obtaining food by dabbling on the surface or just under. The most often seen in the UK are mallard, which are considerably heavier than the others, with males weighing up to 3 lb 3 oz and females 2 lb 2 oz. They usually feed from dusk to dawn. During the day they rest in scattered flocks on open water, swimming gently with their heads drawn back or with their bills tucked into the feathers of their backs. They will sleep on the bank and sometimes a few birds will feed sporadically on the edge of the water. In the evening they will go off in pairs to the ponds and ditches to seek for food, which can be animal or vegetable: their diet consisting of acorns, snails, slugs, worms, insects and berries.

Chapter 10
Rook Hawking

Corvids

This is a generic term for the family but is generally used in a more restricted sense to describe crows and rooks. As a family they possibly represent the furthest stage in avian evolution. Much in their behaviour suggests highly developed mental powers and some species have a complex social organisation. They are highly adaptable and the large number of species and worldwide distribution suggests that they are also very successful.

Most corvids are social, although to what degree ranges from species to species, from the rook with its large colonies but small territories, to carrion and hooded crows which as pairs maintain large territories throughout the year. Many of the species are practically omnivorous, taking both animal and vegetable food. The vast majority of their feeding is done on open ground, though many have predatory habits and will take the young and eggs of other birds. Carrion, insects and vegetable items such as acorns, the seeds of pine cones and sometimes soft fruits are also eaten.

They are strong fliers, capable of dramatic aerobatic flying. Intelligent, wary yet gregarious, these large black birds are common throughout the UK.

There is often a conflict of desire in this branch of hawking. Many falcons readily and willingly chase rooks and crows long before they have been entered at game. If they are successful in their first attempts (which may well be flying at check), they repeat the performance whenever they can. To a falconer wishing to concentrate on game hawking this can be a blow, as whenever corvids are about the falcon is more than likely to give chase when it sees them. However, we have found that as far as grouse hawking is concerned, the falcons that readily fly rooks are almost invariably the ones that will be highly successful on the moor. These falcons show a marked aggression and tenacity that will become valuable assets for us later on.

Rooks are generally plentiful all year round. In the Border country farmers are only too pleased that you have falcons capable of reducing corvid numbers, particularly around lambing time when carrion crows can reap such havoc on newborn lambs, or pre-harvest time when rooks and crows flatten great areas of cereal fields in order to get at the ears of corn.

Hawking during either of these periods is fraught with difficulty owing to the need to enter the lambing fields or crop fields to retrieve the falcon. Far better to attempt constructive culling when they can be hawked making maximum use of the land. These periods are normally early spring, before lambing, or throughout the autumn and early winter.

We normally use saker, peregrine and hybrids for this branch of falconry. Any of these are extremely well equipped and powerful in straight-line pursuit. They will attempt rook at first sighting and providing the slips are within reach they can be very successful first time around.

Rook gatherings, which may well have carrion crows in their midst as well, are best on large open stubble or pastureland. If they are too near to trees or woods they will fly into these immediately they see the falcon and will not be tempted out of them. On the other hand, on very open feeding grounds they will have to make a journey back to the rookery which will provide some excellent flying for the falcon.

We drive round in the car looking at various fields that contain corvids to see which will provide the best slips for the falcon. Once we have decided, the falconer uses the car as a 'blind' to slip out of the vehicle unnoticed. The falcon is unhooded while still shielded by the vehicle so that she has the chance rouse, take stock of her surroundings and gather her wits. Then we hold her out into the open, where she will see the rooks and probably bob her head. If they move because they can see people she may take off after them immediately, or she can be cast in their direction. Whichever – if she is in any degree of fitness she will begin pursuit. Once she is amongst them she will have to decide which one to chase. During autumn flights she will find many young birds in the flock as well as moulting adults and these will give her the opportunity to strike. This is normally done by a simple bind to the quarry, which she then carries down to a secure spot in order to pluck it. Falcons do seem to enjoy eating rook and crow flesh although its dark meat is a bit rich for them.

Spring rooks are far more tricky as quarry because they are extremely fit as flying birds at that time of year and the falcon needs to have been wedded to them in the course of the previous autumn. Secondly the falcon needs a great deal of time to get fit enough to take on long, demanding flights. We prefer not to use falcons that have spent time in aviaries for spring rooks because their fat reserves would take too long to break down. Instead we use eyases from the previous year who have proven themselves in the field and have remained in a state of flying fitness throughout the winter, or experienced intermewed falcons that remain in hunting condition throughout the winter and into the spring.

Fitness is important for this hawking because it is often so windy at this time of year. The falcon will need to be capable of 'into the wind' slips, and the rooks or crows may well challenge her by flying hard and fast in that direction, too. If there is a fair degree of ground to make up before she gets to them, her fitness is all the more important; you don't want to run the risk of her giving up halfway. As they spiral and tower away from her she has to be able to rise with them and preferably get above them so that by stooping she can be selective on her quarry. Corvids taken from high-mounting flights such as these are really spectacular. As they wheel and whirl about her it's difficult even to know which is rook and which is falcon. As she stoops they may side-slip or outmanoeuvre her with their excellent flying skills. If she strikes one from this position and goes down to begin to pluck it, you need to be pretty quick off the mark in running after her, as the rest of the flock will descend rapidly to attack her if she's exposed in the open fields.

Corvids have powerful, dagger-like beaks. If they get a chance they will stab at any part of the falcon's anatomy, particularly round her eyes, and can inflict crucial wounds. Crucial because if the wounding she receives from them is too much for her she will stop flying them. Peregrines seem to take umbrage the most at attacks inflicted on them by corvids. Sakers are more capable of resisting them because of their longer reach of leg. Perhaps the most efficient of all falcons are the hybrids, particularly saker x peregrine, prairie x peregrine and gyr x saker males. Hybrids have a manic approach to their adversaries and the combination of heterosis and aggression makes them excellent for this type of demanding hawking.

Hawking from Horseback

Care are useful for getting you round to see fields of rooks, but inevitably they are a problem if you are miles away from them or you cannot get your falcon to the best areas for flying. Horses are the answer. Providing you have some degree of proficiency riding overland, this is far and away the most dramatic and exciting way to hawk rook.

There is nothing new about this. The horse was still a means of transport at the turn of the century. Today it is still useful over big country that vehicles simply couldn't get into and is exhilarating in the speed of the hunt and flying falcons in their most natural style.

Horses need to be carefully selected as hawking mounts. The most important quality is the right temperament. The ability to accept the close proximity of the hawk is vital, but most horses of a kindly and quiet nature can be trained to accept the unfamiliar experience of flapping wings; indeed, some will be unmoved from the first introduction.

The horse should be responsive and not easily agitated, as a good deal of the riding will be done one-handed. Its build is not of great importance but ideally it should be sixteen hands or under, as quite a lot of mounting and dismounting can be involved. Well-boned horses are best over heathland and fell country. A good jumper is almost a must for the competent rider as the pursuit of hawk and quarry can be quite fast. (For the more leisurely approach there are usually handy gates which one can walk through!) The horse also needs to be patient when you're dismounted, and stand still until you've picked the falcon up from the lure or her kill.

Not all horses will tolerate a falcon flying round them, nor will they tolerate you holding the bird on the glove while mounted. Horses have to be thoroughly schooled with hawks in exactly the same way as you would begin to train a gundog or the hawk itself. Horses that are stabled during the summer months may well have swifts or swallows nesting in the rafters of the stable, so they become familiar with the flapping of wings around them. Some old falconers deliberately used to keep pigeons in the stables for the same reason.

One of the techniques that need to be mastered in horseback falconry is mounting with the hawk on the gauntlet. The smaller the horse the easier this is, but it still takes practice, and some people prefer to reverse the usual principle and mount from the right-hand side, carrying the hawk on their left. Others simply hand the falcon to another mounted rider and take it on board when they are perfectly seated themselves.

The falcon has to be trained to accept riding at speed while on the glove and to ignore the presence of the horse and other riders when the hood is struck, so that she can continue to concentrate on the rook gatherings in front of her.

When hawking on horseback we generally use falcons that are already skilled in flying and have had previous success at quarry. They are conversant with hawking and the use of dogs, which makes them more likely to accept the presence of another

Traditional falcon. The peregrine. *(Richard Edmead)*

Traditional hawk. The goshawk. *(Steven Shaw)*

The Harris hawk: the versatile all-rounder. *(Steven Shaw)*

The red-tailed hawk. *(Richard Edmead)*

The prairie falcon. *(Philip Norgale)*

Gyr x peregrine hybrid.

Lanner falcon.

Gyr x saker hybrid.

animal. When horse and falcon are introduced for the first time, the falcon is taken back to basics and expected to come for the garnished lure which the falconer drops out in front of the horse. As she begins to realise there is nothing to be alarmed about in this large animal, so you can shorten the distance each day until she is capable of flying directly underneath the horse if need be to get to her lure.

She will also need to learn how to balance whilst the horse is walking and trotting and in particular when it is in full gallop. We practise this in the calmness of the home paddocks so that both horse and falcon learn without dangerous distractions such as cars, dogs or loud noises.

Hungarian horsemen, when training falcons to fly heron on the state fish-farms, taught their sakers to fly from one mounted falconer to another in a circle of cantering horses. We teach our falcons this skill as it improves the balance of the rider, who is riding with only one hand on the reins, educates the horse to falcons flying alongside and up on to it and lastly allows the falcon to become bold and self-assured with a continuously moving perch onto which she must alight to feed. Horses for their part need to be reassured that falcons will do them no harm and are not to be shied away from. For the horses' basic training we use the ever-faithful Harris hawk, which, being large and slow, is an ideal bird for the horses' first experience of this type of work.

The hawks are called from a post so that they land on the falconer's fist, approximately 20 yards in front of the horse. Meanwhile, the rider keeps a check on the horse's reactions. If these are not too traumatic then the hawk is called from trees or other objects so that it is flying directly at the horse to its falconer. Once the horse accepts this calmly, the falconer mounts the horse and calls the hawk to him while he is seated on horseback. If this goes smoothly, the falcon is flown from the saddle to a second falconer. The falcon will literally fly over the horse's neck between its ears in a flight line to the lure. A properly trained horse will be unperturbed by this and at this point horse, rider and falcon are forming a partnership.

The corvid family are far more approachable from horseback, which makes the strategy of flight easier to negotiate in the first instance. The field of riders needs to be in a position to cast the falcon into the wind with few if any natural obstructions en route. The horses are stood still as the falcon's hood is removed. She may rouse, or simply leave the fist immediately she sights the gathering. The rooks will be unaware of her approach for a moment, but as soon as they notice her they lift and wheel into the wind to evade her. Flights such as these can bring instant success; alternatively they may involve the field in a stern, hard chase as falcon and rooks career across country.

If the flight is taken out of sight before the mounted field can reach the falcon, then telemetry will be needed fairly quickly. This equipment and further falcons waiting for flight are kept in a vehicle that is in touch with the field via two-way radios. This back-up is important, as much of the equipment that one would normally carry on foot is far too cumbersome to be carried on horseback. Equally handy vehicles are Quad bikes. When it's not raining we occasionally use these as well to keep up with the field and carry the telemetry.

This branch of falconry is one of the most demanding practised today because of the skills and techniques required. Riding out into the field and navigating so that the horses and falcons can be in a commanding position for flight is exciting and exacting. Horses contribute to mobility which is an asset to this branch of the sport. The falcon reverts to what she does naturally, that is straight, level pursuit. Waiting-on is not important and is often quite superfluous. The fact that the falcon is carried at a higher elevation gives her a slight advantage as she speeds forwards and upwards to catch her rook. She needs to get above strong-flying corvids, and it may take her a mile or more to accomplish this.

Keeping the horses just behind the falcon will enable the riders to see all of the flight. Sometimes as the flight heads towards woods or copses it is easier to watch the final approach through binoculars. If she catches her rook then the field can ride speedily towards her; if she misses, her falconer can begin to lure her back.

As often as not ditches, fences and walls intersect the ground that is being flown. Horses that can jump will be better able to follow the flight in a direct line than ones that cannot. However, once you've effectively taken your eyes off the falcon it's often difficult to relocate her. With a little practise, fairly good guesswork comes into play, especially if the rooks or crows were already heading for woods: generally speaking that's where the field will find her.

Rook hawking is available most of the year. It can be practised by any variety of powerful long-wing and with the added dimension of horses remains a branch of falconry with tremendous scope and enjoyment.

Chapter 11
The Game Fair and Display Hawk

The last decade has seen a growing interest on the part of organisers of public events in the inclusion of free-flying demonstrations by birds of prey in their main arenas or display areas. These people seem to have become aware that the public is captivated by raptors and the birds are a top attraction because the crowds will pay to see them fly. There is no doubt about it, a well executed demonstration of tactics and flying techniques is an exciting spectacle; and as a bonus the birds themselves seem to have an exhibitionist streak and play to the gallery.

If you have aspirations to this field of work then you need to watch a number of major free-flying demonstrations in order to see how the experts handle the hawks and how they handle their commentary. A high standard of presentation is an absolute priority: being in love with your hawks is not a good enough reason for entering a public arena to show other people your pride and joy. Your objective must be that what you are about to do is educational and that you wish to state the case for falconry and conservation; you must also be familiar with how these birds are adapted to their environment and conversant with current legislation governing them.

Hawks and falcons are trained specially for such events and are definitely not giving an exhibition of falconry. Any hunting falcon given the opportunity would leave the arena and actively search quarry to pursue. This would obviously disrupt the display and break the continuity and flow for the other hawks that were to fly. However, many of the disciplines needed for falconry training are very relevant in the training of demonstration hawks.

Many falcons will adapt very easily to lure flying and show both style and ability. Harris hawks and common buzzards will also accept the presence of a crowd and demonstrate their abilities well. But the single most important factor that makes them so watchable is the skill that has gone into their training.

Falcons are the highlight of the general display and to get them to a peak of excellence means giving them vast amounts of *recreational* flying. This cannot be stressed too strongly. Their natural ability to chase a lure is an inherent characteristic in their desire to hunt, but schooling them in this manner *ad infinitum*, will merely bring their pitch down and turn them into stereotyped flying machines.

Recreational flying should ideally be done in open spaces, particularly where there are hillocks or steeper slopes that have favourable winds blowing into them. If that is not possible, letting them hack around will not only muscle them up but will give them an interest in their surroundings. What this type of flying produces is a falcon that, when released in the arena, can go looking for lift and height and can then put in spectacular, hard-driving stoops. It will also be very fit which means that the commentator will have time to talk about the falcon's performance, while it is flying around enjoying the day.

Hawks need plenty of free-flying time as well. They enjoy flying into and out of trees and this type of exercise helps keep them well muscled; it also enables them to use the available space around them. Harris hawks are the exception to the 'no hunting' rule in that they are equally good for large group work if they too are hunted. They are quite capable of co-operating in both spheres and in my opinion this is far more satisfactory for the hawk. Consequently the Harris's recreational flying time should be spent in the hunting field.

All this handling will make them very familiar with you, and this in turn will give them that vital composure in the weathering or static area. Falcons and hawks that are nervous with you will also be nervous when exposed to hundreds of people and will be highly unlikely to want to co-operate.

Well-trained flying birds are what people have come to see and between yourself and the organisers a lot of work must be done prior to your arrival at the showground. For most of the day the display hawks will be on view to the general public. They need to be contained in a weathering ground that should have been erected by the organisers and large enough to contain six birds, so that they cannot reach each other from their perches and the public can view them without getting too close. An area 30 feet square is the minimum requirement. It must have shelter that can block out extremes of sunlight or rain. This can either take the form of permanent wooden weathering (usually erected at very large shows) or a suitable large broad-leaf tree in the enclosure. Alternatively, bring you own portable canopy (which can be purchased through many good camping stores). Two of these will be enough and protect a display team.

Can you speak in public? What you say matters. Today most people are better informed than ever before about ecological and conservational issues. They are fed enormous diets of this on television and through the rest of the media. They can reason and evaluate whether what they have seen and heard is in the interest of raptors' welfare. You must have enough background knowledge to be prepared to answer a vast variety of questions on falconry and legislation.

Choosing a Display Bird

Six birds, possibly all of different species, are ample for displays that involve travelling. The logistics of transporting more than this means that larger vehicles need to be used, and this may be impractical. Carrying boxes for six birds can be housed comfortably in an ordinary estate car. In addition all these birds can be flown in the course of the event. As previously mentioned the Harris hawk and buzzard are well disposed to demonstrating. Their larger cousins, the red-tail and the ferruginous, are less suitable, as they are more aggressive and very often temperamental. The ferruginous also requires a good deal of space to show its flying skills well.

Accipiters such as the goshawk or sparrowhawk are not suitable either. Their frenetic disposition means that crowds and densely populated environments are strictly not for them. More than any other species they would find such occasions highly stressful.

Lanner falcons, sakerets (males sakers) and luggers are particularly well suited to displays as their light wing-loading gives them the ability to get up and get a good pitch over the arena, while enjoying the opportunity to chase the lure.

Peregrines take a great deal of work to keep them fit and on hot days their heavier wing-loading means they will have to work harder to get up. Without a wind to help them this may be impossible to accomplish and so they may go and sit on the nearest obstacle and refuse to co-operate.

Prairie falcons need an experienced hand to fly them and although they have a lighter wing-loading than the peregrine, it requires a great deal of effort to keep them fit and attentive to the job at hand.

Female sakers are as good as the males, but once again their size is such that they require lots of recreational flying to maintain fitness.

There are of course infinite varieties of falcon that can be flown, but they all require specialist experience. Sticking to the most reliable species will produce the best results in the demonstration.

One falcon that is rarely used for demonstration is the kestrel. This little falcon is probably the one which budding hawk-keepers will focus on, no less delicate than merlins or hobbies it requires experienced handling: that may be a difficult point to get across in the context of a spectacular flying display.

Owls are often used by display givers, the most eye-catching being the eagle owls and horned owls. Smaller owls are not suitable for a number of reasons: they have no connection with the past or present development of falconry and consequently look totally out of place in a display area; and their endearing appearance often encourages people to want them as pets which they most definitely are not.

Eagles are occasionally used by peripatetic display givers, the most often seen being the Tawny eagle. Buoyant and of an easy-going disposition they can on favourable days give an impressive account of themselves. However, eagles are for the most part not able to show their natural ability to soar and stoop in an arena and consequently will be shown flying on the horizontal plane rather than the vertical one. To accomplish flights in this way they, too, need to be very fit and like falcons and hawks will require a great deal of attention to recreational flying.

Social imprints and parent-reared falcons and hawks make some of the very best display birds because they are particularly well-adjusted characters to start with. Full imprints are tolerable in the falcons, often putting on a very good display, but in hawks are to be positively avoided as these birds have little fear of anyone or anything and short-duration teamwork in the arena often stimulates 'temper tantrums', because you are not devoting enough of your time to feeding them. They may well decide to do something about this by launching an attack at you. This aggressive behaviour doesn't need encouraging. In other words, don't use them for this kind of work!

Equipment

Blocks and bow perches should be specially kept for the job of displaying the birds. Nothing looks smarter than hawks, falcons and eagle owls on perches that are immaculate and can show the birds off to their very best advantage. Blocks should be of the correct diameter for the species sitting on it and should have trauma-resistant surfaces such as astroturf on block tops and well-padded leather- or synthetic-bound bow perches.

You should provide signs that tell the onlooker what species the bird is and are legible from outside your enclosure. Where a show may be of two or three days' duration, it is often a good idea to have display boards not only showing the species of bird graphically or photographically but giving information as to where it can be found worldwide and a brief description of its lifestyle.

Leashes must be clean and preferably once again kept for the purpose of showing the bird. Jesses should be well greased or renewed if they show signs of stiffness. All falcons, hawks and owls must be in aylmeri jesses, not traditional jesses. Before flying, replace their mews jesses with field jesses just as you would if you were hunting them.

Baths need to be available for the birds to use, especially on hot days. You will need a bucket or some similar container to carry water from the taps on site.

Hoods should be well fitting and professionally made. Falcons and hawks should not be left sitting in the weathering with these on for any length of time, as clearly people appreciate their beauty more when they are not wearing a hood.

Food will need to be convenient. Skinning a rabbit or plucking a quail just before you are due into the arena is a non-starter! Ideally the food will not require casting. Fur or feathers can be tricky if you want to get the falcon or hawk off the glove or lure. If it is totally preoccupied plucking the object and has no intention of leaving it, you may well have to waste a great deal of your display time coaxing it away from its food source.

Skinned rabbit or beef is perhaps the best on these occasions as they are comparatively clean foods and can be tied down very firmly onto lures or held tightly in gloves for feeding purposes. They also make good bechins (titbits) for garnishing gloves with. Of course this food is chosen purely for convenience on the day: no falcon, hawk or owl should be kept on such an unbalanced diet on a regular basis.

The Showground

It is absolutely vital to arrive in plenty of time. Many shows open their doors by 9.30 a.m., which means the public are already up and about at that hour. You will need to be on site early enough to set up and to position your vehicle so that if you are using it in the arena you can get to it at all times.

Hawks appreciate as much time as possible weathering before they are flown; they also like the opportunity to bathe. By arriving early you will be able to check that the static area is the size you requested and that the fencing round the enclosure is high enough and secure. It needs to be people proof and dog proof.

Laying out the weathering, getting water for the baths and putting shading up, display signs and generally getting organised may take some time. In addition there may be a trade tent for your photographic display or equipment sales and setting these up will equally take time.

When all this is done to your liking, you will need to make sure that *you* are presentable for your public. The vast majority of people who go to outside events where some aspect of country sports is being conducted will expect to see you in country clothing. Your image is very important, particularly if you are to be the main feature of the day and all eyes are on you.

The numbers at these events will vary depending on the kind of event it is. But in any gathering from small to large, people are fascinated by birds of prey. Questions will be fired at you all day long and you will need to be able to answer them with great patience. Occasionally you may be asked deliberately provocative questions by someone who is clearly opposed to country sports. Becoming involved in a public argument is unlikely to resolve anything. Far better to suggest that the matter be taken up privately.

Having previously arranged how many displays you will be providing you will need to check in the programme for the event that times are as agreed. This is important when allowing time to set up telemetry, put food into bags, check lures, etc. You may also need to be by the arena before your event to have a radio mike fitted for the commentary.

Assistants

By now it will be apparent that there is a lot of work involved in displaying, and it would be extremely difficult to manage by yourself either in the arena or out of it. Assistants need to be conversant with the hawks and falcons, capable of explaining about them to the public and generally taking over if you're not there. If they are actively involved in the flying routine you are about to undertake it should have been worked out and practised beforehand. Should one of the hawks decide to leave the flying grounds, a responsible person must be left in charge of those remaining while the other takes the telemetry to go and look for it.

No display bird should be left unattended so that it becomes vulnerable to others that are flying. Any bird that is not flying should ideally be in its carrying box in the car while the display is in progress.

At the end of the event you should seek out the organising officials to speak to them before you leave. This is not only a matter of courtesy; it can give you an opportunity to ask how they felt the demonstration went and listen to any sensible suggestions that could improve it for the following year.

Filming and Television Work

In the course of their work, film and TV programme producers may well decide to incorporate some aspect concerning a bird of prey. They might contact you directly or through an animal acting agency of which you are a member. They will enquire whether you have a certain species of bird and what it will be required to do in the filming.

More often than not the person responsible for getting you on site will be the prop manager. Do not assume they know anything about birds of prey and how they behave. Often the sequences that they will need the bird to perform are too difficult to put into practice.

Outside locational work obviously suits hawks, owls, eagles and falcons as there is more room to interpret the producer's script and for the bird to relax in a familiar type of environment.

Studio work is far more difficult as the geography of a set is made up of props and lighting, which is not only at floor level but also multi-lit from the roof with vast arc lamps hung from steel hawsers. Staff and crew members are everywhere. As specialists they all have a job to do and this will involve them being tightly grouped around you when filming commences.

If a bird which the producer would like in the programme is unsuitable for the conditions of filming you should say so. For instance, an inside set which requires a peregrine to fly round in it is a problem before you start. It is not that it couldn't be done, but it involves a considerable degree of difficulty and risk for the bird.

For this type of work a comprehensive collection of raptors would need to be flown and handled so that they were 'bomb proof'. You may be asked for any type of raptor and only relaxed, confident birds can adapt to film work. Occasionally you may be able to visit the studio beforehand to see for yourself what they would like you to do. That makes it much easier to decide how you will tackle the scenes involving your bird. If this isn't possible, make sure that you have a detailed description on what is required so that you can practise any difficult manoeuvres at home before you get on set.

Film or television work usually means very long hours. Flying sequences may take quite some time to perfect, so, coupled with all the other scenes that the actors and film crew must perfect, you might have to be available for anything between eight and twelve hours.

If a bird simply has to sit on a prop or with an actor this should be comparatively easy and will not take so long, but generally speaking producers like actors of all description to be on call from early morning onwards.

If your bird is required to do flying scenes and they are to be 'shot' in the morning, you will need to have had plenty of practise beforehand to make sure they will fly on cue. This is important as most raptors are flown much later in the day and if they are into that routine then they are not going to change their habits overnight.

Nothing will please a producer more than an animal 'actor' which will oblige with a perfect performance and truthfully nothing is more rewarding than watching your own hard work being put into practise and that well-trained bird turning in a star performance.

Radio
Clearly there is nothing visual involved here, but sounds and voices are important. If you are asked to appear on radio, it will probably take the form of an interview: they will be asking you questions about keeping birds of prey and expecting you to contribute in a very informed manner. These are often live recordings and you need to be conversant with various facets of your subject. Flying, management, hunting, displaying, breeding and legislation are just some of the topics that can be thrust at you and you will need to be able to speak fluently on these issues. Nothing comes across more clearly than a radio conversation, probably because the listener has no visual distractions and can concentrate on the spoken word. Mistakes in this medium become glaring ones.

If you are asked to do this type of interview but feel uncomfortable about it, you should elect to have a speaker who is experienced and competent there with you, so that they can do at least some of the talking. This may make it more interesting for the listener, and certainly less demanding on you.

Chapter 12
Dogs for Falconry

The variety of gundogs available for the hunt is legion. In this country some thirty-one breeds are recognised by the Kennel Club, producing an average of 74,000 registrations per year. Puppies abound everywhere and with so many breeds to consider what is a falconer to do?

The various breeds are divided into specialist categories. They can be purely hunters, or exclusively pointers, or retrievers. They may be also a combination of all of these called hunter-pointer retrievers (HPRs or continental gundogs.) The numbers registered each year do not reflect the number of sportsmen and women in the field, but do to a large extent illustrate what a growth industry dog shows are.

This accessible pool of dog potential needs some careful consideration. First and foremost, which dog is for you? The answer depends on your hunting environment and your ability as a trainer.

Hunters

The first step is to assess how useful a dog will be as part of the falconry team. Let's start with the hunters, by which I mean the spaniel family. These are all foot-scenters. There are nine differing types, some of which are unsuitable for work purposes. In the UK the American cocker and American water spaniel (rarely seen) are purely show dogs. However the remaining spaniels can be found as working dogs. The complete family comprises American cocker, American water, clumber, cocker, English springer, field, Irish water, Sussex and Welsh springer spaniels. Of these the most commonly used in the field are English springer and cocker followed by a minority of clumber.

The usage of field, Sussex, Welsh and Irish water spaniels was at its height around the turn of the century. As the English springer and the cocker became more popular they displaced those that had previously been in fashion. The former breeds can still be seen in small numbers today and are eligible for field trials that exclude cocker and English springer spaniel. The American cocker and American water spaniel are token gestures to the working gundog. They are purely for show and the voluminous coats which need hours of grooming would not endear them to any self-respecting falconer. There is no doubt that they filled a very important niche in the development of gundogs in North America, but the advent of more adaptable breeds simply relegated them to showing status, where today they can be seen and admired.

The spaniel is fundamentally a hunter who flushes or 'springs' the game once it has made contact with it. The springer spaniel is aptly named. It is an energetic, fizzy, medium-sized dog which remains enthusiastic about its work at all times. It is used primarily in cover, which can be very dense, and with its thick coat as protection it moves fur and feather for the attention of hunters.

Its smaller cousin the cocker has the same qualities but was developed specifically to flush woodcock, hence its name.

The clumber has always been a much slower, more ponderous hunter. Although it is very capable, it went out of fashion once the springer and cocker became more popular. Almost stifled by showing fanatics (who pay little attention to working genes), it has had a very encouraging revival in a newly formed club, the Working Clumber Spaniel Society, of which Her Royal Highness The Princess Royal is President.

Retrievers

Retrievers are used exclusively within the shooting world. Invaluable as an aid to recovering shot game, they are not expected to hunt in a direct sense and they do not point. They are calm and collected dogs, capable of remaining still for long periods at the shooting stand (or peg) or at flight ponds at dawn and dusk, or picking up at the end of a long drive. Their retrieving skills are highly developed and in this field they excel. As falconry dogs they are non-starters.

Pointers and Setters

These galmorous gundogs are bred to search for game as rapidly as possible by air-scenting. When a dog locates a scent it draws onto a point. Originally bred as a slower running dog that could also retrieve, today its speed and nose are its designer qualities. Popular breeds in this group are the smooth-coated pointer, the long-coated English setter, the Irish red setter and the black and tan Gordon setter.

Hunt, Point and Retrieve breeds (HPRs)

This category, also called continental gundogs, represents the newest dogs on to the UK gundog scene. They started appearing just after the Second World War and were designed to eliminate the need for the specialist breeds mentioned above. Versatility is their strong point and there are nine different breeds. The smooth-coated ones are Bracco Italiano, German short-haired pointer, Hungarian vizsla and Weimaraner. Those with a dense wire coat are German wire-haired pointer, Hungarian wire-haired vizsla and Italian spinone. Long coats are the Brittany and large Munsterlander.

Spaniels, setters and pointers have historically been featured in falconry in one way or another, often as combination kennels, meaning that as an individual dog had to fulfil its specialist task, it was quite common to see kennels of springers, pointers and retrievers, all important aides to hunting, housed together. (It was quite usual for a falconer to shoot as well as to hawk, so he would need retrievers.)

Falconry through the ages concentrated on specialist quarry and techniques to succeed with it. This approach prevailed right up until the Second World War and as the seasons revolved so one needed to use the dogs accordingly. For instance, red grouse hawking requires fast, mobile dogs that can work well out in front and point birds; partridge hawking on the low ground is the same. Here the pointers and setters were put to work. Once winter hawking began, the goshawk came on the scene, and the spaniels, the 'maids of all work', could flush fur and feather with equal vigour. Inevitably one would be invited to a day's shooting and the retriever would need to accompany its master.

Keeping so many different types of dog that spent only a small proportion of their calendar year in the field was a costly business. It is no coincidence that the HPRs began to have an enormous attraction to falconers and shooting men alike. Once the various breeds started arriving in this country they were put to work. Initially they were expected to perform each task as well as the specialists and indeed early field trials had them running against pointers and setters, and being compared to spaniels. But this was the result of ignorance of how they were trained in their home countries. Today HPRs are recognised as fulfilling the role that they were bred for. This group has had the most dramatic rise in modern falconry and we shall look at how it fits the bill compared to traditional breeds.

The deciding factor in most cases is the look of the dog. In this, you can be spoilt for choice as they come in smooth varieties, long-hair and wire-hair. Any dog you choose *must* come from working stock – that is, parents which work in the field with many others in its pedigree having done the same. Unfortunately many working dogs have been contaminated by breeding from purely show strains. There is a commonly held belief among show people that a gundog is a working dog forever. The fact that they never work them seems an irrelevance. Yet once a breed is selected purely for cosmetic and glamorised features, the working ability fails to surface. If you like, the working gene is diluted.

Working dogs should be mated to working dogs in order to compound this heritable factor and to allow for a maximum number of pups in the litter to have inherited this characteristic.

A litter cannot provide a hundred per cent top quality dogs. In a litter of ten, two may well be outstanding. Six may be average while two may be below average. It is not possible to pinpoint how eight-week-old puppies will develop. What can be said is that if a dog is bred with the working aspects first and foremost in the breeder's mind, then you the purchaser have a good chance of getting a youngster that will prove to be an asset.

Habitat Requirements

For many falconers today the immediate environment is where they are going to hunt and for the vast majority that means on low ground. although more and more falconers are becoming migratory with the start of various game seasons, the 'field next door' is still where you will be most of the year. In the majority of cases these will be fairly small fields, with borders or woodland and/or hedges which do not call for wide-ranging, fast-running dogs. Although you may well be going to fly a falcon as well as a hawk this does not need a commitment to two different breeds of dog.

Those who fly exclusively falcons need bird dogs: pointers and setters. If this applies to you, then your flying will be done on the largest open space available. Whether on downland, fell country or moorland, the sheer expanse of ground on which ground-nesting species of game birds live means that the fastest dog possible, and one with a good nose, is imperative. Little has changed in this sphere. Setters and pointers have always done this job with grace, pace and style. They are beautiful to watch once you have achieved the necessary communication and rapport to make the dog part of the team.

However the majority of modern falconers prefer to have a varied and full hawking calendar which incorporates much flying during the winter months and indeed the early summer months too.

If you are likely to be flying in a variety of demanding habitats – one that may be impenetrable for large dogs, or cover too great an area for smaller breeds to cope with; marsh or river basin which require powerful swimmer-hunters, or mountain and moorland – you should ideally have a dog that will be effective no matter what habitat it is called upon to hunt in. That means the HPRs.

Let us look now at another way of considering traditional breeds: they can be divided into upland or lowland hunters.

Upland Dogs

Modern pointers have evolved over the past 200 years. They are descended from the old Spanish pointer, which was a dog of great scenting powers but no particular speed; its job was purely low-ground work on red-leg partridge. They were imported into this country by British officers in the 18th century after the Treaty of Utrecht, following the War of the Spanish Succession. Their ponderous approach to pointing soon demanded a dog with more running power.

It was Colonel Thornton who pioneered the outcross with the old English foxhound which was to be the basis of the modern pointer. The initial breeding programmes were fraught with problems. The foxhound is a foot-scenter whereas the pointer is an air-scenter. The style of the pointer was at risk to the development of speed and greater pace. Selective breeding began to see positive results and coloration started to play a major part. It is said that Joseph Lang, the gunmaker, was responsible for introducing the lemon and white coloration by outcrossing with a lemon and white hound which originated from Château Billy in France, where they specialised in stag and boar hunting.

No doubt Colonel Thornton saw the immediate advantages of his pointing dogs. He would have put them to good use in his falconry calendar. His fellow officers also saw the advantage of shooting over them. Up until this period it was customary to keep the dog on point and draw nets over the dogs to trap the partridge. For this purpose setters were used. However, around this time it became fashionable to shoot birds on the wing.

Grouse hawking with dogs was unknown at this time: the partridge had the bird hunters' undivided attention. Not surprising when you consider that most landowners had their own estates on which partridge were well distributed and a gentleman would have little need to venture beyond his own boundaries for maximum sport. Shooting was purely and simply a pastime, possibly involving two or three guns, for which the pointers worked amply well.

The pointer and setter were initially developed for falconry. Although shooting could make use of their skills as well, it wasn't until around the turn of the last century that grouse hawking began its meteoric rise to popularity. Suddenly large tracts of heather demanded good running, air-scenting dogs. At the time there were some outstanding kennels of all the composite breeds in the UK. Such large territories needed large numbers of bird dogs for the job. It wasn't unknown to have twelve dogs from novice to fully trained making up the hawking team.

The colour of the dog was determined during the early breeding programmes of Colonel Thornton. No doubt he and subsequent other breeders used foxhounds and Spanish pointers that had as much white on as possible to enable them to see the dog easily in the field, in preference to liver or dark-coloured dogs.

In later years there simply was every colour imaginable, from almost completely white to the Duke of Kingston's remarkable blacks. The latter were highly prized and were considered superior to all others being bred at that time. However breeders soon found a greater consistency in their pups; the present day colours of liver and white, orange and white, lemon and white and black and white are the result.

One of the features of the newly evolving pointer was its comparative ease of training. It might be used purely as a pointer, but it would also retrieve. With its fine coat it did not possess the glitz and glamour of the setters and was generally relegated to the status of 'work horse'. A good middle-sized dog that would suit all uses, capable of both speed and endurance, became the preferred animal. Anything smaller couldn't cope with moorland and anything larger (more towards the foxhound build) was too heavy to run for long periods of time. Today's pointer has changed very little.

While the pointer was developing, the setters were already being used solely for low-ground game birds. Like the pointer's, the setters development needed a sound working dog that could be bettered. Land spaniels featured in their early breeding and they were also of Spanish origin. Setters were used to locate quail and partridge, crouching or 'setting' to indicate that birds were in front. The fowler, as he would have been known, opened and spread his net, which would have been arranged for capture. The dog would then be signalled to go forwards carefully and at the moment of flushing the birds would burst upwards and forwards into the net. This practice was well known in Elizabethan times, as indeed was the breed of dog that performed these tasks. These land spaniels or their derivatives were very similar to today's springers, heavier built and with more leg, but with the same exuberant attitude to work. It is well documented that some of these dogs were capable of assisting with netting and during Elizabeth I's reign they were alluded to as setters.

Setters became a necessity with the advent of the gun. Shooting flying birds, although a new concept, gained rapidly in popularity. It is thought that in this country the deliberate use of a dog to 'sett' was developed by Robert Dudley, Duke of Northumberland about 1550.

The setter was recognised for its superb 'nose', its ability to discriminate delicate scent, and its willingness to crouch down once close to the quarry. This last quality was probably the reason for the introduction of the pointer. In the transition period of netting and wing shooting, the requirements for a dog to stand on point for the gun were obvious, particularly in root crop. The modern setter, of course, stands equally well to the point and in fact the advent of diverse game crops caused the emphasis on crouching to be of less importance. Even today every working setter will from time to time show the 'classic' stance that gave it its name.

Once the pointer arrived on the scene the setter's fortunes waxed and waned, but during the latter half of the last century it was the most popular pointing dog and with its three distinctive coat colours it was an obvious choice for its beauty alone. Its coat gave it resilience against the weather while its thickly padded feet provided it with protection in all forms of rough shooting, making it a better candidate for broken ground and extremely hard work. However in hot weather it became fatigued more easily and this was where the pointer, with its short coat, came into its own.

Today both setter and pointer have their *aficionados*. Little has changed in their structure, but if anything they have a slighter frame, all the better for running. At the turn of the century the top dogs on the moor were members of the setter family. Today it is more likely to be the pointer. Their excellence of breeding and field performance have been kept very much alive by field trial enthusiasts and if high-ground work is all you will ever have time to pursue, then these dogs are the ones to go for.

Low-Ground Dogs

The spaniel seems to be the mother of invention. Featuring strongly in setter breeding at its earliest point, it was also a well-established hunting dog in its own right. In the past there were two categories of spaniel, the water spaniel and the land spaniel. In 1697 Nicholas Cox wrote in *The Gentleman's Recreation*: 'How necessary a thing a spaniel is to falconry and for those that delight in that noble recreation, keeping hawks for their pastime and pleasure, I think nobody need question as well as to spring and retrieve a fowl being flown to the mark and also divers other ways to help and assist falcons and goshawks.'

Spaniels have been around a very long time. Their current breeding has provided a small compact dog that is fearless in cover with a good coat to sustain the very roughest wear and tear. Their tails are docked, a practice known to Nicholas Cox, who curiously thought that it prevented worms from breeding there! But in addition it saved the tail from damage while working in heavy cover. Spaniels are energetic, busy workers with a constantly wagging tail and never seem to tire. Used in the shooting field today they are expected to retrieve as well as to hunt. Once they are on to a 'hot' scent with game location, their job is to flush the quarry out of cover for the hunter. Their range of work is about 15–20 yards from the handler and they must be trained to be obedient to the flush by not attempting to chase whatever they put up. They are capable of working root fields, hedges and ditches, water meadows and deciduous woodland. They can also retrieve under direction over long distances.

From the onset the spaniel was subdivided: the springing, hawking spaniel or starter and the cocker or cocking spaniel have been known for hundreds of years. The former was a much leggier version than today's. While falconry was at its height these dogs excelled. However, with the advent of the gun, they were found to be too fast and wild and of course too difficult to manage – hence the development of the shorter-legged modern spaniel.

Woodcock were very popular as a sporting game bird and the cocker spaniel (a cross between the springer and the water spaniel) was an important part of the kennel. More compact than the springer but in many ways a miniature version, it was capable of going into small, tight areas of cover, particularly bramble and briar, to flush woodcock.

During the early 19th century, the springer was used as a finder or starter to the greyhound. It had to locate hares for the greyhound to pursue, and seemed to enjoy the chase as much as the greyhound did. Fortunately for the sanity of the owners, by the middle of the century this use of the springer had gone into decline.

The springer is highly adaptable and early writings on the breed remarked on its faithful disposition, good coat, enthusiasm in the hunt and ability to enter any form of cover.

At the turn of the 19th century there were distinct variations of land spaniel – the clumber, field and Sussex. Of these the most popular was the Sussex and represented a very old branch of the spaniel family. One of its attributes was that of giving tongue when working. This of course was ideal if you happened to be in an impenetrable jungle of undergrowth, but already the idea of cultivating birds to shoot was taking seed and modern coverts with rides cut out were far better for the slower, silent clumber.

The clumber could be classed as the aristocrat and one of the oldest in the family of spaniels. Its ancestry is definitely continental, but its English origins can be traced to Clumber Park, estate of the Duke of Newcastle. Historically it had been connected to the old setting dog, but in the field it was purely a dog for coverts. It was a highly prized gundog, but because its original breeder would not allow offspring outside his estate it became highly inbred. It became all the more celebrated by subsequent patronage by Earl Spencer, the Earl of Abingdon, the Duke of Norfolk and the Duke of Portland.

The clumber was known for its mute qualities when hunting which allowed it to get very close to the game; kennelmen put bells on their collars so that the guns would know where they were. Far and away the heaviest of the spaniels, the clumber's weight probably gave it its steadiness while working.

The field was a comparative newcomer and thought to be a direct result of Sussex outcrosses. Predominantly black it had an enthusiastic following and redeemed itself well in root crop and woods. However, its colour was not ideal for shooting over and its popularity began to wane.

As these breeds began to decline in favour of the modern springer, they did from time to time feature in falconers' kennels for use with sparrowhawks and goshawks. Inevitably the more highly adaptive springer simply took over. Today, although still used in conjunction with hawks, the springer has steadily lost ground to the HPRs, which have one major asset. Although springer-like in their enthusiasm and attitude to work, they are able to point and can give the falconer time to get the hawk into position.

Tradition played a major part in the dogs available in the field: pointers and setters or springer spaniels; distinct demarcation between upland and lowland work. Not until after the Second World War did that situation change and with the rapid rise of the modern falconer, so there was a rapid rise in another family of dogs, the HPRs.

The HPR: The Dual Purpose Gundog

While Great Britain developed its own specialists over the centuries, the same development was going on throughout the Continent. Britain had in fact taken freely from dogs abroad in order to achieve goals in the field and to this end the continentals led the way. Some of their own breeds were documented in writings as early as 1582 and are recognisable of the breeds they are today.

Like the British, the Europeans looked primarily to the spaniel family to provide the base for the extended family tree of dogs used for hawking and the gun. Germany alone has thirty-two types of dog used either as gundog specialists or as tracking dogs in conjunction with the rifle. Of these the first dog to make a significant impact on these shores was the German short-haired pointer (GSP).

Brought here in small numbers after the war it began to gather a growing number of enthusiasts. The steady growth in the population coupled with more leisure time meant there were more people interesting themselves in shooting. Housing was in a boom time and land which had previously been held by single landowners now became accessible. Rough shooting was on the increase. For centuries spaniels had held the elitist position in this sphere. Their effective working in coverts had provided birds for the guns.

In the rough shooting field the HPR began to challenge the traditional breeds. Designed to do many jobs, it could hunt the cover, it could locate fur and feather and if the ground was open or broken it behaved like a pointer and could quest well out for birds. Being far taller than the springer, it could clear obstacles such as fences and drystone walls with comparative ease when being sent for retrieves. It wasn't difficult to see why these dogs might catch on.

The spaniel had worked to flush game where it was easy to find. Now the HPR could work where game was scarce, over any type of terrain and once the game was located could hold it on point, until it could be reached by the handler/gun.

It is curious that, with the number of breeds available on the continent, the early input into importing them here should have been predominantly the GSP. The growing numbers of falconers in the UK who would have liked to experiment with different breeds would have to wait until the mid-'80s to have access to the greatest variety of working HPRs.

HPRs are truly versatile dogs. Primarily designed for multiple duties in the field, it had to be friendly and protective as well as a companion. It had to be capable of tracking wounded predators such as fox or wildcat and trailing wild boar, deer and rabbits. It also had to be able to point and retrieve all variety of game birds as well as wildfowl. Many of the breeds that became the foundation stock were specialists in some of these categories but not all of them. The German wire-haired pointer took the concept of an all-pupose dog even further. It evolved in the late 19th century and was a mixture of the finest wire-coated breeds. It was a true hybrid in the dog world and by 1926 it accounted for more half of the dogs listed in Germany's field-dog register, a situation which still exists today.

Nowadays they are seen in low-ground work, pointing rabbit, hare, partridge, pheasant, duck, woodcock, snipe and lark, while with their long legs they are also seen more and more often on the grouse moor in which they are highly adaptive pointers. Furthermore they adjust to changeable environments with ease and can equally alternate between the hawk and the gun.

The German Wire-Haired Pointer (GWP)
During the early 19th century, attempts began to produce this ideal dog. While these early experiments progressed, various other breeds began to evolve into the modern style that we can see today: the German short-haired pointer and long-haired pointers, the Weimaraner, the wire-haired pointing griffon, the pudelpointer and the stichelhaar. The latter three breeds had strong wire coats which were preferred by many sportsmen

The gyr falcon.

The saker falcon.

Our young trainees are kitted out in a well fitting hood. *(S. Rudy)*

Hawking from horseback. *(S. Rudy)*

as they allowed the dogs access to dense, punishing cover. These three would be instrumental in the formation of the GWP.

The fact that cross-breeding was a paramount importance to achieve the desired results evoked criticism and controversy. The breeders remained undaunted. They justified their moves by stating their motto: 'Take the good where you find it, breed as you like, but be honest about it; and let the results be your guide.'

The primary emphasis was on performance. Next would come conformation, but the performance dominated their breeding and to this end they would utilise whatever bloodlines they deemed necessary. In this case the end did justify the means. This new wire-haired breed began to evolve as an animal that exhibited no deficiences in natural ability, temperament or trainability and through judicious breeding remains the same today.

Its use in UK falconry was first seen in Michael Woodford's book *A Manual of Falconry* (1960). Although some falconers were experimenting with this breed it was not until a photograph of Woodford's own working dog appeared that falconers realised this could be the type of dog they were looking for. But they would be extremely difficult to find. It would be a further fourteen years before any quantity of breeding stock arrived in Britain.

Up until this time it was the German short-haired pointer which had gained ground. These dogs were featured in many shooting and falconry homes and had established themselves in their own field trials.

In 1978 the GWP bitch Wittekind Blanche, owned and trained by ourselves, was precocious enough (at twenty-two months) to be entered in field trials. Within the space of three trials she had already eclipsed all other continental breeds and won an Open Championship Field Trial on grouse. During the following decade she and many of her progeny were to epitomise just what constituted good breeding, winning trials here and in Ireland. Wittekind Blanche became the foundation bitch for the 'Wiggmansburg' kennels which specialise in imported German dogs for both falconry and shooting. As no other wire-hair kennel has such as illustrious background and as I have had almost a falconry lifetime association with this breed, it will feature very strongly in the ensuing chapters as the guide to dog training.

This medium-sized dog with coarse wire coat, docked tail and full beard seems a paradox in the gundog world, yet its ability and intelligence is the basis for their all-round versatility on low-ground or upland game-hawking as well as making them the ideal 'any weather' dog.

The German Short-Haired Pointer (GSP)

From the 17th to the 19th centuries, the GSP was heavy and slow. It was composed of hunting hound bloodlines (Deutsche Bracke) and that of the Schweisshund (a small, painstaking, trailing hound). In addition it was made heavier by being crossed with the old Spanish pointer. It was not until the middle of the 19th century that sportsmen realised the need for a lighter framed, versatile gundog. With the connection between the British royal family and the German House of Hanover came the influx of the smarter, more elegant British breeds, particularly the pointer, into Germany. This gave rise to the modern German short-haired pointer.

Again a medium-sized dog, it comes in the same colour phases as the GWP: liver and white ticked, black and white ticked, and solid liver. With its short coat it is a more elegant animal and has a lighter frame than its heavier-built cousin, the GWP.

During the years when wire-haired pointers were unavailable we used exclusively GSPs. In the early '70s they were still being bred from imported bloodlines, primarily for the field. The dogs that we worked from 1971-1979 were of outstanding quality and were proficient on lowland and upland hawking. However with their short coats they weren't suitable to the extremes of outdoor living in our Scottish climate. They also had the habit of whining continuously, which was one of the factors that contributed to our changing breed.

Hungarian Vizsla

An aristocratic dog owned and worked by the sporting nobility of Hungary, the vizsla was originally bred to scent and search for birds, like the old setting breeds, using nets or in conjunction with falcons. Towards the end of the 18th century a variety of breeds were brought into Hungary and were purposely bred to the vizsla. Hungarian aristocracy had a passion to have in their employ English gamekeepers, who naturally brought their own gundogs (retrievers) with them. These bloodlines were infused with the native bird dogs and in 1880 English and Irish setter dogs were also part of the breeding make-up. As in many continental breeding programmes, the desire was to create a dog with increased hunting quality while keeping the traditional characteristics of the native vizsla. The modern vizsla evolved in the 19th century, having been selectively bred for its improved qualities.

We have trained many vizslas throughout the years for shooting clients and have found them to be good pointers and retrievers. Their gentle nature is very akin to the pointer. Like the GSP they have short coats not suitable for our climate requirements. By comparison to the GWP and many GSPs we also found that they lacked drive and determination on the hawking field.

A medium-sized, smooth-coated dog with a magnificent russet colour, the vizsla is lively and intelligent, obedient but sensitive, and very affectionate.

There is also a wire-haired Vizsla which, like its smooth-haired counterpart, has a glorious russet, hard wire coat. This coat derivative was evolved from outcrosses to German wire-haired pointers.

Weimaraner

Grey or silver grey dogs occurred in the foundation breeds of the four oldest varieties of French hounds, notably in the ownership of Prince Rupprecht as shown in a painting by van Dyck (1631). A short-haired grey sporting dog is also to be seen in Wurttemberg, represented on a large painted ceiling around this era.

Breeding for type began around the end of the 18th century and was centred at the court of Weimar, from which the breed eventually took its name. Most of these dogs are short-coated, but long coats exist in the breed too.

The weimaraner is a tall rangy dog, somewhat larger than other HPRs. The eye colour is unusual in that it has shades of amber into blue-grey, but are all part of the overall look of this stunning grey dog.

Italian Bracco
This breed has only recently arrived in the UK and is an unknown commodity as far as falconry is concerned. It was evolved by crossing the old native breeds of hounds of Italy with indigenous gundogs in the early 18th century. The Bracco is less temperamental than the gundog but less independent than the hound. Nevertheless a long-established gundog, heavily and powerfully built, physically resembling older species of hound.

Italian Spinone
This is the wire-haired answer to the Bracco. Both were designed for slower scenting location work, particularly where marsh or woodland was typical. Very similar to the clumber spaniel in their methodical approach to work, they lack the turn of speed required for open country. Both Spinone and Bracco are the largest of the gundogs, standing up to 27½ inches at the shoulder. The wire coat sustains it in the hardest of cover and weather and it is most often to be seen in the distinctive white with orange markings. In its roan colours it resembles the GWP. This is a long-established Italian breed which originated in France in the district of Bresse and from there spread to Piedmont in north Italy. The Barbet, the Procelain and the French griffon are mentioned among its forebears.

Having worked one of this breed I can highly recommend them if your hawking does not required strenuous work. These giants of the HPRs have very good noses and are good retrievers. Their weight makes them far from agile and ours had the greatest difficulty scaling dry-stone walls or jumping fences of any height. However they are great swimmers and can be of excellent use where streams and rivers need a good flushing dog along their banks. With their tough dense coats they can survive the hardest winters. But they are definitely not upland work material as they simply have the wrong build.

Brittany
The French produced a whole series of breeds by crossing the Spanish pointer with various kinds of hounds. From the activities in this field of breeding came the Brittany. The long-coated French gundogs had a distinct connecting link with the *chiens courants* or hounds. Exactly how they arose is not clear, but they undoubtedly had the working ability instilled through the Spanish *perdiguero* (partridge pointer). Crossing with the English setter had the effect of improving their aptitude for general field work, but reduced their great love of water. The French consider this breed to be the fastest of all the continental gundogs. Standing maximum at 20 inches at the shoulder, it is workmanlike, compact and lively and comes in every shade of colour and self colours. It is the only breed that can produce pups with a naturally-docked tail.

Large Munsterlander
This breed is the 'youngest' in terms of modern development and became stylised in its distinctive black and white silky coat in 1908. In former times little importance was

attached to colour. The original ancestors of both the large and small Munsterlander and indeed of all the German breeds of long-coated spaniels and pointers were the old 'hawking dog' and the land spaniel. The Munsterlander's close relationship to the French *épagneul picard* is apparent, as here it would have found its blue and black roan colour with its long coat and feathered tail. With its infusion of German long-haired pointer it became particularly suitable for working in coverts, woods and water.

Again, we have trained a large number of this breed for shooting clients. Their setter appearance belies their true speed, which is much slower. They are very methodical workers in woods and dense cover, far slower than either GSP or GWPs. They are certainly good pointers and retrievers with a tremendous capacity for swimming. This breed still has a good influx of imports available for breeding working dogs.

All of these breeds have been developed for the field in conjunction with the gun. That they were all bred to perform a multitude of tasks is the reason for their being. Today in the UK some of these breeds do the job eminently better than others. This is generally a direct reflection of the number of dogs that have been bred for non-working purposes.

To be an asset to the falconer they must:
1. Be of proven hunting bloodlines by import or home breeding.
2. Hunt with drive and determination.
3. Face cover and water.
4. Most important of all, be biddable. There is nothing worse than a working dog that is not obedient to command.

Within these reqirements we have found the following to fit the bill very well: German wire-haired pointer (GWP), German short-haired pointer (GSP), Italian Spinone, Hungarian vizsla and large Munsterlander. Of these I personally have had the most success with the GWP and GSP.

The Brittany has an ardent following and is certainly to be seen far more frequently in the hawking field. However it is too small for mixed contour work (low-ground to upland hawking) and would not be the dog to choose if you were intending to work large falcons over vastly mixed terrain. To date I have no experience of working this breed, but have judged them in the field trials.

Chapter 13
Puppies

There is nothing like a litter of puppies to convince you that you could not be without one. An energetic group of playing brawling youngsters that absorb you into a total state of time-wasting!

For the vast majority of dog owners this is how it all starts. Having decided on the breed you want to specialise with, it then becomes necessary to locate very good litters to look at.

Many of the leading shooting magazines and journals will have advertisements in their classified section for a wide variety of breeds. Alternatively the Kennel Club Year Book lists societies registered at the Kennel Club. To obtain information and addresses of breed secretaries you can write to The Kennel Club, 1 Clarges St., Piccadilly, London W1Y 8AB or telephone 071 493 2001.

A further source of information is to visit a major championship dog show. This not only allows you to see the most glamorous animals in your chosen breed, but it is also the place to ask breed club officers how to get in contact with *working* litter breeders.

The very best way to view your breed is through field trials. Although this is strictly the 'high art' of competition it will allow you to see top dogs at work and to get to know more about bloodlines and *all* kennels that contribute enormously to producing excellent dogs for the field. Good breeding comes from knowledgeable breeders, people who know their dogs and consistently produce animals that are suitable for the job, as well of sound temperament which means they are a pleasure to have in your company.

In order to assist the would-be buyer there has been a great deal of emphasis from the Kennel Club and the British Veterinary Association in testing dogs and bitches for severe and debilitating hereditary diseases which can terminate the working life of the dog or worse. Within this sphere are two schemes which are of benefit to you the buyer if you know that the stud dog and bitch have been tested.

Hip dysplasia is a term used by dog breeders to cover a number of abnormal conditions of the acetabulum (the cup-shaped socket of the hip joint that receives the head of the femur) and the head of the femur. Dogs and bitches are scanned under anaesthesia by their own vet who sends the resultant radiograph to the Kennel Club, where it is examined for the degree of dysplascity. The results are published in the Kennel Club Breed Records Supplement and are given as a score for each hip. The *lower* the score the less the degree of hip dysplasia. The maximum score possible for poor hips is RH 53/LH 53 Total: 106. The score for perfect hips is 0:0.

Examination for eyes is done jointly by the KCBVA Eye Scheme. One of the most debilitating eye diseases is progressive retinal atrophy or night blindness. This involves progressive degeneration and the dog eventually becomes blind. Once again the results are recorded in the Breeds Supplement and are classified as *affected* or *unaffected*.

There are specific breeds within the HPR group which seem prone to these conditions, but at present seem little affected by either of them.

Litter watching is important as you will be able to take note of the interacting puppies and to assess which of them are bold, which are timid and which are dominant with their siblings. You should take the pup away from the litter when it is about eight weeks of age. It has been seen through various experiments that if you leave it later than this, i.e. ten to twelve weeks old, the pup's role of dominancy may well have been determined. As dogs are naturally pack animals they need to ascertain at an early age the 'pecking order' within their ranks. Puppies that are already demonstrating a continuously bossy attitude to their litter mates will be the ones that are striving for dominance and may well wish to assert that on you, the trainer. These 'Alpha' animals are best left to more experienced trainers. What you want is a pup with an outgoing personality who is prepared to make a fuss of you and is neither shy nor retiring.

Whether you have a dog or a bitch is purely a matter of personal choice. There is absolutely no difference in their working ability. If anything bitches are at a premium as they tend to be subservient and consequently easier for the less experienced to train.

However they do have regular seasons which means they come into oestrous or heat every six months. Unless kept confined a bitch will wander away from home in order to seek male suitors. Males may also become unwelcome visitors to your property around this time, which lasts between nine and eighteen days. It can be particularly vexing if you were intending to travel to a field meeting or to be with friends over the weekend to go hawking, to find the bitch is in heat. She simply has to stay at home and you could be dogless for some time. As a temporary measure she can have her oestrus suppressed by the use of Ovarid (the equivalent of the pill for the dog), but she cannot be maintained on it indefinitely. Male dogs by definition are available and ready to go hunting all year round!

Once the pup has been decided upon you need to prepare your living quarters for it before you bring it home. Even if it is eventually to live outside in kennels it cannot possibly be expected to do this at the tender age of eight weeks. We like to have our pups in the kitchen at this time where they are readily open to socialising and we provide an enclosed kennel for them to retire into out of harm's way and of course to give them somewhere to sleep when they get tired. These kennels are portable, can easily be dismantled for cleaning and fit into cars. They will require bedding in them and one of the most recent and excellent materials is a product known as Vet-bed, which is synthetic and looks like a sheep's fleece. It is very easy to wash in the machine and has the added benefit of being thermally stable. In other words a puppy will be kept snug and warm on it. To help the pup to adjust to his/her new surroundings you will need to take this sterile piece of bedding and let his dam and siblings lie, play and sit on it to infuse it with their scents. This will not stop the first night's howling, but will help to provide some comfort in those first few days and nights.

Puppies of eight weeks old should be completely weaned. That is they should be capable of eating solids and drinking from a bowl. It is very important that you acquire from the breeder the food that the puppy has been eating so that you can continue this regime. To alter its diet now would in most cases induce diarrhoea, which would stress the pup all the more while it is getting used to its new surroundings. The diet you wish to feed it on should be introduced slowly with its previous one until the processs is complete and its gut can tolerate the change. Although the puppy has milk teeth at present it should not be fed quantities of milk as this also acts as a laxative. If milk is given at all it will need to be semi-skimmed. Meals should be given three times a day. As pups, up until now they will have been kept scrupulously clean by their dam and do not dirty their 'nest'. They will need to be put out after each meal to defecate and urinate. Male pups need to urinate approximately every two hours when they are very young. A good supply of newspaper is required which they can be taught to use until they are capable of 'holding on' until you let them out.

The youngster will need to be wormed and vaccinated against parvo-virus, distemper, leptospirosis and hepatitis. During the period of vaccination it will need to be kept confined to the house. In an 8-week-old pup this period is longer than a pup who may have been vaccinated at 12 weeks of age. The younger pup will have fewer antibodies and will require the greater isolation period away from adult dogs.

A pup will thrive on social stimulation. It needs very much to be a member of a pack. It doesn't matter how small this pack is, it could be just you and it, but at least you're there. Even at this early age some degree of training needs to be initiated. They're never too young to start.

During the early months puppies cannot be left alone for long. You cannot leave a pup for your eight-hour working day and expect all to be well on your return. As long as someone is in the house during the greater part of the day this will stop vices such as howling and barking developing, and you will not have a destructive dog that wrecks everything in sight in an effort to get out and find you.

As they get older, so the knowledge that people may well be absent for some time becomes acceptable to them.

Now supposing you don't want all this hassle of bringing up a pup, what are your alternatives? Many gundog kennels today are able to provide a small number of fully trained adults or part-trained sub-adults. This avenue of approach has several advantages in that the dog is already kennel/house-trained, will accept being left in the confines of the kennel or house, knows the hunting business and can be of immediate assistance in the field. It is also fully-grown and sensible!

All of this can be yours at a price. Trained dogs are at a premium. In the HPR category these will be animals approaching two years of age or over, dog or bitch. From a gundog kennel they will have had one season's shooting over and be proficient in hunting, pointing and retrieving. At the top end of the scale they will be of field-trial standard, having at least been entered in trials and been placed.

If they are privately owned they will be very proficient in the field, acquitting themselves on all counts in every aspect of hunting and retrieving and although of field trial standard may or may not have been entered. This quality of dog will be hard to find. Very few come on to the market, which is not surprising as they take so long to get to this standard. Naturally this will be expensive.

The next category, part-trained sub-adult, may well be easier to locate. These young dogs will be over fourteen months but under twenty-four months old. They will have had either a part or a full season in the shooting field depending on their age. They will be responsive to hand signals, obedient to the whistle, drop to fur and feather and be steady in the field. Again an expensive commodity, but not as expensive as the former.

In both categories, the trained dog can at any time give a demonstration of what it will do so that the prospective purchaser can see it in action.

So, if you are in the position of not having to worry how much a dog will cost and you don't want the trauma of bringing on a pup, then these last two types will suit you.

Once again, just as if you were purchasing a pup, you will need to pursue all the avenues of breeders and gundog-training kennels that will either supply the end product or put you in touch with people who can.

Kennelling and Housing

It is easier to keep gundogs kennelled outside than inside. However if you only have the one dog, then it is infinitely better to have it inside where, as part of the 'human pack', it will integrate far better. It is noticeable that dogs kept inside are more at home with people and probably by and large mature at a faster rate because of their greater contact time with people.

If they are to be kept in the house several points need to be adhered to. The pup needs to have a definite place that is strictly his own. So that when told 'bed', he can go there and lie down. There are times when it is inconvenient for the youngster to be round your feet. When you are eating he shouldn't be round the table and if you are sitting down relaxing he shouldn't be fighting with you as to which chair he's going to have – should be told 'bed'.

The designated area can be the portable kennel or one of the collapsible see-through wire cages, or perhaps a permanent dog bed in another part of the room or a separate room. Whichever, he must at all times be firmly taken there until he can be commanded to go by himself. If the house has young children it will often be for his own safety that he goes there! Children can be intolerant of a pup's needs and very young ones are capable of hurting pups as they view them as just another toy, albeit an animated one. So the pup needs to be rescued for its own good and it is beginning to learn how to function in the human pack.

If the pup is eventually to be kennelled, then the transition from house to kennel can be learnt slowly so that undesirable habits are eliminated. A pup will not be able to live outside before it is five months old. This move is taken very well if there are older dogs for company, but if it is to be the only one, then as it gets to the age of twelve weeks and onwards it should be possible to put it into the kennel at one of its meal-times and expect if to stay there for a short period. Initially fifteen minutes is quite long enough, but this can be extended a little each day. To settle it after it has eaten, take it for a small walk/playtime and then put it in its kennel bed compartment to sleep. It may howl and make all sorts of protest when you leave but if you've tired it out well enough it will settle down to sleep.

The kennel should be in view of the house so that the puppy can see people. It should have a secure, draught-free sleeping area and a good concrete run which is totally enclosed by weld mesh linking. In the run should be a water bowl and a bench raised off the ground which all dogs love to use as sun beds. Ideally the kennel should be south facing. If outside accommodation is the priority, then a puppy bought in the early springtime is going to fit in well with your needs. At our kennels here we breed pups only for this time of year, which means they will be able to fit in with the milder and pleasanter time of year. In addition they will be ready for basic training in the field at the time of year when game birds will be abundant.

For some owners the house is a no-go area for dogs. They will be in the kennel from the start. These pups will more than likely be part of a kennel already and have the companionship of older dogs to help them adjust to their new accommodation. Generally owners with previous experience opt for this housing as they are already able to help a new pup adjust. Secondly their daily routines evolve round the kennel and the pup soon becomes familiar and adaptive. Regular walk times, feed times and play/handling times means it quickly gets the hang of how its environment functions.

Kennelled pups need a lot of time spent with them. Socialising is not so easy if they are not under the same roof as you and time *must* be set aside for this daily. You cannot give them too much, and in return the bonding that is vital for that rapport between you is developing.

Basic Training

In many ways an eight-week-old puppy is like a very young child. It needs to spend periods of time in active bursts of energy then long periods of sleep. Its powers of concentration are very limited, but even so lessons of the most simple kind must begin to feature every day from now on.

No doubt you will have chosen a suitable name for the pup and you will expect it to learn that this name is a word that relates to it alone. If it is a house pup then you will have plenty of opportunity to call its name and reward it by stroking and patting and fussing it. Kennelled pups may not be quite so quick on the uptake, mainly because they are more likely to be outside running around and the myriad distractions around them mean they don't realise you are talking to them. If they don't pay attention then offer an alternative to what the pup is doing. Clap your hands or pick up some item of play and encourage the pup to join you, calling its name at the same time. Pups seem to grasp that this word means them from approximately ten weeks onwards. Once there is a response to the name or the fact that you are calling them, catch hold of them when they arrive and gently push them down into the sitting position with the command 'sit'.

Youngsters will find this far too much of a game and will want to wriggle away and be off immediately. Be firm; hold them in the sit position and if needs be to give them a little reward of food, then make a really big fuss of them once they have done it. It doesn't take them very long to realise that if they come up to you when you call and sit attentively, you will do something very pleasurable for them. 'Sit' soon becomes compulsory to the pup when food is on the go. It will sit in rapt attention while you hold the food bowl temptingly out of reach, with the command 'sit', before putting it on the ground and allowing it to eat.

Puppies can't take too much in their daily lessons as they soon become disheartened by constant pressure to do as they're told. These formative training times need only be five to ten minutes spread throughout the *whole* of their day.

One of the lessons they hate the most is learning to walk on the lead. To be shackled to something is anathema to them, particularly when they are used to going out of the door and running around freely, doing their own thing. One way round this problem is to get the pup to start to learn to wear a collar for short periods during the day. The sensation of something round its neck will not be quite so bad when you attempt to take him for a short walk. Quite often pups find collars irritating and spend some time sitting down trying to scratch it off. With the lead attached begin your first walk. Not far to start with and if need be have someone in front whom it knows so it will automatically pull on to get to them.

Although you don't want a pulling dog, don't worry at this point – training for manners on the lead will come later. Lead training, the most elementary of lessons, can become one of the very worst for the owner. Pups that do not like being on the lead will develop the infuriating habit of not coming in when called to go back on the lead, or worse still will stand just out of reach and circle round you so that you cannot get hold of them to put them back on it.

Once the daily routine of being on the lead is in progress, out on the walk it makes sense to call the pup back to you at regular intervals – mainly for a pat which establishes continuous recall and reward, but also you can take these opportunities to slip the lead on and walk further on, then let the dog off for another romp around. This firmly establishes that leads do not signal the end of 'the best moment of its life', but that there is more to come because you will let it off again.

Patience is a learned art. It is also a discipline that you, the trainer, will need to adapt to.

Cars also are the bane of a pup's life. They inevitably make it car sick. In order to allow the pup to get used to the motion of the vehicle, take it for short rides very early in their training. An eight-week-old pup will adjust far better and find it less traumatic than a sixteen-week-old pup. Try to avoid taking them directly after a meal. A short trip will allow them to be out of the vehicle in comfort, that is before they climb over the car seats to demonstrate the art of projectile vomiting!

It is even better if the pup can be taken to fields or areas where other dogs do not go, to be let out for a little romp around. Remember that if has probably just had its inoculations and must not come into contact with other dogs at this stage. The ideal of cars leading to playtime means that the pup very quickly becomes more than keen to get into the car, rather than seeing it as an object of torment.

As much as the youngster gives pleasure, it can also be very naughty. Nothing is more likely to get your blood pressure rising than to see it ripping your best falconry glove to pieces, devouring the entire hawk food contribution for the day or playing leap frog over the Harris hawk out on the bow perch! All of these it will do if you let it.

One of the other words it will learn is no. Rapping this out in a stern voice is generally all that is needed for a pup to take note and realise that this behaviour is just not on. Older pups take more telling. In their case immediately you spot incorrect behaviour grasp hold of the pup round the scruff of the neck, shake it and tell it no.

However, do not do this unless you catch the pup in the act. Its powers of memory are not able to relate to something it did a short while ago, so it will not understand why you are now punishing it.

This emphasis on training works well providing the rest of the household fit in with your scheme. A pup should not be given commands by others as it will eventually become brainwashed into thinking that all humans run around yelling commands and it doesn't matter if you follow orders or not. Houses are areas of feudal conflict when it comes to whether the kids or the dog should be doing this, that or the other. This is one of the main reasons the most trainers elect to keep dogs kennelled: they can't be corrupted so easily. Only one person will be giving the orders and the pup's allegiance will be only to that person.

As the pup gets older it will need to know 'stay', 'heel' and 'down'. Once again 'stay' can be implanted into its memory banks when food is present. From the age of sixteen weeks onwards it will have enough poise to be able to *stay* in the *sit* position while you walk back two or three steps holding its dinner bowl. Count to five, then put the bowl down as a reward. The waiting time can be increased as the pup becomes competent at doing this, so that you can first put down the bowl with the command *'stay'*, count up to ten, then command the dog in to eat. As ever. Command then reward.

'Down', is not quite so easy. This is a subordinate position which dogs do not take kindly to. However the great virtue of this command is that from this position it is more difficult to get up and chase (as we shall see in Advanced Training) and is far easier for you to control the pup in the down position in later lessons with the hawk. To achieve this tell the pup to sit, then place you hand on its rump so that it remains down. With your other hand draw both of its legs out in front until it is in the down position. To stop it attempting to rise, keep you hand firmly over its shoulder blades, repeating the word 'down' *and point to the ground directly in front of it*. Count to three. Then praise the pup by making a big fuss of it.

Initially you will need to go through this procedure each and every time you want the pup down, but eventually by repetition it will go down on the given word, with your hand pointing to the ground.

'Heel' is best taught on the lead. The youngster should by now be able to walk on the lead but is highly unlikely to be capable of this off the lead. From now on you will need to use a steel check chain which will have the power to enforce your message. It is advisable to tutor the pup on the right and left side, but primarily it will need to be good to command on the right as you will have the hawk on your left. When the lead is on and the pup gets out in front (beyond your knee), tug the check chain firmly with the word 'heel'. Very shortly it will find that 'out in front' can be extremely unpleasant and it is better to be as close to you as possible. This lesson can of course, be enforced every time you go for a walk. Once the pup is fluent in this you may remove the chain and, giving the 'heel' command, walk him for short distances off the lead but to heel. It will if you use a wall or hedgerow or some obstacle which is on the dog's side so that it is not tempted to break away from you and disobey the control command.

With consistent training a pup should have mastered these basics by the age of twenty to twenty-four weeks. However, some youngsters are more advanced than others and seem to mature more quickly. Although the above are well tested training programmes, it must be understood that pups are very individual and no two will respond exactly alike within any given time span.

Having got the pup familiar with our spoken commands, we are going to introduce another element, the whistle. This device more than any other will give greater control over larger distances. We use a black Acme 210½ pitch dog whistle. These can be purchased from pet stores or from any of the well-known dog-training suppliers. If you need to find them, look once again in the shooting papers and journals.

Now the pup is going to hear the verbal command followed by a whistle command and this will be endorsed by a hand signal.

Sit. One long blast. Right hand is raised like a policeman stopping traffic. Give the command 'Sit'.

Heel. Lots of short, sharp, staccato blasts on the whistle. Hand points to the ground at your heel. Give the command 'Heel'.

The pup will gradually become familiar with your commands and obey them when you ask. When it is capable of co-operating with you at this level it will be time to look towards some advanced training.

Chapter 14
Advanced Training

This is without doubt the most exciting time for the trainer, one which can reap the greatest rewards or most monumental disasters. The young pupil must now advance into the world of hunter, pointer retriever. Anyone who can train a dog to this level should have no trouble training either hawk or falcon successfully.

Many people believe that a dog's retrieving instinct will encourage it to retrieve the hawk, and that it would be dangerous to teach the dog this discipline. As we have seen, pointers and setters were during their earlier times retrievers as well. The fact that today they specialise as pointers has not diminished their will to retrieve. I might say here that if we were not careful one of our best pointers (English) would attempt to snatch the grouse from the falcons and didn't give a hoot how she did it. A risky business, particularly as in an untrained state for retrieving she wouldn't be persuaded not to do it. As we will see, retrieving is a vital component to training and is an asset in the HPR.

Now is the time to learn about hunting and pointing, quartering and the use of wind, retrieving, swimming, jumping and above all steadiness.

Young dogs often have a Jekyll and Hyde approach to the environment. On the one hand they can be paragons of virtue when out for a walk, yet when in the hunting fields become total strangers, not listening to commands and running wild. To avoid what would otherwise be serious confrontations between you and the dog, the basic training must have been ingrained to such an extent that such behaviour can be minimised and can indeed be used constructively.

If you acquired your pup in the months of February or March, by the start of the partridge season it will be eight or nine months old. This is a good time to start work on its pointing skills and indeed partridge is the finest of low-ground birds to begin the lessons on. HPRs have a natural instinct to point. It is not something you can teach. But you encourage them to begin by allowing them to hunt.

It should not begin pointing on rabbits. For one thing rabbits will teach the dog to keep its head low to the ground, which may affect its bird-locating ability, and secondly you are likely to end up with a full-blown coursing event that gives the dog immense pleasure, but does little for your blood pressure.

A pup may well have shown distinct signs of aberrated pointing from a very early age, suddenly freezing when it sees a little bird, or perhaps one of its brothers or sisters or some inanimate object before it. Fixing them with its gaze it may begin a deliberate, slow stalking, then in the last few paces rush forwards in an attempt to catch its 'quarry'. In these few moments it has the rudiments of hunt, point and retrieve.

When working for a point it will be necessary for the dog to quarter across territories that may hold game which it will need to locate. For this we need one more whistle discipline – 'Turn'.

Caution the dog with its name. Give two pips on the whistle and put out your left arm. Start moving across to the left, which effectively takes the pup with you. As it continues and runs on past you, stand still and let it run to the distance you require. Now repeat this procedure, going out to the right.

Always run a novice dog *into the wind*. Firstly it will make maximum use of available scents. Secondly, with game that may be difficult to sit to the point, it will have less chance of spooking or 'bumping' them. Thirdly, with the wind in its favour game will be less likely to hear it approaching giving it all the more chance to point.

What exactly is pointing? It is a clear indication by the dog that something is in front, normally in cover. The dog simply comes to a halt. It may have enough time to compose it so that it is in a most stylish point, shoulders back, with long reach of neck and one foot up. This classic stance comes from the animals with great conformation.

I have recently read claims that cocker and clumber spaniels will point. Anyone buying pups on this premise would be sorely disappointed. All breeds of dog will show an innate pointing response to game before them. It is a moment's pause before the next step, the retrieve. It may appear to be pointing, but the unquestioned master of it have been superbly bred for the job. Whether pointer, setter or HPR, nothing matches them in their specialised roles.

While the young dog is casting into the wind, it is important to provide it with margins. These are the boundaries which are suitable for you to work with it. It should not be allowed to work over 40 yards from you. Once it is to that range, give two pips on the whistle and get him to turn in the opposite direction, using your hand signal and verbal encouragement as well if needs be.

Sometimes young dogs seem reluctant to explore their new surroundings and want to hang round you rather than cast on. When this happens, take another person that the dog knows out into the field, stand 40 yards apart and, as you both start to walk into the wind, begin to call it to you. Once it has reached you, your friend should call it across and once it has arrived the process is repeated. These lessons teach the dog confidence and thus begin to show it how you want territories worked. Dogs should not be encouraged to go out as far as possible, as this can be a problem. For the vast majority of your hawking time you will need it fairly close in. If it is going to be used on the grouse moor, then it will be an experienced pointer and range will be within your control. It is comparatively easy to get a dog to run out as far as it can. It is much more difficult to get it to work close.

Partridge and pheasant should be the objects of desire in training your pup. Whether it is 'bird dog' or an HPR, these low-ground nesting species, particularly partridge, produce delicate air scent and give the dog the excellence of 'nose' that they should possess. It is my experience that dogs taken as novices straight onto the grouse moor have no difficulty locating these upland game birds. So strong is the scent of this quarry that they point them very well. However, upon their return to low-ground game birds of which they have no experience, they are quite likely to fare pretty badly and in fact can spend more time blundering into game than pointing it.

Back in the home fields it may not be quite so easy to find partridge. Here pigeons could well be an asset. Dizzied pigeons give the pup an opportunity to locate 'game' and allow you to teach it what to do next. Tuck the pigeon's head gently under its wing and rock it gently on its back. Place it in some tussocky grass or convenient cover and go back to fetch the pup. Pigeons have been known to remain like this for up to fifteen minutes, but it would be wise to experiment with them first so that you know beforehand what they are likely to do.

Try to leave the bird there as long as possible so that maximum scent is emitted; then allow the dog to begin quartering towards it upwind. As it comes into the scent trail it may pause. Caution the pup to be steady and carefully go over to it allowing him to draw closer until it points. If you are in any doubt about the dog's steadiness, always put a check lead on. As it points, stand there and stroke the dog from head to tail with the caution, 'Steady, Steady'. The pup may well be totally mesmerised. Count to ten. Then make it lie down while you stir the pigeon and get it to fly. It will do this as soon as it is touched. Now although you do not want a dog to sit on point, it has already witnessed the next stage of 'sit to the flush', which it will be encouraged to do when it has located game properly. 'Sit to flush' is a vital component of flushing as it deters any pointer from leaping forwards and snatching the quarry.

The recent use of remote-control pigeon-release boxes also facilitates the above; placed strategically and left for half an hour before the dog arrives helps scent to accumulate and also helps to simulate a 'find' to get him to point. Once pointed, pigeons are ejected from the holding box and wing their way smartly and swiftly back to the loft.

Retrieving

This begins at home. From the age of twelve weeks or sometimes earlier, pups will naturally pick up objects and parade around with them. They are not picking them up for you as such, but the instinct to gather something in their mouth is very strong. One thing they are not keen on at this stage is giving their trophy to you! When a pup is young and has 'personal' objects, encourage it to come to you; as it moves within reach gently reach out and pull it close to you. Often in its delight to bring you something it will pick up really awful objects, such as cow-pats or dead birds in an advanced state of rot – in fact anything that attracts its attention. You must grit your teeth and bend down to accept it. *Never* shout at it to drop it. Such unexpected behaviour will deter a young pup from bringing you things in future, and you might inadvertently jeopardise your training programme. As a pup gets older and very confident at retrieving, by all means discourage it from bringing undesirable objects. It will be mature enough to balance positive retrieves against negative ones, which you do not want.

Carefully take the object from the pup's jaws and make it sit. Slowly give the object back. (If it's rotting material, have a dummy in your pocket to replace it with.) Don't allow the pup to leap forwards and snatch your hand in an effort to grab it back. Say the words 'gently, gently' and from the command in your voice plus the slow hand movement it should attempt to take its prize without doing an impression of an alligator.

This begins the important notion that the pup is in a partnership that involves give and take, but it must accept it is to work with you. This will progress to the future date when you will come to rely on this dog's absolute steadiness.

These are very simple little games that the pup enjoys, and should be kept to that. Once you've satisfied yourself that it will retrieve, do not begin lessons in this area until the pup is six months old or more. One of the reasons is that it needs a mature outlook in order to accomplish a task which involves seeing a dummy thrown, marking where it went, sitting obediently until told to go, then going as quickly as possible to the area, locating the dummy, bringing it back and giving it to you. That may be really easy in the local playing fields but more difficult where cover is involved and it needs help to find the dummy, involving hand signals and directions.

Retrieving helps the dog to take hand signals, which command your dog to work in certain areas. These will be of enormous benefit when he is working at a distance from you.

Right and left signals are taught by sitting the dog 10 yards in front of you and facing you. Throw one dummy out to the right on a line with the sitting dog. With your arm outstretched give the command 'lost' or 'fetch'. The dog runs to the fall and brings the dummy to you. To ensure it gives you the dummy and doesn't run around or away from you, try to position yourself with your back to a wall or fence. The dog will need to approach you direct. Bend down and reach out with the word 'dead' or similar. For those perfect moments of poise, make the dog hold the dummy and sit in front of you before you take it. This is getting it composed and teaching it the finer art of steadiness.

Lessons in retrieving are begun on short grass fields so the dog can see clearly what you want. However, it doesn't take it long to grasp these lessons. Sooner or later it will run to the fall and instead of coming back with the dummy will pick it up, throw it through the air, then quite probably leave it there. Boredom . . . to alleviate this situation from now on do *all* your retrieving in long grass or cover so that the dog has to use its nose and concentration powers to locate the dummy. In this way it will become a bold retriever to hand.

Working with a left-hand dummy is exactly the same as for right hand. When the dog completes this, sit it again and place both dummies out, right and left. This time you decide which one to send it for. Now you can begin to see the reason for hand signals and whether the dog will listen to you. Send it for a chosen dummy with a clear hand signal and command of 'Lost'. If it makes for the wrong one, blow the whistle immediately for 'Stop'. As it sits and watches, re-direct it. Should it persist with the wrong direction, blast the whistle for 'Stop', and as it sits shout 'No'. Now send for the correct dummy. Once it has completed this, you may sit it in front and with the appropriate hand signal send it for the second dummy. The purpose of these lessons are right and left direction, which can be extended to cover working out for 30-40 yard retrieves. In these disciplines the dog will begin to see the relevance of taking hand signals at a distance.

Go Back

This lesson teaches the dog to go into another area or return to where it has already been and search it out again. Sit the dog in front *looking at you*. Throw the dummy over its head and behind its back. As it waits for command, put your hand up as in the 'Stop' mode; lean forward as if pushing something away from you and say 'Go back'. The dog should look over its shoulder, spin on its axis and go back for the retrieve. This is a particularly difficult set piece. It needs to be performed on 'tramlines'. Use country lanes with hedges on either side or driveways or fields that have a wall on one side the dog can run along. All of these aids help it to learn to run in straight lines. Once mastered it is a powerful tool in working the dog.

Swimming and Jumping

These are fun lessons for the dog. Swimming should be taught in the summer months and jumping when its bones are capable of supporting its weight, around nine months old.

Water is a great playground for pups. Introduced properly, HPRs are very strong swimmers. They will be an asset to you in locating waterfowl or simply getting across to the other side of a river to hunt the opposite bank out for you. Always choose an entry that has easy access to *shallow* water for a pup. With wellingtons on, go across to the other side and encourage the puppy to follow. As it becomes confident in this element, introduce some basic retrieves over water. Throw a dummy to the far bank, providing it's not more than 12-15 feet away, and get the pup to bring it for you. Since it doesn't require a swim, it'll do it. As you begin over the weeks to build its confidence up, you can go to deeper water with easy access banks and once again get the dog to fetch dummies for you.

Dummy work gives a dog great purpose in the water and allows it to become confident without too many problems.

As it becomes super keen, it must once again be taught composure. Sit it on the bank. Give the command 'Stay'. Make it wait until you tell it to go.

You can also set up right and left retrieves on the opposite bank and once the dog is across the other side give the whistle command 'Sit'. Put out your right arm and get the dog to fetch the dummy. Once it has brought that back, if you feel confident it can achieve a double, send it for the other one too.

The training is beginning to pay off. Our young dog can now locate game birds, will hold a good point, will flush and sit to the flush, and take signals, both whistle and hand.

For many people rabbits are a staple quarry in the field. A steady pointer is an excellent way of finding them even if they've gone to ground as the dog will mark the hole for you to put the ferret down!

One major problem as far as dog training goes is that rabbits rarely sit still for long and their accelerated departure usually has the dog in hot pursuit too. It is here that your training will be tested to the full. *Have you got control?* In other words, if your dog does accidentally break after them, can you stop it? Of course you can and you do this by being in control of the situation before it arises. You will be able to see from the dog's pointing stance and head position that you have ground game in front. Get the whistle in your mouth and move up to the dog diagonally so he can see you. Caution it. As soon as the flush is made, blow for 'sit'. In addition shout the word 'Sit'. This sudden barrage of commands will alert the dog to the fact that if it doesn't sit its world may well fall apart. And that is exactly what will happen if it doesn't obey.

Nothing is more tiresome than an out-of-control dog coursing rabbit or hare which could have been taken by the hawk, or racing in and knocking the hawk off the game because it hasn't been trained to be steady.

Which brings me to one other item of risk to the dog. Steadiness to sheep. Much of the hunting ground from Humberside northwards, and westwards to Cornwall, has sheep on the ground. The chasing of these is a much more serious matter, as a fit young dog can outrun a sheep, bring it down and either attempt to or succeed in killing it. Dogs which kill sheep have no room in the kennel and must be destroyed. This is not something you can train a dog not to do, once it has done it.

Far better to have taken it among sheep when it is young and taught it not even to think about giving them a second look by verbally threatening it and using a willow stick as enforcement to back up your lesson. If this is instilled into them as impressionable youngsters they become a joy to work through sheep and will completely ignore them.

During these formative periods in a young dog's life you must remember to keep training down to time levels it can cope with, i.e. ten to fifteen minutes a day. Above all when it completes its work give it a great deal of praise and then a play period. Nothing will get a dog learning its lessons as well as your praise combined with free play.

No two animals are alike, hence one pup may well be accomplished at twelve months while another will not be until it's eighteen months or older. Probably the most important thing when training is not to overdo any lesson. If the dog gets it absolutely right first time, don't bother with this again until the following day. Whenever the manoeuvre is correct, the dog needs plenty of praise from you. This way it will remember what happened and record it precisely.

The golden rule is: take your time and enjoy watching the dog learn and work, because it is going to be your assistant for the rest of its life, which could be as long as ten active years.

Chapter 15
Dogs and Hawks: Working Together

The very best dogs are those which are fully trained for use with the gun. Falconers of the past knew this and today that still holds true. The majority of dogs in the hawking field will never be used for this discipline, but that does not detract from their ability.

If possible, in your first season try not to fly your hawk over your dog. Instead let someone else fly the hawk and you work the dog. It isn't easy to concentrate on both. After spending so much time on training the dog, now is the time you will make or break it.

The great question really is when do I need to get a dog? The answer is you must get one before you get a hawk. Serious falconry is not a 'chuck it and see' syndrome. It is a structured learning curve towards high-profile hawking utilising both falcons and hawks. It seems an irony that in many cases an inexperienced person acquires a hawk, then realises they need a dog and before you know where you are the dog and the hawk are of a mediocre poor standard because you cannot do both training jobs at once.

As we've seen there is much to the training of a young dog. It will be twelve months minimum before you can use it in the field with confidence (and probably older than that). The person who trains a dog well will also have a hawk worth watching.

Having brought the dog to an advanced standard of work, you can now introduce it to hawking. Initially it may view the hawk with curiosity as its scent emissions (those of a carnivore) will give the dog a clue that this too is an animal of the hunt and not one to *be* hunted.

The hawk will no doubt have distinct aversions to being in such close proximity with another predator. It will require careful work to gain acceptance. One of the first formative steps towards compatibility is in the hawk's manning regime. Here at the Wiggmansburg kennels we always have young dogs out with hawks while they are being carried or walked. No impressionable young hawk will put up with this simply because it has to sit on the fist, so it is very important always to have food available to that it is eating while being walked. The dog should be kept on your right hand side and in the early stages on a lead. Nothing scares a hawk more than a boisterous dog that is jumping and leaping about around you.

From the dog's point of view this is all very basic, so it is likely to have a calm attitude to manning, which is helpful to the hawk's state of mind. As this lesson becomes routine for the hawk, the next step is to have it flying with the dog close by.

The obvious progression here is while the hawk is on the creance. Choose a suitable place where your dog will not be distracted by other dogs appearing and you are unlikely to attract an admiring crowd of spectators.

Find a suitable post to put the hawk on to, or give the hawk to someone else to hold. Lie the dog into the 'down' position and command 'Stay'. It should be behind you, a comfortable distance away, as far as the hawk is concerned (about 40-50 feet). Stand

3-6 feet away from your hawk and call her to the glove for a small reward. Although she may be reticent, the fact that the dog is far enough away should be encouragement for her to make that vital leap towards you. If you have engineered your training properly then she will succeed first time.

From this moment on her fear of the dog will be placated by you, food and learning to hunt. As her training allows you to go further away from her each day, still using the creance you will soon be calling her over 30-40 yards. She will be making a conscious decision to fly to you even though the dog is there, rather than veer off at a tangent looking for the nearest tree. Once she can accomplish this then you will need to bring the dog in closer and in fact she must demonstrate her trust in you and the dog by flying over it.

You may well need an assistant at this point. The creance line may be carried over the dog and you will need someone to help keep it clear. As before, put the dog in the 'down' position. This time you are going to call the hawk over the dog. Stand 20 feet away from the dog, put up your fist and call the hawk for her reward. There should be no reason for her to see this angle of approach to you as any different. She should be confident enough to ignore the predator she is flying over and come when she's called.

Having shown that your training is paying dividends you will now need her to catch the dragged lure. This time, because she's going to have to do all her manoeuvring on the ground, with the dog at this level too, she might have second thoughts about it.

The dragged lure or 'dummy bunny' needs to be taught to the hawk in its initial stages, without the dog being there. Many young hawks take some time to realise that this is a food source. Your bird needs to be competent at chasing, seizing hold of and eating from the lure before you introduce the dog to this discipline.

When she's ready once again the partnership will practice these field moves. In her accustomed field put her on her perch/post and lie the dog in the 'down' position. Now the boot is on the other foot. The dog is about to see something furry being pulled across a field and another animal having fun coursing it! This time it will be *its* training that is paramount. Will it be steady and watch this or will it be so tempting that it gets up and rushes after the hawk, jeopardising the whole of your training?

If you are in any doubt, a few lessons with the dog on its own lying down and having the lure pulled past it, over it and round it will instil into it the need to remain steady.

Training is everything and, as can be appreciated, cannot be rushed. The better the hawk and dog know their jobs, the more exciting days hawking you are going to have. From the hawk's point of view she has gained rewards every time she has completed her work. The dog should also gain so that as soon as the lessons are finished it may be allowed to run freely and play, which it will see as a fair reward for concentration with the hawk.

Finally in these early stages the hawk is ready to leave the creance and begin her work flying free. She should not see any difference in this respect and should find the dog acceptable.

Although as time passes many hawks and dogs work as a proficient partnership and are excellent to watch, it is their formative weeks together in the field that will have a profound effect on the hawk and whether she really can accept the dog.

One of her main worries seems to be that although something exciting is going on, e.g. rabbits are on the loose and she would love to catch them, she seems reluctant, as working away in front is the dog. It seems ridiculous that she should treat this as different, but she does. The dog isn't lying down any more, it races backwards and forwards with frenetic energy. It once again appears to be a threat. Harris hawks and goshawks take a particularly dim view of hyperactive dogs and can let it spoil their day.

The situation need not arise if in the initial stages of hunting the hawk is by herself with you in the field, whether it's for rabbits bolted by the ferret or pastures that have them lying out in tussocky grass, copses or woodland. Once again she lacks confidence. At this stage she cannot concentrate on two tasks at once: hunting and the dog.

Her success at quarry will allow her to focus her attentions on the hunt and once the dog is brought back to joint fieldwork she will be able to equate the dog providing the quarry with her being ever eager to hunt it. It will only be necessary for her to catch a small number by herself – say six rabbits – as by the same token it wouldn't take her long to realise that if you and she can work together there's no room for the dog!

Clearly there will be times when the dog will be superfluous to the day's hawking, but those instance are *far* outweighed by the times you really need a good working dog.

If pheasant, partridge, lark, duck or snipe are to be hunted then you might be lucky without a dog, but with one the opportunities to make your hawk successful are increased dramatically.

In the advanced stage of hunting as a team the dog will need to be in control of many situations: working away from the handler; pointing and waiting for you to get into an optimum position; flushing quarry and not interfering with the hawk. All of these require utmost steadiness which comes from sound basic training and an understanding of what you all need to be achieving in the field.

We have looked at the preliminaries of how to introduce a hawk to our trained dog; the same attention to detail is required with longwings. Falcons by and large are more prepared to tolerate a dog in close proximity. This may relate very strongly to their mode of hunting which utilises the sky rather than the ground. Their natural predators will be other birds of prey, and consequently their aversion to ground predators, i.e. dogs – seems less heightened.

Like the hawk, the falcon will need to be tutored in the field with the dog in attendance at all times. Her lure work demands that she remains on the ground until you come to pick her up. This is the time when she should be taught to eat her food on the lure next to the dog in the 'down' position. It is important to make sure that the food, which ideally should be back of rabbit (as it takes longer to pick at and eat), is secured very, very tightly. The falcon must at no time be able to steal it from the lure and then make it very obvious she is going to fly away with her prize.

The dog who is very close at this point should not have any thought in its head of reaching forwards to steal the food from the lure. It may well be anxious that the bird is getting fed and the dog is not. If it does make attempts in this direction it must be firmly told 'no' and given a sharp shake as an additional reminder. At no time should you feed a dog with hawk food. This will encourage it to go looking for it either in the mews or in your hawking bag, or attempting to steal from around the hawk perches.

While the dog is learning all about the hawk or falcon, so the birds are doing the same. As it becomes a working relationship in the field, this form of mutualism is the hunting harmony you are looking for. Those instances when the hawk or falcon comes looking for the dog because she knows that's where the action is, are symptomatic of excellence of training, opportunity to hunt successfully together and expectation. For the falconer it is the combination that will achieve high-quality falconry. And that is how it should be.

Finally, some hawks and falcons become so 'wedded' to an individual dog that they refuse to co-operate with 'strange' gundogs in the field. If at all possible you should attempt to fly the hawk with other dogs, particularly of different colours to yours. If this becomes a problem, then the only way round it is always to fly over your own dog and no other, as ultimately this will produce the best results every time.

Chapter 16
Breeding or Raptor Propagation

Why did the modern falconer become involved in captive breeding? Why is it necessary? Such questions may be answered today when one looks at the enormous leaps forward this branch of aviculture has achieved both scientifically and as a positive tool for conservation.

The main thrust of the programme to breed raptors began in the late 1960s and early '70s and was as a direct response to the catastrophic effects of DDT in the northern hemisphere. In a developing world human interference has been at the forefront of structural and biological changes in the environment which have caused the demise of a vast number of species of flora and fauna.

In the last 200 years we have lost ten species of birds of prey alone. The most recent of which was the Madagascar serpent eagle, which was extinct by 1950. This is because it was dependent on a specific habitat, i.e. humid rainforests which have been largely cut down and destroyed.

Of the others, six species of owl, one vulture and a caracara were all eliminated because their habitat had been appropriated by man or by his pets and pests.

During the major part of those 200 years the normal method of securing specimens (euphemistically speaking) was by shooting them and having skins sent to the various celebrated museums, which merely added to the speed of their departure. The new technology annihilators, latter day DDTs could have been equally catastrophic, but the modern falconer was evolving as a biologist/aviculturalist technocrat. Falconry was into a new era. Like the phoenix, it arose, this time in the space age.

While DDT pesticides were being used it was becoming painfully obvious that the eggshells of many species of wild birds of prey were thinning. Of the various species affected the peregrine falcons, especially of North America, were in a serious situation. In 1962 Joseph Hickey, a falcon expert, attended the International Ornithological Congress at Cornell University. Whilst there he was made aware by fellow attenders that there did not seem to have been any young falcons fledged in the north-eastern United States or for that matter in south-eastern Canada recently. Surely this couldn't be the case. As a member of the Department of Wildlife Ecology at the University of Wisconsin, Hickey came in contact with a paper written by Derek Ratcliffe of the Nature Conservancy in the UK. This paper spelled out the bare facts. In the UK the peregrine population had collapsed to 328 pairs. Just prior to the Second World War it numbered 820 pairs and was regarded as one of the densest populations in the world. Hickey and Ratcliffe met and collated information to find that egg breaking, death of chicks, failure to lay and failure of birds to pair were endemic in British peregrine populations. By 1965 the situation was revealed as catastrophic in Europe, the USA, Canada, Scandinavia and Australia. Ratcliffe and Ian Prestt (who had recently attended a symposium on organochlorine pesticides and their toxic effects) exposed DDT as the prime culprit.

By 1977 a total ban on the use of DDT was to be seen in all European Community countries. Some countries had banned it considerably earlier. In the UK a voluntary restriction was carried out from 1965-1975, in Canada and the USA by 1970 and '72 respectively.

DDT has residual properties. More complex than first imagined, it meant that in the early '70s the decline of the peregrine was still evident. By 1975 a survey showed that for the whole of North America only 324 nesting pairs of peregrines could be found from previous historic numbers estimated at 7,000 (though the pre-DDT population was poorly known).

The UK, Spain and Australia had fared better. Their populations were now on the upswing. The USA and Canada, by far the worst affected, had to do something to arrest what might well be the extinction of the indigenous peregrine.

The consequence of this destruction was that a whole new form of awareness evolved. Previously regarded as vermin, there was now the need to ensure the survival of threatened raptors. The work that took place to secure the future of the peregrine put it into a spotlight that has contributed more than anything to making so many people 'raptor watchers'.

Just prior to this era it had been customary for falconers in this country to obtain wild falcons under licence. It soon became apparent that they just did not exist in sufficient numbers anywhere to justify this practice, so a voluntary ban was undertaken by falconers not to apply for licences until the situation was resolved and peregrine numbers were on the increase.

In the United States in vast areas of previously occupied territory they had quite simply vanished. For USA falconers this was one of the main criteria for looking at the possibility of breeding them in captivity. It was considered a long shot. Previous attempts had been quizzical rather than scientific and hadn't really established any parameters or common ground to work with. However if it could be achieved it would have to be in numbers that made the efforts worthwhile, as well as providing enough birds for release and restocking previously known sites.

By the early 1970s it was known that falcons could reproduce naturally as compatible pairs within the confines of their breeding chamber and could also naturally rear and incubate their young. Using the methods of poultry breeders, artificial insemination and artificial incubation could double the numbers produced.

The facility that was to be the mecca of this pioneering work was at Cornell University in Ithaca, New York, led by Dr Tom Cade, whose single purpose was to prevent the extinction of the peregrine falcon.

By the mid 1980s it was possible to reproduce virtually all known species of falcon. Furthermore, this enormous scientific and practical input had been the cornerstone for many projects on the continent with access at all times to the considerable information output at Cornell.

The success of this captive breeding programme would not have been so meteoric, had it not been for one vital ingredient: the falconer. The urgency for captive breeding of their indigenous peregrine meant that falconers sacrificed their trained falcons to the breeding chambers, at great expense and effort, in order to re-instate this bird in the wild.

Falconers in Europe did likewise and latterly the same has been done in Africa. Indeed, when DDT threatened Zimbabwe's African peregrines, it was the falconers who brought the problem to the notice of the authorities and falconers who instigated research into environmental pollution, thus initiating their own enormously successful captive breeding/release programme.

That falconers had a vested interest is undenied. That they were gravely concerned about the peregrine's loss from known breeding sites and might no longer be available for falconry spurred on the desire for artificial propagation. Saving the peregrine was the motivation that created worldwide breeding programmes costing millions of pounds and involving several thousand people with support from government bodies, conservation organisations, foundations and corporations. Almost without exception successful breeding in captivity has been created by falconers and their colleagues, who provided sustained motivation and the technical skills to succeed in a very difficult task, which universally cannot quantify the input, time and personal expense involved.

The production of falcons and hawks, although commonplace today, will never produce a magic formula that enable all pairs to breed at any time. Each pair is a special case which requires trial and error to identify their reproductive responses. Through intuitive insight and management from the breeder may come the desired result. As this procedure is both time-consuming and laborious, producing falcons on a large scale is a costly undertaking.

Today the release of over 3,000 peregrines in the USA has put the bird very firmly back in its ecological niche, particularly when one considers that the breeding successes have induced a self-sustaining, self-propagating wild population. On the continent and in other countries previously affected, the current profile is of a comparative success story. The UK today has more than 1,000 breeding pairs, which is in excess of previous figures known. In Europe the total population is at least 4,000 pairs and in North America 500 known pairs nesting in the West. These numbers continue to increase. There is evidence that in America the peregrine should be removed from the endangered species list. It is now felt by scientists involved with its breed/release programmes that there has been a rapid increase in numbers and distribution, showing large numbers of territories in use. There is no sign of any widespread problem for the bird, suggesting that the population is secure for the foreseeable future. Ultimately it would prevent large sums of money being wasted when a favourable outcome for its re-instatment is inevitable.

Today the modern falconer has the knowledge and ability to breed all known species of raptor. Indeed twenty-one species of falcon have so far been bred, along with a great variety of eagles and hawks, and these numbers are growing. In real terms this means that no species of raptor should become extinct. With the advent of successful captive propagation we are now beginning to look positively at domestic populations.

Raptors, like humans, occupy an important ecological niche at the top of the food chain. The work on chlorinated hydrocarbon insecticides put them into a new category, that of environmental detector, or monitor. In this position their status can be used to indicate habitat quality.

Such work is not entirely the remit of the biologist; it is a multi-disciplinary involvement for people whose aim is to secure the future for flora and avifauna, maintaining a natural balance wherever possible.

Captive breeding in responsible projects provides ideal opportunities for detailed biological study in many aspects of a species. Current knowledge in raptor veterinary medicine has been accelerated through the captive breeding schemes, particularly in nutrition, clinical pathology, energetics, physiology and disease. Such information has not only been important within the realm of captive propagation, but equally of relevance in conservation programmes. Management and production techniques developed within the breeding programmes are of enormous advantage in that these can be used for work on endangered species.

Some species, such as the American kestrel, breed very readily in captivity which can permit large numbers to be used for raptor research. It's an interesting thought, but had such captive projects been around in the 1950s, it might be said that the effects of DDT could have been averted.

Educationally, captive breeding has played a very important part in raptor conservation. Public attitudes have changed considerably over the past three decades towards raptors in particular, from the destructive to the protective. This respectful tolerance is one important factor in promoting survival in the wild. As the process of captive breeding provides continued relevant information for maintenance of wild counterparts, it consistently provides a living image of what can be done in the name of conservation. Although its benefactors are many, it is *everyone* who benefits.

Chapter 17
Aviaries

There is no hard and fast rule for the size of a breeding aviary or chamber. But there are minimum requirements which have been evolved from practical experience: if you can enlarge upon these because you have the space, then do so. Hawks and falcons, eagles, owls and vultures, all benefit from space according to the occupant's size. Just as humans, given the opportunity and financial resources, prefer larger homes to smaller ones, particularly if they have gardens and or grounds, so for raptors more space means less stress.

Perhaps one of the most successful constructions and one that is much used in a modified plan throughout the world today, is the Cornell chamber system which is 20 feet x 10 feet x 14 feet high. The height of an aviary is worth considering in that for the majority of breeders it will just not be possible to have tall constructions, whether it's because of neighbours, or building regulations or simply not having the space. We use a modified system which is 20 feet x 12 feet x 10 feet high. A reduced height of 8 feet is possible for small raptors such as merlins or sparrowhawks, but clearly this lower ceiling height is not ideal for larger falcons and hawks as it does not allow for aerial manoeuvrability when flying from one destination point to another, or for aberrated flying displays in the breeding season.

Many aviaries are constucted of wood, usually marine ply, and during the summer are particularly cool. However, our persistent damp climate with its driving rain, gale-force winds and snow, makes this an unreliable material in certain counties because of its limited life. Metal sheeting such as galvanised corrugated sheet or box profile galvanised zinc sheet may be better. These are designed to be rugged and to have a viable life span of at least twenty years. The outer surface can be coated with weather-resistant paint used from a spray machine, and green or brown allows the chamber to blend in with its surroundings.

Metal constructions have one drawback in that they can become very hot in the summer unless a great deal of care has gone into siting the nest ledge and various perches in shade. However they are enormously strong structures and can take the strains and stresses of extremely violent winter weather far better than any other.

The chambers are what are known as skylight/seclusion, which means that the occupants have uninterrupted vision through the roof but cannot be put under stress by the close proximity of the outside world. This may seem improbable in hawks and falcons that have been manned and flown, but experience has shown that when they are given liberty into the aviary and their relationship with you is at a temporary close, then they will revert to wild behaviour if they are not given the concept of total security from within. Furthermore excitable behaviour is tantamount to various levels of stress, which is not conducive to breeding.

The sides of the aviary should be dug into the ground. Ours are let into the ground by 2 feet, as this stops ground predators from digging in. In certain locations, aviaries can also be equipped with an electric double-strand fence which will further stop unwelcome visits from foxes and cats. These are powered by a battery and can be purchased from agricultural suppliers. Rats can also be a serious problem, often finding their way into your secure construction via mole tunnels. Once in, they need to be eliminated as they can quickly colonise.

The roof netting should be of a strength that will not break under pressure from within or without. We use a specially constructed netting from a company that will make any length and width that you require. This comes in several sizes of net square, from ½-inch squares upwards in ½-inch graduations to 3 inches. It is a heavy duty black nylon and is typical of nets used for cricket practice or trawler nets. In addition a bounce net is laid 12–18 inches underneath the main net like a ceiling; this is of lighter construction and less tension, so that falcons and hawks cannot hit the taut main nets, which they could do with some speed and damage their ceres, the cartilage above their eyes and the tops of their shoulders.

At *no time* should chicken wire be used. This is the equivalent of using a vegetable shredder and will do irreparable damage to raptors of whatever species and type.

If metal is to be used on the roof, then plastic-coated chain linking or galvanised weld mesh are the tools of choice. Both are particularly expensive and heavy, and will need roof joists to support them.

Where the nest ledge is situated, a solid roof cover is used as shelter. This should be approximately 3 feet wide and run the width of the aviary. In addition, sheltered perching should be available at the opposite end. This allows for protection from rain, snow and sun.

Snow is one factor that gives a great deal of concern to many breeders. Its annual occurrence is often a surprise. Usually it is not of any quantity to worry about, but you can never be sure when that is going to be. An aviary with a netted roof is highly susceptible as the sheer weight of snow can tear the netting down, allowing the birds inside to escape. The bigger the square on the net, the more likely it is that the snow will fall through. However, you are not likely to have 3-inch squares if you've got merlins inside. We find as a general rule that 1½–1¾-inch squares (suitable for the majority of breeding birds) will allow a certain degree of heavy snow through, although accumulations do occur and with a lesser gauge that this the snow constantly gathers. It will mean that, suitably attired, you will need to go into the aviary with a long-handled broom and gently knock the snow off the roof from underneath. If a broom cannot be found, use any long piece of wood with a cross piece on top which has been covered with foam sponge or a soft fabric. What is very important is not to push the netting so hard and fiercely that it ruptures, leaving gaping holes.

If snow is not cleared then the weight factor can become critical. If it freezes in this state the birds will be in a darkened ice cave until it thaws. The use of chain link and weld-mesh roofing doesn't require such attention as they are load-carrying surfaces which should be able to support tonnage of snow. In these cases snow should simply be swept off the top surface, to allow daylight in.

Location

The siting of the aviary should be such that the nesting area is facing south. This allows for maximum sunlight, which is particularly important at breeding time. The outside wall near the door should have a chute through which food can be passed down to a feed tray inside. This tray should be a surface that can be in a sense self-cleaning. Plastic mesh of the kind used for fencing is ideal as a base as it lets the rain through and allows any build-up of debris to fall to the chamber floor.

If the aviary is to be of the 'barn' variety, that is many chambers side-by-side as one continuous long, low building, then a safety corridor will be important. Access to the doors of aviaries will only be via the corridor which opens at either end. If a hawk escapes out of its front door then it remains safe within the external corridor.

Ideally the aviary should be in a quiet situation. However, it must be said that many hawks have bred very successfully in extremely noisy surroundings. The occupiers that have never been flown or manned are probably better in a quiet situation, whereas those that have been handled are more likely to tolerate peripheral noise. It should not be out of your sight to the degree that you cannot, when standing outside, hear or see what is going on in or round the aviary. Neither should it have been constructed so close to the house that you can go upstairs and look out of the window into it! Seclusion and a great degree of privacy for the occupants is essential.

One other interesting factor is the siting of street lights. If these are shining into your aviaries every night, then eventually the hawks inside will respond to the altered photo period. What this means is that they may start premature breeding rituals and indeed females in this situation have been know to lay infertile eggs, despite being with a known copulating male. Their sychronised breeding behaviour will have been disorientated. Clearly such a location would be inappropriate.

Interiors

The flooring inside needs to be a surface which will remain reasonably clean for up to six months at a time. Earth floors simply become hard-baked in summer, creating dust, and a muddy swamp in winter. Pea gravel has been found to be one of the most suitable surfaces. Certain parts of the country have a shalerock substratum which left as it is makes good flooring. It drains well, allows the minimum of weeds to flourish in the spring and summer and in fact has the preferred properties of pea gravel. Gravel needs to be laid at a level of at least 5-6 inches deep (allowing for settlement). It can, however, be hosed down and is comparatively easy to replace as necessary. If aviaries are on a grand scale, then their natural floor will be quite sufficient, as the area for soiling will not be as critical, as concentrations will not be such a problem.

Perches

These should be designed so that they offer sunlight and/or shade. Hawks prefer to sit as near to the roof as possible in most chambers as this sensation of height is a natural response; indeed in the wild their species cousins would do the same, as this facilitates prime hunting look-outs and positions of safety. One or two perches should be constructed in this manner. They should be 2½ feet from the ceiling, which allows comfort in sitting there. However, should the hawks decide to copulate on this perch there would be the minimum room to do so.

A perch which runs full width can be placed at one end and indeed can also be placed next to the nesting ledge so that it runs to the opposite wall. These perches will be at least three feet from the roof as it is more than likely that they will be used for copulation, and height is important. If the roof is very high then you will need intermediary perches between the floor and top-level perches. This will be of particular benefit to females who are carrying well-developed eggs and are too heavy at this stage to lift their body weight vertically. They can use these like a ladder. Youngsters out of the nest for the first time need the reassurance that they can get back up to the nest and this will assist them, too. For 'branchers' that get onto the floor in our chambers they are all supplied with a 1 foot wide, 8 foot long plank which has wooden rungs screwed on (rather like a ship's gang-plank). This slopes gently to the floor from the nest ledge so that when they eventually get to the floor, as they are incapable of flight, they can scramble back up the plank to safer levels.

Falcons such as sakers and gyrs tend to be somewhat lethargic in aviaries. When they do fly around they also manage to land on their perches with considerable weight, which can induce foot injuries and subsequent bumblefoot. Landing areas should be covered with de-traumatising material such as 'astro turf'. This shock-absorbing surface should be applied on all areas that these falcons can approach with a degree of speed.

Hawks seem to suffer less in wear and tear in this category and benefit from a variety of round, textured perches. Natural wood with its bark attached with various widths from 1½-2 inches in diameter suit the majority of hawks' feet. Tree stumps put into the interior design are also appreciated because they add to the diversity of foot surfaces, which they make use of.

In particularly spacious raptor aviaries, it has sometimes been found that getting up speed involves the risk of collision with static perches (or walls). The majority of raptors have favourite perches or favourite ends of their aviary. Here it has been proved beneficial to provide mobile swing perches. These are attached to the roof and once the bird has landed it has to grip and balance because the perch begins to swing freely. They can be designed to run the whole of the width of one side, set back about 5-6 feet, which allows for swing and for the bird to slow up to land on it.

Bathing

All hawks and falcons need to bathe, some more than others. Bathing also allows them to drink as and when they need to. Although they are infrequent drinkers their requirements for water are such that it should be available at all times particularly during the breeding season. Females have an increased need of water when they are laying eggs. It is quite noticeable that females at this time will stand in their bath scooping large beakfuls of fresh water. This is probably in direct response to the eggs' requirement for water just prior to calcification.

The siting of the bath should be that they will not defecate into it and that you can enter the aviary comparatively easily to clean it out and provide fresh water.

Algae build-up is a problem in the summer in aviary baths. When they are taken out it is beneficial to scrub the sides with Virkon, or a washing soda solution. This effectively kills the microscopic cells which build up and allows fresh water to remain uncontaminated for longer periods. Algae accumulation exists where water remains stagnant and given the right circumstances can be very poisonous. Baths cleaned with any proprietary product should be rinsed out well before re-filling.

Nest ledges

These are usually a box construction for falcons and a corner ledge site for hawks. Falcon ledges are 3 feet x 2½ feet x 4 inch boxes filled with pea gravel. The gravel presents a close proximity to surface material used in the wild and the birds can dig and hollow out scrapes that will cup the eggs while the female is incubating them. The scrapes also serve as a container for the young when they are very small; the rough substratum helps their feet to grip and their knee joints are kept tucked under their body. This stops the youngster from becoming splay-legged, which it may well do on a smoother surface. Alternatively, the ledge can be a continuous shelf that runs the width of the back wall. These take considerable filling with pea gravel, but allow the eyases more room to move, once they become mobile.

   Hawks require something more substantial and a corner shelf unit, sited at the rear of the chamber, will accommodate larger birds and their young. These ledges will have slatted bases with a gap of about an inch between each slat, so that air can pass underneath. The nesting material will need to be sticks and twigs. For goshawks and Harris hawks we provide ¼–½-inch diameter sticks, from which they can construct the base. The nest cup that the female will form should be of soft spruce which she can whip and bend into a tight structure that will safely contain her eggs. Often females will gather foliage growing in the aviary, and thread that into the cup as well.

Chapter 18
The Occupants of the Aviary

For many falconers the decision to put their hawk or falcon into an aviary will arise from the desire to reproduce from their hunting hawk. It is a source of immense pride and pleasure, but the thought of losing it is too great. The prospect of flying one of its progeny is the natural process which will secure your sport in the future.

To gain the necessary experience and background knowledge for more complicated species, buzzards and lanners are excellent birds to start with. Their behavioural reactions and responses will provide valuable data for more complicated hawks and falcons.

However not all birds will breed, despite your best intentions and architectural triumphs. One needs to look carefully at the source your adult bird came from and how it was reared.

There are infinite variations within the practicalities of breeding, but as a beginner you want as few problems as possible.

It is probably true to say that the highest proportion of raptors bred today are from stock that was reared by their parents or foster parents. These young were subsequently taken up by falconers, given full training and then hunted. Such birds receive a level of conditioning that makes them receptive to natural pair bonds. In both hawks and falcons, young females often respond by laying in their second year.

As breeding has become a commercial success, so some of the methods for rearing have been geared to maximising a female's annual laying potential. Many females are quite capable of producing eight or more fertile eggs, but the rearing system may not have the required number of foster parents. Consequently they're reared by hand, using various techniques and these young present the greatest difficulties for natural copulation as they become sexually mature.

Imprints

These are reared by hand during the formative period in which a reversal of identity takes place: they equate the human with an avian, developing a filial relationship in which they identify solely with man and express this identity through vocalising and later sexual bonding. There are a variety of ways of producing imprints, but without fail all have been reared in the presence of man, at an age when dependency was irreversible.

Classification of the degree of imprinting has become confused in many people's minds. The various methods of hand rearing can influence the young bird's basic behaviour patterns and sociable response to you. However, its maternal attachment has been learned and just how co-operative it is going to be with you will depend on whether it was imprinted with a high degree of thought upon its interaction with you, especially where food is concerned, or whether it was reared in the hope that it might identify with conspecifics (its own kind).

Sociable Imprint

This refers to the 'art' of rearing a falcon or hawk as an imprint on man. Isolated from its siblings, the chick is usually hand reared from as early as day one or removed from the aviary nest between its tenth and fourteenth day. It will now be kept in a brooder and later an open-topped ambient air brooder where it will see people at all times. It will learn from an early age (usually around day nine) to feed from a dish. The food is always available and this ad-hoc method allows the youngster to feed as and when, which means that it doesn't need to vocalise to you for food. This is a very contented state and as it becomes accustomed to the human environment, it begins to see the falconer as an additional part of the scene and not simply the food machine. As it reaches 'brancher' stage and becomes fairly mobile, it will often leave the brooder; if you are sitting down it will come and climb over you and eventually lie down to sleep on you or on your hands.

At this stage youngsters can be taken outside and shown their surroundings. On warm days we often take them out into the paddocks where they will later learn their falconry skills and put them onto the dry-stone walls to take stock of their world. By this time both falcons and hawks are beginning to learn to feed on a lure as well, but their food consumption is still very ad lib.

At no stage do these young ever 'scream'. They remain quiet throughout their lives and are not affected by 'screamers' put out onto the same lawn with them, once they are trained.

Young falcons and hawks are identical in their responses and we have reared buzzard and goshawk in this manner. Goshawks are a particular pleasure imprinted in this way as their abundance of aggression is directed to hunting and not to the falconer. Nor do they demonstrate the stereotyped behaviour of excessive mantling and tail breaking that other degrees of imprinting seem to do.

Dual Imprint

These young are often reared by their own mother or perhaps by a foster mother who is likely to be an imprint herself. Dual imprint is a misnomer as no breeder can state such an identity unless these offspring will breed naturally and co-operate fully in an A.I. programme. This will not be known until it becomes sexually mature, which in certain falcons could be as long as five years.

An imprinted female will rear young in the presence of her falconer, allowing him/her to enter the chamber at will. She will feed, brood and generally tend her charges while you are in with her. While the youngster is being reared in this way it becomes familiar with man as well. The end in view is a state of ambivalence, that the birds should be capable of pair bonding naturally, while remaining highly sociable with you, should you require them for A.I. The females will actively solicit copulation when sexually mature and males will solicit courtship even though they are in a chamber with non-duality birds.

That some of these birds do become 'duals' is undenied, but experience has shown that for many breeders the skills needed to bring them to this level are not well enough developed.

Young falcons and hawks are precocious enough to realise from a very early age that you represent no threat when you enter the aviary and also that you always seem to be there with food. Although not obvious at this stage, imprinted behaviour may well arise when the youngster is taken up for flying.

Creche Rearing

This term is applied to a clutch of eyases reared in the nursery system. These young will normally have been hatched in an incubator and will not have the back-up of parental or foster rearing. They are hand reared *en masse* in a group environment. It is imprinting by numbers. There are instances of individuals forming natural pair bonds when reaching sexual maturity, but the majority will respond and behave as imprints.

However, creche rearing, properly conducted, produces excellent prospects for breeding. The idea behind the system is to allow eyases to imprint upon each other without interference imprinting from man. Two aviaries are required. In one aviary will be a pair or single, mature, birds of the same species. The second aviary, directly alongside, will have a full-width ledge with the young on. A food platform will be on

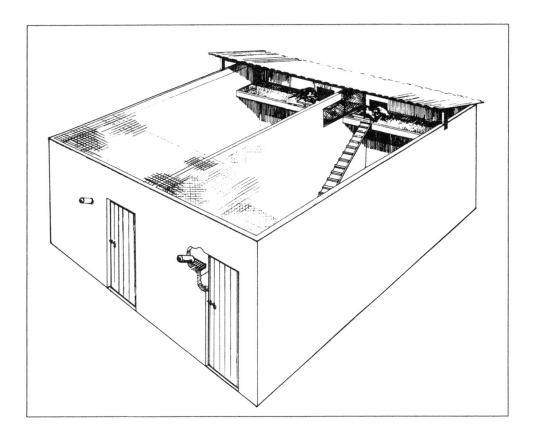

the ledge between both chambers. This platform can see straight into the next aviary. Ideally the partition wall should be see-through as well. Eyases that can eat out of a dish and have developed a good downy coat can be put into their chamber. This will require a heat lamp while they are still very young. To feed them will require a hatchway at the back of the ledge and a corresponding one for the adult aviary. Although at this stage their food is still minced in a bowl, the adults should have their food tied down *firmly* onto a board before it is put onto their ledge.

The eyases will no longer see you. Food will always be available and the adults will be fed at the same time so that they will have to come down beside the young to get their food. As this is tied down it will take longer for them to eat. The eyases will make the transition. They will strongly identify with each other as well as with their own kind. It has been noticed that some adults will attempt to feed the young through the partition as they get a little older. In this situation the young will fledge in a familiar environment, simulating parent rearing.

One thing that eyases are quick to catch onto are your footsteps, heralding the fact that you're bringing food. The walkway to their hatch should be soundproofed. This is one further eliminating factor in the non-imprinting process.

Screaming Imprints

As their name implies, they do just that. The noise level from certain species can often be intolerable. All forms of imprinting could technically produce this effect, if mismanaged. As they sit on their block or bow perch, they drop one or both wings in a partial mantle and simply open their mouths and yell at the top of their voice. We have seen that this type generally emanates from hand-reared young (fourteen days and onwards) put back in with rearing adults in the hope that they will not become imprints. In addition the breeder has periodically given them welfare checks and by going into the aviary, further endorsed imprinting. These same young are often taken out from the aviary as soon as they can fly and weight controlled for training. The moment they are dieted they begin screaming, which is often uncontrollable.

These hawks suffer acute identity crises throughout their lives. They will not relate to their own species, nor will they respond adequately to man in a specialised breeding programme.

Reverse Imprinting

This can be carried out on imprinted females. The female is given a group of eyases to rear. In the group should be a male unrelated to her. He will be kept in with her until well fledged and flying strongly round the aviary. He will then be taken up, manned, flown and hunted and at the end of his season put back in with her. She will recognise him and will tolerate her 'young' in the same territory. He can be taken out and flown each season until he reaches sexual maturity. During this period the imprinted female will maintain the established maternal bonding. When he begins to demonstrate courtship display and breeding rituals, she will respond to him and allow copulation. It is a long process to go through, but may well be worth it in terms of a breeding future for the female.

Imprints can of course be bred from and we shall look more closely at that in the chapter dealing with artificial insemination. For the falconer/breeder who has an aviary the prospect of getting the right occupants can be a minefield. However, falconers are more likely than aviculturalists to establish the psychological suitability of their potential breeding birds because they will have flown them. The rapport that develops in the field will give clear indicators for natural breeding potential.

The majority of hawks and falcons demonstrate sexual responses at the age of three years. Gyr falcons are somewhat later than this (four to five years) while eagles and vultures will be six years or more and small falcons and hawks rather younger (one to two years).

Timing

The occupants of an aviary need to be introduced to each other in October-November. The late autumn with its decreasing light is very similar to the increasing light of spring. Interaction between the pair, no matter how superficial, will start the process of pair bonding. They need to be watched on introduction. This can either be through observation holes, or by close-circuit television cameras.

Springtime is when the males will show a greater degree of interest in the females. To encourage the females to respond, feeding routines are divided into two or three feeds per day. This does not mean increasing the volume, merely providing smaller but more frequent meals.

The quality of feed is important in that maintenance diets of day-old chicks are simply not good enough. Quail, rabbit, pigeon, rat and mice should be given, depending on the species of raptor you are breeding from.

True Hawks *(Accipiters)*

Once the decision has been reached to attempt to breed either goshawk or sparrowhawk, then a great deal of care is required in their introduction and management. With the extreme difference in size between the sexes, if you put them together too early, the female will often attempt to hunt the male by chasing him and may well inflict fatal injuries as he attempts to escape her intimidating behaviour.

These accipiters need to be kept in a double-windowed, duo-chamber. They are adjoining aviaries in which a sliding mesh window is at either end of the central wall, so that they may see each other but cannot enter or put any part of a foot or talon through.

The windows also have strategic focal points adjacent. The idea is that if the bird goes to one of these points it will stimulate behavioural reaction from the opposite aviary. At one window will be seen the breeding ledge (both male and female will have their own) and at the other window, in each aviary, will be a feeding tray.

Initially the windows are covered by a wooden shutter. Neither bird can see into the other's chamber. In the early part of the year, usually January, the wooden shutter at the feeding tray end is opened. Neither can get through as the mesh window is firmly in place. Similarly in February all the nesting materials are added and the shutter at the nest end is removed.

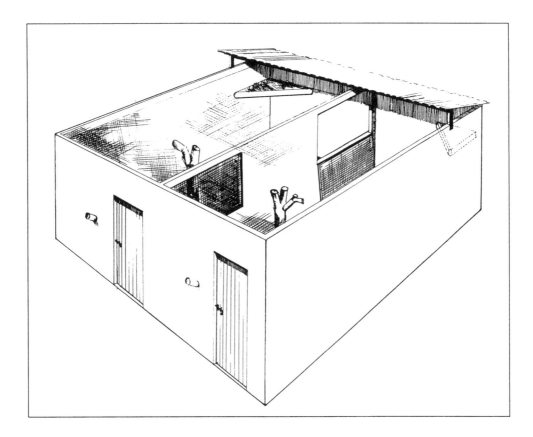

In this manner, you can observe how the birds react to each other's presence. Feeding regimes will usually provide indicator mechanisms, particularly if the male partially plucks and leaves the food in sight of the adjacent female. Additionally, as each individual begins to work on its respective nest, observation will reveal whether the two hawks are synchronising courtship behaviour.

Nest building by both birds is usually a good indicator of heightened breeding intent. During these activities both male and female will 'flash' their white tails under coverts as visual indicators to each other.

You will need to slide the mesh windows open to let the male into the female. They need careful observation now. If she attempts to harass him or if he appears to be confined to one perch and any movement or look from her elicits 'twittering' from him, they should be separated immediately for several days until she has had time to become receptive.

Observation is a major part in success. If you cannot devote a considerable part of the day to it when you are attempting to establish a pair of these hawks, you should not undertake it.

Sexual Dimorphism

In birds of prey this refers to the size difference between male and female. It is evident in all diurnal raptors and as the female is larger and stronger than the male it can present difficulties in the breeding chamber. Generally speaking all non-accipiters will tolerate the close proximity of each other within one chamber and once established as breeding pairs will remain so annually. However, as female accipiters exhibit particularly militant tendencies, they will be separated from their males once again during the late autumn until the start of the next breeding season. Sexual dimorphism in accipiters is far greater than in other species. It is possible that initially the female genuinely sees the male as a prey species, not as a conspecific. His smaller size may well represent the relative size of quarry she would comfortably tackle in the wild. Driven first and foremost by her aggression and egged on by any sudden movement of the male, she will hunt him. Not until she is in an advanced breeding condition will she respond to the male's courtship rituals.

Chapter 19
Incubation and Rearing

The best incubators are the parent birds. No machinery can do it better. Incubators emulate and simulate the brooding parents, and although a degree of skill is required in operating them, they can achieve the end result. So which is the best way of getting your fertile eggs to hatch?

Natural Incubation
A pair of breeding birds in an aviary will, if settled, sit their eggs for the full term. On average this will be thirty-one to thirty-two days, by which time the first egg will have pipped. If the pair are established breeders and have reared young before, there is no reason why they should not hatch and rear their own young.

It may well be that the laying female is not able to sit her own eggs, in which case an alternative species can substitute. This can be another hawk or falcon or even a domestic chicken.

Chickens that are known to be good sitters, particularly of the bantam family (i.e. pekins, cochins, silkies etc) are quite capable when trained for long-term sitting to bring the fertile eggs right on to pip. Hens are chosen because they have previously demonstrated their ability to sit their own eggs to term and subsequently can be trusted with raptor eggs.

Artificial Incubation
Sometimes females will not sit their eggs, or because of artificial insemination you may be taking the eggs sequentially. It is far better for the egg if it receives at least seven days' natural incubation from another raptor or an incubating hen. However sometimes even these are not available and an incubator needs to be used instead.

Incubators have been designed to handle the hatching of multiple-laying birds such as pheasant, partridge or quail. No incubator was designed solely for the use of raptors, although all current models can be adapted to your requirements. You therefore need to have a working knowledge of your incubator before you begin to put falcon or hawk eggs into it.

The optimum temperature for raptor eggs is 99.5°F/37.5°C. This is the same as hens' eggs and although there have been eggs hatched above and below this we have found that this produces maximum hatchability.

The Egg
A typical egg will lose 15 per cent of its initial mass during natural incubation. This loss gives rise to air-cell volume whose functional importance is to assist in the interchange or diffusion of gases.

During the pre-natal period oxygen and carbon dioxide are exchanged across the chorioallantois (placenta) and water vapour is continuously lost. Since the shell is rigid, gas enters through microscopic pores to replace the lost water and forms an air cell at the blunt end of the egg. The air cell increases steadily until it occupies approximately 15 per cent of the internal volume of the egg at the end of incubation.

Much of the embryo's energy requirements are taken from the fat stores in the yolk. For every gram of fat burned an almost equal amount of water is generated.

Metabolic water must be lost in order for the embryo to hatch. Under the brooding female this process occurs naturally. In the artificial incubators, it needs to be monitored so that optimum weight losses occur. Humidity within the incubator room will affect the developing egg. Too damp or too dry an atmosphere may be adverse conditions. These can be controlled by additional incubators which have a micro-environment designed to correct 'heavy' eggs or 'light' eggs, by having one with more water in or one that has silica-gel in to absorb as much water vapour as possible.

For eggs which will receive artificial incubation their weight will be recorded from the moment they enter the system. They are expected to lose 15 per cent of their fresh weight in total or roughly ½ per cent per day, given that the majority of eggs will take thirty-one or thirty-two days to pip.

A graph is required to record daily weights, which must be done accurately on a pair of gram scales.

For eggs that have received some natural incubation, it is unlikely that their fresh weight is known. In this instance the daily weight loss will still be ½ per cent. We have found this to be a reliable guide to weight loss performance on medium sized birds eggs.

Once weighed the eggs are put into an incubator that has no water in it. Here the machine is responding to ambient humidity. Twenty-four hours later the eggs are re-weighed and their progress will determine whether they remain there, or are moved to a wet incubator or a dry atmosphere.

Excessively wet or dry conditions will plunge the egg into an environment it cannot adapt to quickly enough and may well terminate further development. Atmospheric changes must be done gradually over a period of days. This means that monitoring the eggs' weight should be done every twenty-four hours if problems are occurring and every forty-eight hours if the weight loss is on course with your calculations.

Incubation

Whichever system is adopted, you must get to know your incubator. It will need mapping out with a thermometer to know where the optimum, cold or hot spots are. If it is to be turned automatically, make sure that the rolling eggs are not to be nipped or cracked while mobile. All these preliminaries can be done with hens' eggs of the appropriate size. We use modified Roll-X machines. The eggs are turned manually nine times a day and they lie on their side. They will only be turned through 180° on each turn and locational arrows on the egg surface show which turn is imminent.

Sterilising the machine is very important and will be done before egg arrival with potassium permanganate and formalin. Use 0.4 g of potassium permangante and 0.8 cc of formalin per cubic foot of incubator. This is an extremely noxious combination and should be done in a well-ventilated area. To stop the reaction of these two chemicals fouling the interior we put the powder into a small open container such as a sweet tin or tobacco tin and pour the formalin on top, never the reverse.

This works well if you have warmed the incubator up first. Leave the gas in situ for at least twenty minutes, then remove container and flush out residues by running the machine. It will take several hours to clear, but the process can be helped by propping the lid open.

If mercury thermostats are used, the contacts for these will need cleaning with alcohol (medicated swabs, obtainable from chemists) as distortion can occur in temperature readings due to chemical deposits on the contacts.

Once your mapping areas are reading correctly again, the incubator will be ready for use.

Hatching

After thirty or thirty-one days, the egg begins to demonstrate signs of internal change. The use of a suitable candler will show that the developed embryo has now begun to draw down the air sac, which until this point was spherical, so that it is now elliptical. It also occupies a much greater area within the shell. This is the process called internal pipping.

In order to hatch, the chick will require more oxygen than that received through diffusion, so it penetrates the air cell at the blunt end of the shell. This is crucial as it allows its lungs and air sacs, which have up until now been unused, to ventilate and breathe through the air cell. It receives a bulk flow of oxygen and shortly after this it will pip the shell.

The choriollantic (placental) function now goes into decline, but this process is only totally complete at the moment of hatch. The young bird is now in a transition period in which it is developing the strength to break out of the egg.

At pip, the eggs are removed from the forced-air incubators and we put them into a still-air incubator which has had sterile water added for humidity. It will remain here for up to fifty-six hours in order to hatch. A clear plastic collar, 6 inches in diameter, is put round the egg to contain the fresh-hatched young. The floor area is a single sheet of kitchen paper and a thermometer is added to monitor temperature.

It is perfectly possible to hatch in forced-air incubators, but they should not be the same as those with eggs in. This eliminates cross infection and fine feather dust (caused by the hatchling) getting into the fan and motor mechanisms.

In the majority of cases a chick will hatch by itself if its weight loss is correct. It will vocalise during the pip stage and the sound will become stronger as hatch time gets nearer. In the second stage it will form a 'blow hole' through which the egg tooth can be seen. In the third stage it uses the tooth to cut through the shell. If viewed from the blunt end this will appear as an anti-clockwise sawing motion. This may take from twenty minutes to one hour and is punctuated by rest periods. It will push the cap off having turned at least three-quarters of the way round.

Some eggs are problems from the day they are in the system. These become difficult hatchers and may require assistance at birth. However, no egg should be tampered with before fifty-six hours have elapsed. The young still have a very active blood supply and it is all too easy to rupture blood vessels, causing the chick to bleed to death. After that time has elapsed, use a pair of *blunt*-nosed forceps, carefully sterilised, to take a bit of shell away from the blunt end to see why the chick is stuck.

In the majority of cases they are too big to turn and cannot cut through. By giving them a little more room and plenty more time they will be able to cope with hatching, and will often hatch without further assistance up to ten hours later. Patience is needed. Watching the chick to make sure that it is not losing its strength will give you a guide as to whether you will need to help it further.

If embryos and chicks die in unfamiliar circumstances, a post mortem at a veterinary inspection centre will be useful for your future information. Where pathogenic causes are to blame, you need to know so that you can prevent any further occurrence.

Brooding

Once the chick has hatched it should be left to dry out and fluff up. This will take several hours. It can then be transferred to a residential brooder which will be its source of warmth and artificial nest for at least the next five to seven days. These brooders will require a surface bottom which will stop their legs from splaying. We use 4-inch guttering which is the length of the brooder. It has a terry-towelling inlay with kitchen paper on top. This is easy to keep clean and can facilitate mute checks from the young.

During the next few days the chick will find that the original incubating temperature is becoming too hot. The level of heat will need to be very carefully decreased. Indications of how much can be seen from the chick's reactions. If they are too cold they will start to rear their backs, feeling instinctively for their mother's brood patch to keep warm. If they are too hot they will lie out with their legs away from their sides, opening their beaks and panting. In either state they also vocalise, letting you know all is not well.

Observations are very important. During these early days the chick is utterly dependent upon you. These altricial young require constant heat and feeding, none of which they are capable of controlling themselves.

Feeding

The quality of food is very important. A diet deficient in nutritional requirements will lead to poor quality young. Quail have become staple dietary feeding for a wide variety of raptors and in our project remain the sole diet until twelve days, when additional foods can be made available.

The first feed will be a small sliver of breast of quail which has been dipped in a warm solution of Lectade. Additionally, prime the food with a pro-biotic (by Vetark) which stimulates the production of gut flora. This is done approximately six to eight hours after hatching. Any chick that does not want to feed must not be force fed. Leave it and try again later.

Give two or three pieces of prepared food. To get the young to feed you will need to mimic adult 'eechup' calls, which stimulate the young to beg. At this point it will not have developed muscle strength to support its head, so you will need to hold its body and support its head gently while you offer the food with tweezers.

We usually feed every fours hours, but increase this to every three hours with smaller hawks and falcons. That is between 7 a.m. and midnight: they are not fed during our sleeping hours.

At this stage it is easy to overfeed them. If you look at their crop area you will see a small rectangular panel which becomes dark with food content. This should not be crammed or overloaded. Chicks are very delicate at this stage and the crop is only just starting to function. Overloading will lead to problems you do not need. It is a question of common sense as to volume, so that it can put this over by the next feed time. This newborn young has to make the transition from feeding on a yolk supply to the enormous change of receiving meat protein. If this is overdone, the gut simply cannot cope.

After the first three days, in which you will also notice an increase in their food intake, they will need to have calcium added to the diet. This is best done using a hand mincer and grinding a whole, skinned quail. Remove the intestines but not the other organs. Take off the feet, head, wings, neck, crop and tail. This will be fine ground and can be stored with cling film in the fridge for the day's use. This mix is now more tacky to eat. Ensure that Lectade (or failing that previously boiled water which is body warm) is available for dipping your portion into. This helps it to slip down as well as providing essential electrolyte activity and fluid intake.

The food should be warmed, especially if it comes out of the fridge. Each day fresh quail are minced up. Casting should not be made available until they are fourteen days old, by which time they are capable of making a pellet.

Chapter 20
Growing Up: Fledging and Dispersal of Young

Once the chicks have approached day seven, you will need to have made a conscious decision as to what you intend to do. Although still vulnerable and very dependent on you, the chick requires its own mother or foster mother to cope with its next stage of rearing. This will ensure it learns behavioural responses that will provide the greatest chances for future natural breeding.

Young accipiters, buteos and parabuteos have what may be termed altricial precocity. Their ability to recognise you by sight and sound develops at a faster rate than young falcons. By day two they are aware of your presence and by day three or four can climb over siblings in order to establish feeding priority.

These young, if kept in the residential brooder system for longer than nine days, may well learn patterns of behaviour that could stimulate imprinted responses when they are later handled and flown.

Stimulated to react to your presence, they react equally to the movement of each other. In buteos and parabuteos this leads to sibling rivalry and combats – a sort of Cain and Abel syndrome. In the brooder they will need to be segregated as one can seize hold of another and throw it around with force.

This behaviour has also been witnessed in the nest when young have been put back with their mothers and although they have not killed one another, those that are being harassed have lain down with their heads out of the way, not moving until the aggressor decides to stop.

Sibling aggression within these species seems to wane by the fourteenth day. However, they need to be monitored in this period as continuous physical assault on individuals may weaken them and they will not thrive. If necessary remove them from the nest for several days, then return them: this will normally solve the problem.

Close Rings

The fitting of metal close rings to domestic bred hawks, falcons and eagles is a requirement by law. When you have a clutch of eggs the Department of the Environment needs to know. Currently the only exceptions to this rule are owls and old world vultures. It is important that the breeder fits his/her own rings to prove identity.

The following is reproduced by kind permission of the Department of the Environment and is the exact procedure to follow.

Wildlife and Countryside Act 1981: Section 7 and Schedule 4 1993
Breeding Season for Registrable Birds
Ringing and Registering Chicks
Registration Procedures Reminder

Once again we are at the start of another bird-breeding season. If you intend to breed any registrable birds this year please read the enclosed **"Close-Ringing of Captive-Bred Schedule 4 Birds – A Guide for Keepers"** very carefully as some of the procedures have changed since last year.

Each year, at the beginning of the breeding season, all keepers are sent a reminder of the ringing and initial registration requirements. This year we have taken the opportunity to enclose some additional information in the hope of clarifying some other areas of the registration system which are sometimes queried by keepers.

I hope you will find the following notes helpful.

Change of Address at which Birds are Kept
Keepers should note that a registration document can only be amended to show that a bird is housed at a different address from that of its registered keeper if it is still being tended on a day-to-day basis by that keeper. **The bird will otherwise need to be registered by the new keeper if it is not returned to its registered keeper within three weeks, as in effect, a transfer of keepership will have taken place for which a fee is payable. Keepers who return registration documents for such amendments should attach a letter to explain the circumstances under which the bird is being moved**.

Date that Birds are Acquired
When applying to register a transferred bird, keepers are required to **fully** complete the reverse side of its registration document giving the **exact** date, i.e day, month, and year that the bird was acquired. **Applications not bearing an exact date will be returned to the applicant** and registration will therefore be delayed.

Dead, Released, and Exported Birds
Registration documents should be returned **immediately** with the relevant box ticked.

Lost Birds
Keepers should contact their Case Officer **immediately by telephone** when a bird is lost. Under the terms of the Departments' Data Protection Act entry **we are unable to release your name, address or telephone number to the finder of any lost bird without your prior agreement**. This can lead to delays in reuniting bird and keeper. It would be helpful if, either when reporting a lost bird or when next writing to us, you could tell us whether you would wish to disclose your details. **You may withdraw your permission at any time by telephoning or writing to us**. Registration documents should be returned if a lost bird is not recovered after three weeks.

27

Illegible/Lost Rings

Birds that have lost their rings or are wearing rings that have become illegible **automatically become unregistered** even if their registration documents have not expired. As it is a keeper's responsibility to ensure that their birds are correctly registered at all times, **rings should be regularly checked and replacement cable-ties applied for if necessary**.

Licensed Rehabilitation Keepers (LRKs)

LRKs are reminded that they can hold a wild disabled bird for **six weeks only** from the date it was taken into their care, after which, they must either release or apply to register it.

Prompt Registration

Just a reminder to all keepers obtaining new birds – **remember to register your bird(s) as soon as they come into your possession**. Late registration is treated seriously and is always pursued since possession of a non-registered bird is an offence under the Wildlife and Countryside Act 1981.

Finally, we wish you every success during the breeding season. Any queries regarding the above points or any other registration matters should be addressed to your Case Officer at the above address. The Case Officers are now as follows:-

Case Officer	Keeper (by initial letter of surname)	Telephone No (using Bristol code **0272**)
Mr Davis	A–D	218695
Mr Liebert	F–K	218649
Mrs Noakes	L–P	218692
Miss Millard	Q–Z and E	218120

Wildlife and Countryside Act 1981: Registration of Schedule 4 Birds – **Schedule of Fees Payable**

The registration fees are currently under review but until further notice remain as below.

CATEGORY 1 BIRDS

Zoos (see note 1)
Renewal of properly registered birds: £7 per bird

Registration of new birds: **£14 for every monitored (see note 2) £7 for every non-monitored**

Transfers (payable by recipient):   £17 for every bird received from non-NFZ members; no charge if received from NFZ members.

Recognised club members (see note 3)
Renewal of properly registered birds: £7 per bird

Registrations of new birds: **£14 for every monitored (see note 2) £7 for every non-monitored**

Transfers (payable by recipient):   £17 for every bird

Non-club members
Renewal of properly registered birds: £9 per bird

Registration of new birds: **£20 for every monitored (see note 2) £9 for every non-monitored**

Transfers (payable by recipient):   £17 for every bird.

CATEGORY II BIRDS
Renewal of properly registered birds: £1 per bird up to a maximum of £25

Registration of new birds: **£6 per bird**

Transfers (payable by recipient):   £6 for every bird

CATEGORY III BIRDS   No fees payable
SEE NOTES OVERLEAF

Notes
1. To qualify for reduced registration fees zoos must be members of the NFZ and be willing to participate in the inspection scheme. For qualifying zoos the maximum renewal fee payable is £360.

2. The monitored species are **Golden Eagle, Merlin, Gyr Falcon, Peregrine Falcon, Barbary Falcon, Hobby, Goshawk and hybrids of these species**. Other species may be monitored from time-to-time; keepers will be notified of any changes before the breeding season each year.

3. Members of such clubs must be participants in the club inspection scheme; members of such clubs who do not wish to be included in their club's inspection programme must pay fees at the non-club rates.

Licensed Rehabilitation Keepers (LRKs)
The fee for the LRK licence is £33 for the registeration period 1 November 1993 to 31 October 1995. This fee will need to be paid **before** any licence is issued.

Permanently Disabled Birds
Some birds taken in by LRKs will be permanently disabled and unsuitable for release back to the wild. No fee will be levied on LRKs for retaining such birds, nor will any fee be charged for transfers of such birds to LRKs. However, if the bird is passed to a non-LRK a transfer fee will be payable by the new keeper. The progeny of disabled birds will attract the normal registration fee.

IMPORTANT ANNOUNCEMENT

Wildlife and Countryside Act 1981
Registration of Imported Schedule 4 Birds
Changes to Import Regulations

Keepers who frequently import birds should have received notification from the Department's Cites branch detailing changes to the controls on trade within the EEC. From 1 January this year it has no longer been necessary to obtain an import (or export) permit/certificate for birds imported from other EC member states.

While the import of birds from EC countries no longer requires a permit/certificate **keepers should note that the need to register such birds promptly remains. Any keeper failing to do so would be committing a non-registration offence. The previous "safety net" for keepers, of reminder letters from the Department chasing up late notification is no longer possible for imports from EC countries. You are therefore urged to contact your Case Officer as soon as the quarantine period is over.**

LICENSING REQUIREMENTS

UR (UN-RINGED) LICENCE REMINDER
There are various reason why a bird may need to be kept without it wearing either a closed ring or a cable-tie. The two most common reasons are when a bird persists in pecking off cable-ties, and when a bird's injuries prevent it wearing anything on either leg. In these circumstances keepers are required to apply for a UR licence, in order to keep the bird legally unringed.

Most UR licences are valid for a maximum of 12 months. It is therefore necessary to re-apply each year and to give sufficient reasons why the bird remains unable to bear a cable-tie. It is not possible to wait until the bird's re-registration date, as this is renewed on a 3-yearly basis. **You should therefore check any UR licences you have for birds in your keepership. If the licence has expired the bird is unregistered, even if the registration document has not expired. If a bird is passed to another keeper, that keeper will need to apply for their own UR licence as the previous keeper's will be invalid.**

SALE
Keepers should remember to check **BOX 6** of their registration documents before selling birds as they may need an individual sale licence to do so. No licence is required to give a bird away.

Any queries regarding licensing matters should be addressed to:-
   Licensing Section, Room 8/09, Tollgate House, Houlton Street, Bristol BS2 9DJ Tel: (0272) 218693

Wildlife and Countryside Act 1981 – Section 7
Close-ringing of Captive-bed Schedule 4 Birds
A Guide for Keepers

NOTE: Please read this document carefully and keep in a safe place for reference. The guide is not intended as a comprehensive explanation of the law. Any enquiries about the content of the guide should, in the first instance, be directed to your Case Officer.

1. Introduction

1.1 All registrable Category I and II Schedule 4 birds hatched from 1983 should be fitted with a uniquely numbered ring issued by this Department. For captive-bred birds, this will usually be a close ring.

1.2 All keepers who intend to breed any registrable birds in captivity should read this guide carefully. It gives details of how to request close rings and register the chicks. **It also describes certain changes in procedure introduced since last year.**

2. How to Request Close Rings

2.1 There are two ways in which close rings can be requested; by telephoning the Case Officer, or by sending a completed ring request form, copies of which are available from this office at any time. The Department hopes that most keepers will find it easier to telephone their requests as this is a quicker and more efficient method.

2.2 Telephone Ring Request

Ring requests for **both** Monitored Species and Non-Monitored Species should now be made **as soon as the completed clutch of eggs has been laid** unless you are already certain that all the eggs are infertile.

2.3 When a telephone ring request is made all the following details must be given.
  (i) your name and ID number;
 (ii) ring numbers of both the parent birds;
(iii) number of eggs in clutch;
 (iv) date last egg was laid.

If your Case Officer is not available, one of the other Case Officers will be able to take down the details you provide.

2.4 Once this information is received the appropriate close rings will be dispatched within 24 hours. Rings requested late on a Friday cannot, however, be dispatched until the following Monday.

The Case Officers are now as follows:

Case Officer	Keeper (by initial letter of surname)	Telephone No (using Bristol code **0272**)
Mr Davis	A–D	218695
Mr Liebert	F–L	218649
Mrs Noakes	M–P	218692
Miss Millard	Q–Z and E	218120

2.5 Written Ring Request

By this method, a ring request form, completed in full, will need to be sent to the Department **as soon as the full clutch of eggs has been laid**.

2.6 Whichever method is used to request rings, the aim is to ensure that close rings will be available in time for the chicks to be correctly ringed. The Department should be contacted by telephone if there is any delay in receiving rings. To avoid delay in the issue of the rings, please inform us of any special arrangements which you have for the breeding season, especially where chicks which require ringing are being kept at different addresses.

2.7 It should be stressed that it is the responsibility of the person who requests the rings to ensure that the birds are ringed as required.

3. Witness of Ringing for Certain Species

3.1 The Department will continue the practice of allocating one of its inspectors to witness the ringing of the following species:-
Goshawk
Golden Eagle
Peregrine Falcon
Barbary Falcon
Merlin
Gyr Falcon
Hobby Falcon
First and second generation hybrids of any of the above.

3.2 The registration application form and appropriate rings will be issued to the Inspector who will then contact the keeper to arrange a convenient time to witness the ringing of the birds. It is important that the keeper provides as much notice as possible in these cases as it may take some time for an inspector to arrange a suitable time. **Keepers are reminded that Inspectors are not able to assist with the ringing of birds and if an assistant is required keepers must make their own arrangements.**

4. Registration, Transfer and Sale of Chicks

4.1 As soon as rings have been fitted to the chicks you must complete and return form DOE 14088 (a registration application form) **along with the appropriate initial registration fees.**

4.2 The registration application form and rings will be issued for a specific clutch of eggs and must not be used for any other. The form will have printed on it the numbers of the close rings enclosed with it, and details of the parent birds for that particular clutch. It will also bear a 'batch' number in the top right hand corner which you should quote if you need to contact the Department regarding a specific clutch.

4.3 Please read the notes before the registration form is completed. If applications are not completed correctly or are accompanied by incorrect fees there may be some delay in issuing bird registration documents. All birds must be ringed and registered **within two calendar months of the date the rings were issued**. You should not wait until the end of the breeding season in order to submit all your applications together. Failure to comply may leave keepers open to prosecution for keeping unregistered birds. **Make sure that any unused rings are also returned and that the boxes concerning the fate of each ring have been ticked**.

4.4 On receipt of your completed DOE 14088s and fees, bird registration documents will be issued within three days.

4.5 The Department is aware that to promote successful breeding, parent birds and/or their eggs are sometimes moved away from their registered keepers. **Please note that closed rings are always issued to the person who will have possession of eggs when they hatch, even if that person is not the registered keeper of either parent bird**. That person is then required, under the above Act, to initially register each bird in their own name before they are passed on to a second keeper, even if that second keeper is the registered keeper of one or both of the parents. That second keeper would subsequently incur transfer fees in the normal way.

Anyone who passes on a bird for which they have been issued a ring before they have initially registered it, EVEN IF NO SALE TAKES PLACE, should be aware that they may be breach of the regulations governing registration.

IF YOU HAVE ANY DOUBTS ABOUT LOANS AND FOSTERING PROCEDURES PLEASE CONTACT YOUR CASE OFFICER FOR ADVICE.

4.6 NOTE: (a) Category I birds hatched from 1983 onwards which are fitted with either close ring of a larger size than recommended, or a cable-tie, cannot be sold under the terms of a general licence. In these cases, a keeper must first apply for an individual licence **before** he can sell, or advertise the bird for sale.

(b) There are no general sale licences for Category II birds. An individual sale licence would be needed for each bird before it could be sold or offered for sale.

Application forms for Individual Exemption Licences can be obtained from:
Licencing Section, Room 8/09, Tollgate House, Houlton Street, Bristol BS2 9DJ Telephone (0272) 218693 or 218694

5. Return of Rings to DOE

5.1 The Department issues rings on the basis that they will be fitted to the clutch of eggs for which they were requested. It is not acceptable for keepers to use rings intended for one clutch for an alternative clutch of eggs, except in special circumstances, and with the **prior** approval of the Department.

5.2 If any eggs prove infertile or a chick dies before it is close-ringed, any unused rings must be returned to the Department immediately, together with form 14088 issued with the rings. The rings and form should **not** be retained for any other chicks.

5.3 After close-ringing, should it become necessary to remove a ring to prevent damage to a chick, the Department should be contacted immediately. In some cases a keeper may need to remove a ring before he can do so. In every case the ring should be returned, with an explanation of the circumstances. If it is necessary to remove the ring of any "monitored" bird, please contact the Department at once so that arrangements can be made for a Wildlife Inspector to witness the removal of the ring.

5.4 If you are intending to apply to export a close-ringed bird, the Department would advise against removal of the ring before export as many importing countries require a close-ring to be kept on a bird as evidence of captive-breeding.

6. Rings and Ring Sizes

6.1 A list of the ring sizes recommended for Category I and II birds is attached to this guide. Ring sizes will **normally** be issued in accordance with the list. It is accepted, however, that certain birds produce chicks for which the recommended ring sizes would be incorrect and a smaller or larger ring needs to be fitted. If this is the case, when a ring request is made you should give the reason for not requesting the recommended size. Your Case Officer will then send a letter along with your rings to confirm your request. If requesting a larger size ring, bear in mind the Note in para 4.6 above.

6.2 All rings issued **remain the property of the Department. Attempts should not be made to enlarge them, alter their shape or interfere with them in any way**.

6.3 If there are any reasons why the fitting of a DOE close ring is considered inappropriate, the keeper should contact the Department immediately.

7. Double Ringing of Chicks

7.1 For certain species of bird the Department recommends that two different-sized rings should be fitted, one ring for each leg. This is to take account of the variation in leg (tarsus) size between the male and female of the same species, since it is often impossible to sex chicks before they need to be ringed. The inappropriate-sized ring can be removed at a later stage, once the sex is known. Keepers should, however, be aware that it is **not** compulsory for 2 rings to be fitted, but please see Note at end of para. 4.6 above.

7.2. If it becomes necessary to remove either ring for any reason the ring should be returned to the Department, with the bird registration document and an explanation. See para. 5.4 above.

8. Fitting of Close Rings

8.1 Close ringing of chicks normally takes place between the 8th and 14th day following hatching, with all chicks from the same clutch being ringed at the same time. For some species or certain individual birds, however, ringing may need to take place as early as the first day after hatching. It is the **keeper's responsibility** to ensure that close rings are fitted at the time which will best achieve humane and effective ringing of the chicks.

8.2 Close rings fitted at the correct time will be a snug fit when the bird's foot is passed through. Undue force should be avoided and it may be helpful to apply a lubricating gel or soap to ease fitting. If you have any difficulties or queries, your Case Officer may be able to help.

9. Fees

9.1 The initial registration fees for the current period are:-

Category I Birds – (diurnal birds of prey)
Club members and Zoos
Monitoreds	£14 per bird
Non-monitoreds	£7 per bird

Non club members
Monitored	£20 per bird
Non-monitoreds	£9 per bird

Category II Birds – (non raptors which must be ringed)
All birds	£6 per bird

9.2 Members of recognised clubs (British Falconers' Club, Raptor Breeders' Association, Hawk Trust, Northern England Falconry Club and Welsh Hawking Club) who participate in their club's inspection scheme are eligible for the concessionary club rates.

9.3 The transfer fee for a Category I bird is £15 and for a Category II bird is £5. No registration fees are payable for Category III birds (registrable birds which are not required to be ringed). Keepers should note that it is not always possible to deal promptly with applications for registration which are not accompanied by the correct fees.

PLEASE DO NOT SEND CASH OR OPEN POSTAL ORDERS. All cheques and postal orders should be made payable to "DEPARTMENT OF THE ENVIRONMENT" (not DOE) and should be crossed "NOT NEGOTIABLE". You should retain postal order counterfoils for your own records.

10. Category III Birds

Keepers and breeders are reminded that they are required to keep the Department informed of changes or additions to their stock of birds. The following species are included in Category III:

Avocet	Little ringed Plover
Beet-eater	Common Quail
Bittern	Scarlet Rosefinch
Little Bittern	Red-necked Phalarope
Bluethroat	Green Sandpiper
Corncrake	Purple Sandpiper
Spotted Crake	Wood Sandpiper
Stone Curlew	Common Scoter
Divers (all species)	Velvet Scoter
Dotterel	Spoonbill
Long-tailed Duck	Black-winged Stilt
Black-tailed Godwit	Temminck's Stint
Black-necked Grebe	Black Tern
Salvonian Grebe	Little Tern
Greenshank	Roseate Tern
Hoopoe	Short-toed Treecreeper
Kingfisher	Whimbrel
Leach's Petrel	Ruff
Kentish Plover	

Finally, if you have any queries at all please consult your Case Officer at the address below.
Bird Registration Section, Room 8/09, Tollgate House, Houlton Street, Bristol BS2 9DJ

RECOMMENDED CLOSED RING SIZES

SPECIES (Category 1)	♂ SIZE	♀ SIZE
AMERICAN KESTREL	R	R
BARBARY FALCON	V	W
BLACK KITE	V	W
BRAHMINY KITE	W	W
COMMON BUZZARD	W	W
COOPERS HAWK	U	V
FERRUGINOUS HAWK	X	Y
GOLDEN EAGLE	ZA	ZA
GOSHAWK	V	W
GYR FALCON	W	X
HARRIS HAWK	W	W
HEN HARRIER	R	U
HOBBY	R	S
HONEY BUZZARD	V	V
KESTREL	S	S
LANNER FALCON	W	W
LONG-LEGGED BUZZARD	W	W
LUGGER FALCON	W	W
MARSH HARRIER	U	U
MERLIN	P	R
MONTAGU'S HARRIER	S	S
NEW ZEALAND FALCON	U	V
PEREGRINE FALCON	V	W
PRAIRIE FALCON	W	W
RED KITE	W	W
RED-SHOULDERED HAWK	V	W
RED-TAILED BUZZARD	X	Y
ROUGH-LEGGED BUZZARD	W	W
SAKER FALCON	W	W
SOOTY FALCON	R	S
SPARROWHAWK	P	R
STEPPE EAGLE	Z	Z
SWAINSON'S HAWK	W	W
TAWNY EAGLE	Z	Z

Male ♂
Female ♀

SPECIES (Category II)	RING SIZE
BUNTING, CIRL	E
BUNTING, LAPLAND	E
BUNTING, SNOW	G
CHOUGH	R
CROSSBILL	J
CURLEW, STONE	R
FIELDFARE	M
FIRECREST	A
ORIOLE, GOLDEN	M
REDSTART, BLACK	C
REDWING	K
SERIN	B
SHORELARK	D
SHRIKE, RED-BACKED	J
TIT, BEARDED	E
TIT, CRESTED	C
WARBLER, CETTIS	D
WARBLER, DARTFORD	B
WARBLER, MARSH	C
WARBLER, SAVI'S	C
WOODLARK	E
WRYNECK	G

Amended 12/03/93

Returning to the Nest

When the young are to be returned it may be that this is the first time the mother will have had the opportunity to rear any young at all. This could be a traumatic experience for her if it isn't engineered correctly: she may reject the young, by refusing to brood or feed them, or she may openly attack them.

While your work on artificial incubation has been in progress, the female will have been sitting 'pot' eggs. These are replicas of her own made out of kiln-fired clay or resin. A dedicated female will sit full term and longer on these, which will allow you to do the transfer.

Healthy young of nine days old are rather large targets for her to attempt to kill. In her inaugural year she does not want very small young. Put the chicks into a carrying container and have a skinned quail available. This job may well require two of you. Go into the aviary and remove the sitting female. Next take away the 'pot' eggs. Put the young onto the scrape or into the nest, depending on species. They should be placed in the nest cup as a group. Leave the quail on the edge of the nest, go out of the aviary and observe the parent's behaviour.

Nine times out of ten the female may pause for a moment then walk in deliberate fashion over to the group and attempt to brood them. They may have other ideas and attempt to resist her. However they will soon feel the colder air and look for somewhere warm. This will mean snuggling up to her and eventually crawling in amongst her feathers to sleep. The female may be seen touching the young with her beak and gently pulling toes or wings, just checking on what these objects are!

Alternatively the young, on seeing her movement, may instinctively begin to vocalise and beg for food. She may automatically respond and, seeing the quail, pick it up and begin to feed them.

Either way, she is showing positive beneficial response. Even if she broods for a time initially, she will feed them in the end.

However if the timing is wrong and she is still entrenched in egg-brooding behaviour, her desire to adapt maternally to feeding will not be sufficiently developed and she may well attack the young or simply fail to feed them. Rescue the brood immediately, put the 'pot' eggs back in with her and try again the following day. Novice females cannot be expected to want to stop brooding until twenty-one days or more have passed. This allows them to enter the next stage of wanting to feed something.

Fledging

Chicks grow at a tremendous rate, reaching their maximum potential within twenty-eight days. By their sixth week the males will be active and flying round the aviary, with their larger sisters not far behind. The amount of food that a pair requires will be relevant to how many they're feeding. They should be fed three times a day and a variety of diet will be advisable in order to keep pace with demand. Rabbits, quail, chicks and rats all have value in feeding as a mixed diet. Rabbits from the wild must have been shot with a rifle and not contain shotgun pellets.

As the fledged young become more active they may well need to be separated from their parents and put into a flight by themselves. Some youngsters develop filial aggression. Quite simply they torment their parent for food and if the parent bird does bring a food item towards them it is met by the offspring lashing out with its feet, stealing the food item and mantling over it. Youngsters left in for long periods will (with nothing better else to do) harass parents to feed them. Quite naturally the parents become reluctant to feed them as the young are quite capable of finding food for themselves.

Not all young are aggressive in this manner and some will maintain a docile state with their parents *ad infinitum*. However, as time passes and the young are still in with them at the onset of autumn, the parent birds may well become aggressive to the young. This is particularly true of falcons. These will invariably be territorial reactions from the male. Young birds definitely need removing as the parent male may inflict serious injury.

Dispersal of Young

Each breeding season a wide variety of young stock will be available for sale to falconers. It may well be that your offspring are all spoken for prior to fledging. However, if they're not, you will need to advertise them for sale. This effectively means that you will be competing with many other breeders with your species of falcon or hawk.

If they have had attention to detail in feeding and rearing it is probable that they will sell very promptly. One way to avoid disappointment in selling your good stock is not to overproduce. If you have a good pair of birds capable of rearing their own young and you can send them to their new homes when they're physically and mentally ready, this makes far more sense than having more young than you can cope with, financially and practically, and needlessly saturating a market in which there are not enough experienced owners.

Clearly if you do produce very good stock you will soon build up a reputation, so that people requiring young will be recommended to you. Breeding has come a long way in the last ten years. More and more people are capable of producing birds for falconry. Not all breeders are falconers and consequently their criteria for breeding may be a far cry from what a falconer requires in his hunting bird. Breeding from unrelated bloodlines that have no known defects, who were themselves flown and/or hunted, is the goal that one should ultimately be striving for.

Chapter 21
Artificial Insemination

In every system there soon arrives a spanner to upset the works! In raptor breeding this is when a bird of either sex will not copulate with its mate. In the case of falcon females, they will more than likely lay eggs and appear to interact with their male, but the eggs will be infertile. Equally the male may well go through all the breeding rituals and show well-defined responses to his female, but refuse to copulate with her. Without some visual help here it would be difficult to know who is the odd one out. Ideally close-circuit TV cameras will help solve the mystery; so will plain old-fashioned observation from you through the spy holes in the aviary.

When this problem occurs there is probably a strong degree of imprinting in one of the birds (and occasionally both of them), even though it may not be apparent. In their first laying season you may well need to double clutch them in order to be sure that they will not produce fertile eggs. Sometimes what may be a lack of synchronised behaviour can correct itself during courtship second time round. Also if you race into AI the pair, either or both, may be completely put off any further interaction as a result.

Artificial insemination is labour intensive and is no substitute for naturally copulating pairs of falcons or hawks.

Practise first of all on chickens or quail or pigeons. AI should not be performed at any time on falcons or hawks unless you have mastered some of the techniques beforehand. There are dangers in the mishandling of male or female which could have profound effects on either of them.

In addition AI cannot be done by yourself. You will require an assistant who is capable of helping you on all occasions and preferably performing the same procedure each time so that you work as a team.

AI has a constructive role to play when females that are known imprints are put into breeding chambers with the strong chance that they will lay eggs and that you may be capable of making them fertile. These females are put in by themselves and from that point in time will interact with you. There will need to be a donor male in his own aviary who has been reared as an imprint and who will co-operatively provide semen. The very best males and females are always those that have been flown and hunted. Such individuals are very well disposed to people and good at interacting with them.

Males can be trained to deposit semen on specially designed hats from which it can be collected as illustrated in *Falcon Propagation**. The females meanwhile will actively solicit copulation, which is the ideal time to deposit (smear) semen samples. Both male and female will form strong sexual bonds with the falconer and in their respective aviaries will interact on the nesting ledge with you on any occasion that you go in with them. The more frequently you do this, the greater their desire to display to

*Falcon Propagation, a Manual on Captive Breeding, p. 24. Available from the Peregrine Fund in the USA.

you will be. This will effectively raise their hormone levels and improve their chances of fertility.

Quality food for both male and female is important and the feeding can be staggered throughout the day so that going into the breeding chambers with food encourages food passing and plenty of vocalising. In fact the whole sequence of inducing male or female into breeding condition is attempting to emulate the behavioural activity within the breeding chamber of a normal copulating pair.

Interesting as AI work may be, it involves long hours of observation of females which may mean AI'ing at night and very early mornings. Just because you have a donor male doesn't mean he will produce semen when you want it. This can be particularly difficult in the situation of continuous smearing of the female as large quantities are needed to ensure fertility.

However not all AI is conducted with co-operative males and females. The alternative requires a degree of skill in taking semen from the male. Males caught up and physically handled in this manner are usually short-term donors. They may give good samples of semen initially, then quickly peter out. It is a reaction to handling that is the prime cause.

Females that are AI'd in a non-voluntary status will require the sample deposited into the oviduct by manual eversion. The glass capillary tubes that are used for semen collection should not at any time be used for inseminating into the female. These delicate tubes break very easily and could do so inside the female. The sample will need to be transferred to a large glass tube called a cannula which has a syringe top for depositing. This has a specially rounded end which simply cannot damage her.

All semen samples are examined microscopically for motility and maturity. They ideally should be used fresh, not stored.

A female that is AI'd in this way will need constant watching as the eggs are laid. She will need to be AI'd after each egg and the time allocation for that will be between one and three hours after the egg is laid. It is always better to pull her eggs sequentially if possible to maximise on the flow of potential semen, but some females simply will not be manipulated in this way and will lay a clutch of four or five eggs, then stop. They can be recycled and whether or not you do this will depend on whether you think semen will still be available in fourteen days' time.

Chapter 22
Conservation and Education

Birds of prey are a part of the natural world. Like us they kill other animals for food and in some shape or form they are in evidence day and night. In the past twenty-five years great efforts have been made to secure their future, through extensive scientific studies showing factors that can affect their status, protection of eyrie sites from interference and laws to protect them.

However, none of these measures can remain constant unless there is an appreciative audience who remain sold on the idea of wanting to continue to conserve them. Getting across the point of the need to share our environment and tolerance of habitat requirements is but one of the tasks that education has as its daily role.

It was something that I was inherently aware of as a teacher. Often at weekends I would take a large group of children out on field trips into their immediate surroundings that for them were quite an eye opener. Frequently accompanied by the pointing dogs, we were able to see game birds, rabbits or hares in fields where previously to them had been nothing but grass. The richness of bird and mammal life was all around them, the way it evolved and survived was now worth a second look; it didn't have to be such a mystery or taken for granted.

How birds of prey depended on this rich source was wonderfully illustrated through the classroom window one afternoon, by a sparrowhawk we all saw taking a small bird. What might normally have been an immediate interest for just one or two had the whole class buzzing. Through their field work they could identify very strongly with the role of predator and prey. These were children from a socially deprived background, who were already making that important positive step into observing and relating to their natural world.

Children are our next generation of conservation 'ambassadors'. They will become the decision-makers who will manage our wildlife resources. Such eminent positions require non-emotive, rational practitioners whose ground work should have begun at school. Looking after our natural heritage is as much about communication as it is about conservation. How this is best achieved is within the realms of education, through creating an understanding between the interests of man, wildlife and species management. Educationalists need to take a refreshing look at philosophies and policies concerning species management without emotive overtones and to understand that hunting is often the main reason for a species' survival.

Falconers today have achieved enormous success in the domestic breeding of raptors for release schemes, re-introduction programmes and falconry. Such dedication and commitment is a direct result of concern for species' stability in the wild and is in keeping with many modern ecological management techniques. Conveying this to the general public is a continuous process. This may be achieved through public demonstrations, through visits to schools or in our top category falconry centres. It also has not lost sight of the fact that falconry is the taking of quarry with a trained hawk or falcon. Within each falconer is a dedicated wildlife manager whose ultimate goal is the maintenance of suitable habitat where quarry species may flourish so that the hunting raptor can remain part of the natural interaction between predator and prey.

Bibliography

BAILEY J., *How to Help Gundogs Train Themselves* (1993) Swan Valley Press, Oregon, USA

BEEBE F.L., *Hawks, Falcons and Falconry* (1976) Hancock House Publishing Ltd, USA

—— *The Compleat Falconer* (1992)

—— *A Falconry Manual* (1992)

BLOME R., *Hawking or Faulconry* (1929) Thames Valley Press

BRANDER M., *The Roughshooters Dog* (1971) Gentry Books Ltd

BROWN L. & AMADON D., *Eagles, Hawks and Falcons of the World* (1968) Country Life Books

BURTON R., *Egg, Natures Miracle of Packaging* (1987) William Collins Sons & Co. Ltd

BURTON P., *Birds of Prey* (1989) Gallery Books, Madison Avenue, New York

CADE T.J., *The Falcons of the World* (1982) William Collins Sons Ltd

CAMPBELL B. & LACK E., *A Dictionary of Birds* (1985) T. & A.D. Poyser

CHAMERLAT C.A. de., *Falconry and Art* (1987) Sothebys Publications

CRAMP S., *Birds of Europe, the Middle East and North Africa* (1980) Oxford University Press

DAY D., *Vanished Species* (1989) Gallery Books, Madison Avenue, New York

DURMAN-WALTERS et al., *The Hunter-Pointer Retriever* (1989) edited by Tony Jackson

—— *The Complete Gundog* (1990) edited by John Humphries. David and Charles

—— *A Green Guide to Countrysports* (1991) edited by J.N.P. Watson, Redwood Press Ltd

FISHER J., *Thorburn's Birds* (1967) Jarold and Sons, Norwich

GLASIER P., *Falconry and Hawking* (1978) B. T. Batsford Ltd

GONDREXON A. & BROWNE I., *Guide to the Dogs of the World* (1986) Elsevier Publishing Projects

GOTTLIEB G., *The Hungarian Vizsla* (1985) Nimrod Book Services

HAAK, B.A., *The Hunting Falcon* (1992) Hancock House Publishing Ltd

HARTLEY R., *Falconry in Zimbabwe* (1983) North American Falconers Association. Journal. vol. 22. 84-91

HARTING J.E., *Bibliotheca Accipitraria* (1964) Holland Press

HICKEY J.J., *Peregrine Falcon Populations* (1969) University of Wisconsin Press, USA.

HOHENSTAUFEN Frederick II, *The Art of Falconry* (1969) translated by Casey Wood and F. Majorie Fyfe, Stanford University Press

HOSKINS E. & D. FLEGG J., *Birds of Prey of the World* (1987) Pelham Books Ltd

INTERNATIONAL ZOO YEAR BOOK (1984) edited by P.J.S. Olney. vol. 23. Zoological Society of London

JOHNSGARD P.A., *The Grouse of the World* (1983) Croom, Helm

MACLEAN G.R., *Roberts Birds of South Africa* (1985) John Voelker Bird Book Fund Trustees

MAVROGORDATO J., *A Hawk for the Bush* (1960) H.F. and G. Witherby
—— *A Falcon in the Field* (1966) Knightly Vernon Ltd

MEYBURG B-U & R.D. CHANCELLOR, *Raptors in the Modern World* (1989) Lentz Druck, Berlin.

MITCHELL E.B., *The Art and Practice of Hawking* (1964) Holland Press

NEWTON I., *The Sparrowhawk* (1986) T. & A.D. Poyser

SALVIN H. & BRODRICK W., *Falconry in the British Isles* (1970) Tabard Press

SCHLEGEL H. & WULVERHORST A.H. VERSTER de., *Traite de Fauconnerie* (1973) Chasse Publications, USA

SCIENTIFIC AMERICAN, *Birds* (1980) W. H. Freeman and Co

SCHNEIDER-LEYER E. Dr., *Dogs of the World* unknown publisher

SHAW. Vero K., *The Classic Encyclopedia of the Dog* (1881) Bonanza Books

SKUTCH A.F., *Parent Birds and their Young* (1979) University of Texas Press

STEPANEK O., *Birds of Heath and Marshland* (1962) Spring Birds

STEYN P., *Hunters of the African Sky* (1990) The Struick Winchester Group Ltd

THE KENNEL CLUB'S ILLUSTRATED BREED STANDARDS, (1989) Bodley Head

THE PEREGRINE FUND INCORPORATED, *Falcon Propagation. A Manual on Captive Breeding* (1983) edited by James D. Weaver and Tom J. Cade, Peregrine Fund Incorporated, USA.

THOMSON R., *On Wildlife Conservation* (1986) United Publishers International

UPTON R., *O For a Falconers Voice* (1987) University Printing House, Oxford
—— *A Bird in the Hand* (1980) Debretts Peerage Ltd

VESEY FITZGERALD B., *The Domestic Dog* (1957) Routledge Kegan and Paul

WEICK F., *Birds of Prey of the World* (1980) in collaboration with Leslie Brown and Paul Parey, P. Parey, Hamburg and Berlin

WOODFORD M.H. MRCVS, *A Manual of Falconry* (1960) Unwin Brothers Ltd

Glossary

ACCIPITER: sometimes used in North America as a vernacular term for ACCIPITER spp., 'hawk' having there a wider connotation than in Britain. Generally used to describe 'true hawks' such as goshawk and sparrowhawk.

ASPERGILLOSIS: a disease caused by species of *Aspergillus*, marked by inflammatory granulomatous lesions in the skin, ear, orbit, nasal sinuses, lungs and sometimes bones and meninges. Frequently seen as a disease of the upper respiratory tract in raptors.

AUSTRINGER: used to describe a person who flies only short-winged hawks. Rarely used today.

AYLMERI: anklets made of leather secured by a brass eyelet through which the jesses are passed.

BATE: to attempt to fly from the perch or fist either at quarry, or the lure, or from something which has caused alarm, whilst tethered.

BECHIN: titbits or small food items which are placed on the gauntlet in order to call the hawk onto the glove.

BEWIT: small leather strap used to secure the hawk bell onto the leg.

BIND: to sieze the quarry firmly in the feet.

BLOCK: wooden post-like perch used for falcons to sit on either outside or inside.

BOW PERCH: semi-circular hoop with spiked feet made of steel with padded top for hawks to perch on whist weathering outside.

BOX CADGE: a heavy lidless box with padded rim to which hooded falcons are tied whilst travelling in the car.

BRACES: leather straps used to open and close the hood.

BRANCHER: Young hawk which has just left the nest.

BREAK IN: when a hawk or falcon begins to eat the quarry it has caught.

CALL OFF: to call the hawk onto the fist from a post or tree or from the lure.

CARRY: when the hawk or falcon flies off with the quarry. This is a vice.

CAST.1: to hold down a hawk for the purpose of some operation, eg, imping. 2. ejecting a pellet.

CAST: two falcons trained to hunt together.

CASTING: the pellet of fur or feather ejected from the crop.

CAST OFF: releasing the hawk for free flight.

CERE: the fleshy part of the top of the beak

CHECK: to ignore the quarry intended to chase, generally easier quarry.

COPE: to trim the beak or talons

CRAB: fighting or squabbling between two hawks generally whilst in flight.

CREANCE: training line attached to hawks in preliminary lessons of flight to the glove or lure.

CROP: sac-like storage area for food near the front of the thorax.

DECK FEATHERS: the two central tail feathers, usually the first to be moulted.

ENTER: the introduction of a hawk to her quarry.

EYAS: a young hawk or falcon. Usually refers to one taken from the nest.

EYRIE: traditional name for a falcon's nest in the wild.

FALCON: bird of prey with long narrow wing, dark eyes and a notched beak for dispatching quarry. Also used to describe female peregrine.

FALCONER: strictly speaking one who trains only falcons. Today is used generically to describe anyone who trains a bird of prey.

FALSE POINT: where the dog remains staunchly on point at the spot where game has previously departed.

FEAK: to wipe the beak in order to remove pieces of food either on the glove or on the block.

FEATHERS IN THE BLOOD: new feathers that are growing down which are enclosed in a waxy sheath with their own blood supply.

FEED UP: to allow the hawk or falcon to consume its quarry or the total daily food requirements.

FLIGHT FROM THE HOOD: once the hood is removed the falcon initiates a direct chase at quarry, usually rooks and crows.

FOOT: striking the quarry.

FRET MARKS: hunger or stress marks visible as lines or scores across the feathers.

FROUNCE: or pigeon canker is a disease caused by a protozoan parasite (*Trichomonas* spp.) transmitted by pigeons which have been freshly eaten. It is characterised by deposits of necrotic lesions of white or yellowish 'cheese like' growths in the mouth, pharynx, oesophagus and crop.

GORGE: to give the hawk a full crop of food.

HACK: a period of time devoted to rearing eyases which allows them liberty from the time they can fly until they are caught up for training.

HAGGARD: generally speaking a wild-caught hawk in adult plumage.

HARD PENNED: when all new feathers have reached their final point of growth and are no longer in the blood. Usually refers to a young hawk of the year but is also used to denote completion of the moult.

HAWK: a term used to describe short-winged raptors such as goshawk or sparrowhawk. It is also used generically to describe both hawk and falcons.

HIGH: this describes the condition of a hawk whose flying weight is far above the desired level.

HOOD SHY: any trained hawk or falcon that will not allow the hood to be placed on and repeatedly bates away from every attempt to be hooded.

IMP: to repair a broken feather by adding a new piece using imping 'needles' of flexible steel, carbon fibre, fibreglass or bamboo.

IMPRINT: a young hawk raised by hand that forms a psychological bond with its falconer.

INTERMEWED: any hawk that has been kept through the moult.

JESSES: 1. leather straps attached to the hawk's leg through the aylmeri. 2. traditional jesses are attached directly to the hawk's leg.

LEASH: the long nylon lead by which the hawk is tied to the block or bow perch.

LONG-WING: a true falcon.

LOW: a physical condition that describes a hawk that has lost too much weight.

LURE: a dummy bird or rabbit that is used to call the hawk down from a tree or the falcon from the air.

MAKE IN: to approach a hawk that has just killed.

MAN: the process of taming a wild hawk by carrying.

MANTLE: spreading the wings and tail in order to cover the food or quarry.

MEWS: a building that houses hawks or falcons.

MUSKET: male sparrowhawk.

MUTES: the droppings of falcons.

PASSAGE: a wild hawk in immature plumage, caught on migration.

PITCH: the height that a falcon attains in the sky. When the falcon has reached optimum pitch, it climbs no higher, rests on its wings and fans its tail. This is the point when you can bring it into position by waving your glove and calling.

PLUME: to pluck the quarry.

PUT IN: to chase quarry into cover.

PUT OVER: to have digested its crop contents.

QUARRY: the game that the falcon or hawk is flown at.

RAKE AWAY: to leave the flying area and career away down wind.

RANGLE: small round stones the size of a pea given to falcons for casting after the moult. Supposed to put an edge on her appetite by breaking down the fat in the crop.

RAPTOR: used to describe all birds of prey.

RINGING FLIGHT: a direct chase of quarry into the air from the fist, usually executed by merlins.

RING PERCH: a circular metal perch padded at the top for the use of short-winged-hawks and buteos.

ROUSE: to raise and ruffle the feathers quite vigorously, usually prior to flight or as a sign of well being.

SCREEN PERCH: a horizontal perch, padded and mounted at chest height from the ground. A taut canvas or hessian screen is hung directly below to enable the tethered hawk to regain the perch by climbing back up if it jumps off. This is a dangerous form of perch and not to be recommended.

SERVE: to flush quarry under the hawk.

SHARP SET: hungry and keen.

SHORT-WINGED HAWK: true hawks. Those with short wings, long tails, yellow eyes and toothless beaks.

SLICING: excrement from a hawk which is ejected with some force and volume away from the perching area.

SLIP. 1. to release the hawk from the fist at quarry. 2. to slip out of the hood at crows and rooks.

SOARING: effortless flying of hawk or falcon on updrafts of favourable air or thermals.

STAND: to take stand, is to remain perched in a tree or on some form of construction either through disobedience or in anticipation of being served with quarry.

STOOP: to descend with wings closed from considerable height in pursuit of quarry.

STRIKE: impact or hitting quarry.

STRIKE THE HOOD: to open the braces to remove the hood.

SWIVEL: made from stainless steel they are either figure '8' shaped or 'D' ring shaped. Designed to allow the movement of jesses so that they do not tangle up with the legs or with the leash.

TELEMETRY: modern electronic tracking device which consists of receiver, transmitter and directional antenna by which a lost hawk can be retrieved.

THROW UP: to mount steeply on outstretched wings especially after a stoop.

TIERCEL: proper term for the male peregrine. Today it is used to describe any large long-winged male falcon and male goshawk.

TIRING: a tough piece of meat which has little food on it: either rabbit back or pigeon's wing which will keep the hawk occupied for some considerable time whilst it is being walked unhooded. Used to assist in the manning process.

WAIT-ON: when falcons have reached their pitch they will circle high over the falconer awaiting the flush.

WASHED MEAT: meat soaked in cold water then wrung dry so that most of the nutritional value is removed.

WEATHER: to place the hawk or falcon unhooded on its perch in the open so that it can benefit from the elements, bathe and preen.

WEATHERING ENCLOSURE: is an all-weather stall which is covered to provide protection from the worst of the elements and enclosed by security fencing to eliminate people and predators such as dogs, cats, mink, stoats, weasels and foxes.

YARAK: an eastern expression to indicate that the short-winged hawk is in a state of keeness and eager to hunt. This is used particularly when the goshawk has erected all the feathers on her crown and nape whilst slightly spreading her wings when sitting on the glove.

Game Seasons

The Birds and Animals shown in this table may be taken and killed as indicated.
All dates are inclusive

Species Designated as Game Under the Game Act 1831.

Grouse	12th August to 10th December
Ptarmigan	12th August to 10th December
Blackgame	20th August to 10th December
Partridge	1st September to 1st February
Hare	No close season

Species Designated Under the Game Licences Act 1860.

Snipe
Woodcock

Birds in Schedule 2 of the Wildlife and Countryside Act 1981

which may be killed or taken outside the close season and which may be sold dead
from 1st September to 28th February (or as indicated).

Capercaillie	1st October to 31st January
Coot	1st September to 31st January
Common Snipe	12th August to 31st January
Woodcock	1st October to 31st January
Golden Plover	1st September to 31st January
Tufted Duck	Above the high-water mark of ordinary
Mallard	Spring tides 1st September to 31st
Pintail	January. Below the high-water mark of
Shoveller	ordinary Spring tides 1st September to
Teal	20th February.
Wigeon	

Birds in Schedule 2 of The Wildlife and Countryside Act 1981

which may be killed or taken outside the close season but which may not be sold dead.

Canada Goose	Above the high-water mark of ordinary
Gadwall	Spring tides 1st September to 31st
Goldeneye	January. Below the high-water mark of
Graylag Goose	ordinary Spring tides 1st September to
Pink-footed Goose	20th February.
White-fronted Goose	
(not in Scotland)	
Moorhen	1st September to 31st January.

Birds for which there is no close season and which may be killed or taken by Authorised Persons at all times.

Note that only Feral and Woodpigeon may be sold dead.

Crow	Magpie
Collared Dove	Feral Pigeon
Greater Black-backed Gull	Rook
Lesser Black-backed Gull	House Sparrow
Herring Gull	Starling
Jackdaw	Woodpigeon
Jay	

Useful Addresses

CLUBS AND SOCIETIES

The British Falconers Club
J.R. Fairclough,
Home Farm,
Hints,
Nr. Tamworth,
Staffordshire B78 3DW

The Welsh Hawking Club
A. Williams,
Maendy Farmhouse,
Church Village,
Nr. Pontypridd,
Glamorgan.

The Northern England Falconry Club
D.J. Chadwick,
31, Northorpe Lane,
Mirfield,
West Yorkshire
WF14 0QJ

The Irish Hawking Club (North)
D. Watson,
81 Moyallan Road,
Portadown,
Co. Armagh BT63 5JY

The Irish Hawking Club (South)
P. Fogarty,
89 Foxfield Road,
Raheny,
Dublin 5

North American Falconers Association
J. Hegan,
820 Jay Place,
Berthoud, CO 80513
USA

The British Field Sports Society
59 Kennington Rd.
London SE1 7PZ

The Kennel Club
1-5 Clarges St.
London W1Y 8AB

The Hawk and Owl Trust
The Secretary,
c/o The Birds of Prey Section,
London Zoo,
Regents Park, London NW1 4RY

The Hawk Board
Secretary Mrs S. Dewer,
6, Glendevon Road,
Woodley,
Reading,
Berks RG5 4PH

*The International Council for Bird
  Preservation*
32, Cambridge Road,
Girton,
Cambridge CB3 0PJ

The Department of the Environment
Tollgate House,
Houlton St.
Bristol BS2 9DJ

FALCONRY EDUCATION

The British Falconers Club
(see Clubs and Societies p.168)

The Scottish Academy of Falconry and
    Related Studies,
Hyndlee,
Bonchester Bridge,
Hawick TD9 9TB.

VETERINARY SURGEONS

Greenhalgh and Heal,
78, Yorkshire St,
Burnley,
Lancashire BB11 3BT

Mr N.A. Forbes and
    Mr Greg N. Simpson,
The Clock House Veterinary Hospital,
Wallbridge,
Stroud,
Gloucester GL5 3JD

Mr J.R. & Mrs R.E. Best
32, West Hill,
Portishead,
Bristol BS20 9LM

Mr N.H. & Mrs F.M. Harcourt-Brown,
30, Crab Lane,
Harrogate,
Yorks HG1 3BE

CENTRES FEATURING BIRDS OF
    PREY

The Scottish Deer Centre/The Scottish
    Academy of Falconry,
Cupar,
Fife KY14 4NQ

The British Owl Breeding and Release
    Scheme (BOBARS)
Tony Warburton,
The Owl Centre,
Muncaster Castle,
Ravenglass,
Cumbria CA18 1RQ

The Whitbread Hop Farm,
Beltring,
Paddock Wood,
Kent TN12 6PY

The National Bird of Prey Centre,
Newent,
Gloucester GL18 1JJ

The Hawk Conservancy,
Andover,
Hampshire SP11 8DY

The Yorkshire Dales Falconry and
    Conservation Centre,
Crows Nest,
Nr. Giggleswick,
Settle,
N.Yorks LA2 8AS

VETARK Products Ltd,
P.O. Box 60,
Winchester,
Hampshire SO23 9XN

TELEMETRY SUPPLIERS

Custom Electronics of Urbana,
2009 Silver Court West
Urbana,
Illinois 61801,
USA

Louis Luksander,
P.O. Box 247,
Mahomet,
Illinois 61853,
USA.

Audio Precision,
36, Tathan Crescent,
St. Athan,
South Glamorgan CF6 9PE

**FALCONRY FURNITURE
MAKERS**

Ben Long Falconry Originals,
Ruthin,
Clwyd LL15 2PS.

Falconry Furniture,
Mr M. Jones
The Lodge,
Huntley Manor,
Huntley,
Gloucester GL19 3HG

Falcon Leisure,
Woodside,
8, Lorraine Road,
Old Dean,
Camberley,
Surrey GU15 4EF

The Falconer,
Walton Way,
Walton Road,
Wellesbourne,
Warwick.

Ray Prior Falconry Equipment,
4, Hackney Bottom,
Hampstead Norreys,
Newbury,
Berks RG16 0TU

MAGAZINES AND JOURNALS

*The Falconer and Raptor Conservation
    Magazine*
20 Bridle Road,
Burton Lattimer,
Kettering,
Northants NN15 5QP

Cage and Aviary Birds
Kings Reach Tower,
Stamford Street,
London SE1 9LS

The Field
Astley House,
33 Notting Hill Gate,
London W11 3JQ

*The Scottish Sporting Gazette and
    International Traveller*
Market Brae,
Inverness IV2 3AB

The Countrymans Weekly
Yelverton,
Devon PL20 7PE

Index

accipiters 132–4, 140
Africa 22–3
African goshawk 22, 23
African hawk eagle 23
ailments and diseases
  aspergillosis 51–2
  bones in the crop 53
  bumblefoot infection 49
  constipation 49, 53
  diarrhoea 49, 53
  digestive problems 53
  fits and seizures 49–50, 60
  foot infections 48–9
  kidney problems 49, 53
  respiratory infections 50–2
  sour crop 49, 53
  wings 49
altali falcon 39–40
American kestrel 122
Anderson, John 18–19
apprenticeship schemes 13
artificial insemination (AI)
  appropriate situations for 156
  inducing breeding conditions 157
  inseminating the female 157
  obtaining semen samples 156,
    157
aspergillosis 51–2
Australia 22
aviaries
  baths 126–7
  construction materials 123
  Cornell chamber system 123
  deterring predators 124
  feed trays 125
  flooring 125
  interior 125
  location 125
  nest ledges 127
  perches 125–6
  reducing infection in 52
  roof netting 124
  safety corridor 125
  size 123
  snowfalls, dealing with 124
aylmeri 55

Ballantine, Peter 18, 19
Baptiste, Steve 12
Barr, John 21

Barr, Robert 21
Barr, William 18
Bastyai, Lorant de 24
bathing 126–7
bechins (titbits) 57, 86
Bekkers, John 18
bells 55, 63
black grouse 73
Blaine, Colonel Gilbert 22
blocks and perches 85, 125–6
Bond, Frank 12
Botts, Jean 20
breeding
  accipiters 132–4
  artificial insemination (AI) 156–7
  courtship rituals 133
  creche rearing 130–1
  eggs 135–6, 137–8
  hatching 137–8
  imprints 128–32
  incubation 135
  incubators 135, 136–7
  nest building 133
  pair bonding 132
  readiness for 132
  sexual dimorphism 134
  timing 132
  see also chicks
breeding programmes 12, 120–2
British Falconers Club 22, 23, 24–5
British Field Sports Society (BFSS)
  25
Brittany 99, 100
buteos 140
buzzard 83, 84

cable-ties 145
Cade, Dr Tom 120
Carnie, Kent 12
Champagne Hawking Club 21
chicks
  altricial precocity 140
  brooding 138
  dispersal 155
  feeding 138–9, 154
  fledged young 154–5
  hatching 137–8
  returning to the nest 154
  ringing and registering 141–53
  sibling aggression 140

cloaca 53
conservation 122, 158
continental gundogs see hunt, point
  and retrieve breeds (HPRs)
corvids
  characteristics and habits 78, 79
  rook hawking 78–82
creance 57
crop 49, 53

Daims, John 18
DDT pesticides 119–20
De Arte cum Avibus ('On Skill with
  Birds') 15, 16
dead birds 141
Department of the Environment 25,
  140
diet
  best food sources 52
  chicks 138–9, 154
  nutritional supplements 52
  quality of food 52
digestive system
  changes in appetite 53
  imbalances in 53
  monitoring 52, 53
  see also diet
disabled birds 142, 144
dogs see gundog puppies; gundogs;
  training the gundog
ducks 76–7
Dutch falconers 18, 20

eagles 85
education 158–9
eggs 135–6, 137–8
exported birds 141, 149
extinction of raptor species 119
eyases 18, 19, 130, 131

Falcon Propagation 156
feet
  bumblefoot infection 49
  foot infections 48–9
  punctured feet 48
ferruginous hawk
  characteristics 35, 84
  females 35
  flying skills 35–6
  flying weight 35

males 35
    quarry 35
    range 35
film and television work 87–8
fitness, achieving 67
Frederick II of Germany 15–16, 26
free-flying demonstrations
    assistants 87
    choosing a display bird 84–5
    dealing with the public 86–7
    eagles and owls 85
    equipment 85–6
    standards of presentation 83, 84,
        86
    training for 83–4
    weathering ground 84
French Falconry Club 12

Gabar goshawk 23
game fairs 83–7
game hawking
    basic quarry 55
    telemetry 63–6
    training the falcon 55–60
    training the hawk 60–3
    see also lowland hawking; upland
        game hawking
game seasons 168–9
German short-haired pointer (GSP)
    96, 97–8, 100
German wire-haired pointer (GWP)
    96–7, 100
goshawk
    BFC breeding programme 24
    breeding 127, 132
    characteristics 28, 29, 84
    females 30
    first kill 62
    flying skills 29
    flying weight 28
    hooding 61
    hunting techniques 29, 30
    imprints 129
    males 29, 30
    manning 60
    quarry 29, 30
    range 28
    response to lures 30
    ringing 147
    weight range and area of origin
        29
    working with dogs 29, 61,
        62
grey partridge 74
grouse hawking
    black grouse 73
    ptarmigan 73
    red grouse 70–3
    suitable dogs for 90
gundog puppies
    basic training 105–8

car journeys 106
    diet 102–3
    kennelling 104–5
    lead training 105–6
    living quarters 102
    locating sound litters 101
    selecting 102
    social stimulation 103, 105
    whistle discipline 107–8
    worming and vaccination 103
    see also training the gundog
gundogs
    buying part-trained sub-adults
        103–4
    buying trained dogs 103–4
    desired attributes 100
    diseases 101
    field trials 101
    habitat requirements 91–2
    hunt, point and retrieve breeds
        (HPRs) 90–1, 95–100
    kennelling 104
    low-ground dogs 94–5
    pointers and setters 90, 91–4
    retrievers 90
    upland dogs 92–4
    working with hawks 115–18
    working stock 91
    see also gundog puppies; training
        the gundog
gyr x peregrine falcon
    favourable weather conditions for
        45
    females 45
    flying weight 45
    hunting techniques 45
    quarry 45–6
gyr x saker falcon
    favourable weather conditions for
        46
    females 46
    flying weight 46
    maiden flight 59
    quarry 46
    rook hawking 80
gyrfalcon
    ailments 42
    characteristics 42
    colour variations 41
    favourable weather conditions for
        41
    fitness requirement 41, 42
    flying skills 42
    flying weight 41
    handling 42
    hooding 42
    hunting techniques 41, 42
    males 41
    quarry 41–42
    range 41
    ringing 147

hacking 67
Harris hawk
    characteristics 37
    co-operative hunting 36
    females 37
    first kill 62
    fits and seizures 50, 60
    flying akills 37
    flying weight 36
    free-flying demonstrations
        83, 84
    hooding 60, 61
    horseback, flying from 81
    hunting techniques 37
    males 37
    manning 60
    quarry 36, 37
    range 36
    recreational flying 84
    weight range 36
Hawk Board 25
health
    daily assessment 48–9
    digestive system 52–3
    external appearance 48
    general behaviour 48
    mutes and pellets, examination of
        49, 53
    physical examination 48–9
    respiratory system 50–2
    veterinary care 53–4
    see also ailments and diseases;
        diet
heron falconry 18, 20
Heural, Francis van den 18
Hickey, Joseph 119
hip dysplasia 101
history of falconry
    Asiatic origins 15
    Dutch falconers 18, 20
    in Europe 15–16
    exotics and hybrids, introduction
        of 26–7
    introduction to Britain 16
    modern falconry 21–2, 26
    nineteenth-century decline 20–1
hoods and hooding 55, 60–1
horseback, hawking from 80–2
Hungarian vizsla 98, 100
hunt, point and retrieve breeds
    (HPRs)
    attributes 96
    breed varieties 90, 96–100
    origins 90, 91, 95–6
hybrid falcons
    desirable factors 27, 44
    gyr x peregrine falcon 45–6
    gyr x saker falcon 46, 59, 80
    introduction to Britain 27
    naming 44
    peregrine x prairie falcon 44–5

prairie x peregrine falcon 12, 27,
    59, 80
and rook hawking 80
saker x peregrine falcon 80
hypocalcaemia 50
hypoglycaemia 50

imperial falconers 15–16
imported birds 145
imprints
    breeding from 132, 156
    characteristics 69
    creche rearing 130–1
    degree of imprinting 128–9
    dual imprints 129–30
    free-flying demonstrations 85
    reverse imprinting 131–2
    screaming imprints 131
    social imprints 68, 85, 129
    tame hacking 67–9
    training 68–9
Irish Hawking Club 24
Italian bracco 99
Italian spinone 99, 100

James I of England 16, 17
jesses 19, 55, 86

Kennel Club 101
kestrel 85

Lang, Joseph 92
lanner falcon
    characteristics 43
    co-operative hunting 43
    flying weight 42
    free-flying demonstrations 84
    hunting techniques 74
    limited success with 43
    partridge hawking 74–5
    quarry 43
    range 42
large munsterlander 99–100
Lascelles, Gerald 21, 22
leashes 19, 86
licences and registration 141–5,
    148, 150–1
licensed rehabilitation keepers
    (LRKs) 142, 144
Loo Hawking Club 20
lost birds 65–6, 141
lowland hawking
    ducks 76–7
    partridge 74–5
    pheasants 75–6
lugger falcon 43–4, 84
lure work 57–8, 116

Manual of Falconry, A (Woodford)
    97
merlin
    characteristics 31

flying skills 31–2
flying weight 31
hunting techniques 31
males 32
quarry 31
range 31
ringing 147
training 32
Mollen, Aidrian 120
Monson, Sir Thomas 16
mutes 49

National Centre for Birds of Prey 23
Newcome, Edward Clough 21
North America 23–4
North American Falconry
    Association (NAFA) 12, 23–4

Old Hawking Club 21–2
Ovambo sparrowhawk 22
owls 85

parabuteos 140
partridge 74–5, 90
passage hawks 18
pellets 49
Pells, John 18, 19
peregrine falcon
    breeding programmes 120–1
    characteristics 27, 28
    duck hawking 76
    favourable weather conditions for
        28
    females 28
    flying skills 27, 28
    flying weight 27
    free-flying demonstrations 85
    hunting techniques 27, 28
    males 28, 75
    manning 57
    partridge hawking 75
    quarry 27, 28
    range 27
    ringing 147
    rook hawking 28, 78–80
    speed in the stoop 27
peregrine x prairie falcon
    characteristics 44, 45
    favourable weather conditions for
        45
    females 44
    flying skills 45
    flying weight 44
    hunting techniques 45
    males 45
    quarry 44, 45
pheasants 75–6
pointers and setters 90, 91–4
Poles, Major Eustace 22
prairie falcon
    characteristics 38, 39

females 39
flying skills 39
flying weight 38
free-flying demonstrations 85
hunting techniques 38–9
maiden flight 59
males 39
quarry 38, 39
range 38
prairie x peregrine falcon
    introduction 27
    maiden flight 59
    rook hawking 80
    successful record 12
professional falconers 17, 18, 21
progressive retinal atrophy 101
ptarmigan 73

radio work 88
Ratcliffe, Derek 119
recreational flying 67, 68, 83, 84
red grouse 70–3
red-tailed hawk
    characteristics 34, 35, 84
    colour variations 35
    flying weight 34
    Harlan's red-tail 35
    hunting techniques 34
    Krider's hawk 35
    quarry 34, 35
    range 34
released birds 141
respiratory system
    aspergillosis 51–2
    blocked sinuses 51
    damage to 50
    functioning of 50
    infections 50–2
retrievers 90
Rhodesian Falconers' Club 23
rings and ringing
    double ringing 150
    fitting rings 150
    lost rings 142
    requesting close rings 146–7
    ring sizes 149, 152–3
    unused rings, return of 149
    UR (un-ringed) licences 145
    witness of ringing 147
rook hawking
    culling periods 78
    fitness requirement 79
    from horseback 80–2
    hybrid falcons 80
    spring rooks 79
    suitable hawks for 78–9
    wounding by rooks 79–80

saker falcon
    characteristics 40
    colour variations 39

favourable weather conditions for
    40
females 40, 85
flying skills 40
flying weight 39
free-flying demonstrations 84, 85
hunting techniques 40
maiden flight 59
males 40, 84
manning 57
migratory nature 40–1
quarry 40
range 39
rook hawking 78–9, 80
saker x peregrine falcon 80
sale of birds 145, 148–9
Savory, Allan 22
sour crop 49, 53
South Africa 22
spaniels
    attributes 94
    clumber spaniel 89, 90, 95
    cocker spaniel 89, 90, 94
    English springer spaniel 89–90,
        94–5
    field spaniel 95
    Sussex spaniel 95
sparrowhawk
    breeding 132
    characteristics 31, 84
    females 32, 33
    flying skills 33
    flying weight 32
    hunting techniques 32
    males 32, 33
    quarry, 32, 33
    range 32
    supplementary feeding 33
    throwing 33
    working with dogs 33
swivel 19

Taita falcon 23
tame hacking 67–9
telemetry
    batteries 65
    frequencies 63, 65
    mounting the transmitter 63
    rook hawking and 81
    signal reception 65
Thornton, Colonel Thomas 17–18
tirings 56
training the falcon
    bonding process 57
    dogs, toleration of 56, 58, 117
    for free-flying demonstrations 83
    hooding the young bird 55, 56
    horses, toleration of 81
    hunting skills 59, 60
    imprints 68–9
    lure work 57–8
    maiden flights 58–9
    manning process 55–7
    non-imprints 69
    to fly to the glove 57
    to stand on the glove 55
    to take food from the fist 56
    waiting-on training 59–60
    whistle discipline 57, 58
training the gundog
    advanced training 109–14
    basic training 105–8
    'go back' 112–13
    hand signals 112
    hunting and pointing 109, 110–11
    lead training 105–6
    quartering 109–10
    retrieving 111–12
    'sit to flush' 111
    steadiness to sheep 113–14
    swimming and jumping 113
    use of wind 110
    whistle discipline 107–8, 109–10
    working with hawks 115–19

training the hawk
    dogs, toleration of 61–2, 115–17
    for free-flying demonstrations 83
    hooding the young bird 60–1
    lure work 116
    manning 60
    for vertical flying 62

upland game hawking
    black grouse 73
    ptarmigan 73
    red grouse 70–3
UR (un-ringed) licences 145

Valkenswaard 18, 21
varvels 19
veterinary care 53–4

weight, monitoring and recording
    56
weimaraner 98
Welsh Hawking Club 24
whistle discipline
    dogs 107–8, 109–10
    falcons 57, 58
Wildlife and Countryside Act 1981
    Case Officers 142
    Category III birds 151
    exported birds 141, 149
    game seasons 168–9
    imported birds 145
    licences and registration 141–5,
        148, 150–1
    rings and ringing 142, 146–7,
        149–50, 152–3
    sale of birds 145, 148–9
wings
    examination of 49
    injury to 49
woodcock 94

Zimbabwe 22
Zimbabwe Falconry Club 23